Forty Years at Paisano

A Literary History

Forty Years at Paisano

A Literary History

Audrey Slate

ALAMO BAY PRESS

SEADRIFT•AUSTIN

Cover Art: *Paisano Ranch House Winter Evening,* Jim Bones
Author Photograph: John Slate
Book Design: ABP

For orders and information:
Alamo Bay Press
Pamela Booton, Director
825 W 11th Ste 114
Austin, Texas 78701
pam@alamobaypress.com
www.alamobaypress.com

Publisher's Cataloging-In-Publication Data
(Prepared by The Donohue Group, Inc.)

Names: Slate, Audrey N. (Audrey Nelson), 1926-2017 author.

Title: Forty years at Paisano : a literary history / by Audrey Slate.

Description: Austin, Texas : Alamo Bay Press, [2021] | Includes bibliographical references and index.

Identifiers: ISBN 9781943306220 (paperback)

Subjects: LCSH: University of Texas at Austin. Dobie Paisano Fellowship Program--History. | Authors--Scholarships, fellowships, etc. | Artists--Scholarships, fellowships, etc. | Writers' retreats--Texas--History.

Classification: LCC LD5325.5 .S53 2021 | DDC 378.76431--dc23

This book is dedicated to
the Texas literary community—
to writers and those who support them

Forty Years at Paisano

Forty Years at Paisano

Foreword
by Stephen Harrigan

"In memory," writes Lisa Sandlin, one of the seventy-nine ardently grateful writers profiled in these pages, "I take [Paisano] out like a picture book."

When I came across that sentence, I had the odd sensation of my mind—or my memory—being read. Yes, that's exactly what it's like for us former Paisano fellows, those of us who had the inconceivable good luck at some critical point in our careers to be given months of time—and a whole ranch—to do nothing but write or try to write, to force our minds to focus or just let them wander. Sometimes we can't resist thumbing through the mental picture book that, for many of us, tells the story of the biggest break we've ever had.

I suppose I was reasonably typical: young, sort of starting

out, broke, despairing of ever having the time to write a book or a place to write it in. (This was in the 1970's, long before coffee shops began bestowing work spaces to writers for the price of a Macchiato.) I applied for a Paisano fellowship three or four times before the call came from Audrey Slate — the beloved director of the program and the author of this book — notifying me that I had actually been selected. It was the perfect moment. My writing pump was primed with about eighty pages of a novel that had heartening indications it might actually be heading somewhere, my wife and I were new parents of a six-month old baby girl, and the $1500 a month fellowship stipend effectively doubled my income as a struggling freelance magazine writer.

I was determined not to blow this chance, but I don't remember feeling anxious during our six- month stay at Paisano. I just remember working happily in a dilapidated little shed in back of the main house that has since been torn down. Somebody had painted the walls in that shed a serene shade of blue, and in those days before computers my working tools — black felt-tip pens and composition books embossed with the logo of the University of Texas-- had a restful simplicity. I finished the novel in a rush that never seemed like a rush, and that left time for long walks with my wife and daughter and dog along Barton Creek — which was bone dry that year — and through the grassy tick-filled trail that led to the Hartwig cabin.

I am far from the only fellowship recipient who finished a book at Paisano. And there are many others who got a good start on one, or who in the head-clearing sanctum of the ranch decided to abandon a project that wasn't working and switch over to something new. In any case, a lot of writing has taken place at Paisano during the forty years chronicled in this book, including a lot of writing about Paisano. Looking through these pages, you'll find poems, reminiscences, diary entries and scenes from novels that all deal in one way or another with the profound impact that this 254 acre piece of ground along Barton Creek has had on several generations of Texas artists. Snakes, floods, droughts and solitude are common themes, and there are also encounters with straying longhorns, decomposing possums and the ghost of J. Frank Dobie.

It's no surprise that the people who were given the gift of Paisano have felt an imperative to write about it. For many of us it was more than a ranch, more than a few precious months of time. It was as close as anything to the golden moment of our creative lives, when we were unhurried, unconstrained, and productive. And with each new day, as the morning sun spread across the lawn in front of the long fieldstone gallery, we were full of hope for the work that was to come.

Introduction

SINCE THE SUMMER OF 1967, MORE THAN EIGHTY WRITERS AND A half-dozen artists or photographers have made the trip down Rawhide Trail leading across Barton Creek and up a short rise to a modest frame house whose interior walls go back more than a century to take up residence at Paisano. There they have had a chance to pursue their talents wherever those talents might take them—free from the constraints of a daily job and blessedly free from the sights and sounds of the urban area that surrounds them. "Idyllic," "a paradise"—many terms come to mind.

How this beautiful place and the opportunity offered to those lucky enough to be chosen came about is the subject of this work. It is an ongoing story and one in which many fascinating tales and records of substantial contributions to the literature of the region and the country are being added yearly.

The first three chapters deal with how the project came into being, who the people were who settled the land the ranch encompasses, the character of the land itself, and the elements of the fellowship program. These aspects are inextricably mixed into the activities of the writers and artists at Paisano, the subject of the last five chapters. I believe all these things are responsible for the success of this remarkable venture.

Part One

The Setting

The Dobie Paisano Project

J. FRANK DOBIE

Some people mistakenly believe that Frank Dobie donated the relatively small property (254 acres) on Barton Creek that he acquired in 1959 to the University of Texas at Austin as a retreat for writers. He would have heartily approved of using the property as a place to encourage young writers, but that is not what happened.

During his lifetime, Frank Dobie was probably the most famous writer in Texas. In a bibliography of Dobie's work, Lowell Mick White remarks that "his long career teaching at the University of Texas, his famous feud with the university's board of regents, his newspaper columns, radio commentaries, magazine articles, and books all helped make him the most widely known and influential writer in the state....During his long career Dobie wrote twenty-six books, more than five hundred magazine articles, and over twelve hundred newspaper columns."[1] His friend Lon Tinkle, a longtime professor of French at Southern Methodist University and book editor for the Dallas Morning News, titled one chapter of his biography of Dobie "Mr. Texas," an epithet frequently applied to him.[2]

Gradually, over the decades following his death, Dobie became less and less well known for his writing. His name tended to be associated more with an Austin mall and an Austin middle school. Children recognized him as one of three figures depicted in Glenna Goodacre's sculpture Philosopher's Rock in Zilker Park. Many enjoy climbing over and around the figures of Dobie and his literary friends and companions, Walter Prescott Webb and Roy Bedichek. Even as his importance as a writer waned, Dobie continued to be known as a storyteller. In George West, Texas, site of an annual storyfest, organizers felt it was a good time to reintroduce Dobie's writing to young readers. On November 4, 2011, various Texas authors read their favorite passages from Dobie's writing. Former Paisano fellows Jan Reid and Stephen Harrigan participated with other Texas writers at Dobie Dichos, "a night of campfire cooking, book signing, and Texas authors reading from the work of the master Texas storyteller (Live Oak County born and raised), J. Frank Dobie."[3] Dobie Dichos has become an annual tradition at the festival.

Much debate about Dobie's writing took place in the first decades after his death, such as Larry McMurtry's essay "In a Narrow Grave," but the arguments have largely died down. Instead of arguments, assessments are being made about his place in Texas and national letters. In 2005, a panel at the annual meeting of the Texas Historical Society, "Whatever Happened to J. Frank Dobie?" traced his influence on education, folklore, literature, and political and cultural commentary. A day-long conference sponsored by the Southwestern Writers Collection at Texas State

University in connection with an exhibit of Dobie works in 2006 was titled Mr. Texas. Don Graham, the J. Frank Dobie Regents Professor of English and American Literature at the University of Texas at Austin, wrote in 1988: "His legacy as a literary pioneer seems secure."[4]

Three decades after the Lon Tinkle biography, Steven Davis, Curator of the Southwestern Writers Collection, provided a new assessment of Dobie's life and legacy.[5] The Davis biography and various Dobie events at the Southwest Writers Collection bridge a long gap between the revered "Mr. Texas" and the J. Frank Dobie we recognize now as an important and permanent feature of the Texas literary landscape. Many of his works are now available in the J. Frank Dobie Paperback Library from University of Texas Press.

FRANK AND BERTHA DOBIE'S ORIGINS

Brief historical sketches outlining the lives and accomplishments of Frank and Bertha Dobie were published for a special ceremony honoring them in May 1988 at Southwestern University in Georgetown, Texas, where they both graduated in 1910.[6] According to the sketches, the importance of books and education in their early lives informed their long careers in teaching and writing. "J. (James) Frank Dobie was born on a ranch in Live Oak County on September 26, 1888, the eldest of the six children of Richard and Ella Dobie. He lived on the family ranch of about seven thousand acres until his sixteenth year, attending one-teacher ranch schools built by his father and neighbors. At one time he said, 'We had more books in our house and more flowers in our yard than any other ranch home in that part of the country.'" Similarly, Bertha Dobie was the child of teachers. She lived in several small towns in Texas, chiefly in Velasco, where her parents taught in a three-room school and her father was also superintendent.

Both Dobies majored in English at Southwestern and both later pursued graduate degrees. Frank Dobie taught briefly at Southwestern but then went on to Columbia University, where he received an MA in English. Later he was to receive several honorary degrees. Bertha Dobie received an MA in English from the University of Texas at Austin. She substituted for her husband many times in the course he created in 1930, Life and Literature of the Southwest.

Dobie joined the faculty of the University of Texas at Austin in 1914 and, except for three leaves of absence, he remained on the faculty until 1947. Those periods were for army service, 1917–19; a year managing his uncle Jim's Los Olmos Ranch in Live Oak County, 1920–1921; and two years as chair of the English department at Oklahoma A&M University (now known as Oklahoma State University–Stillwater), 1923–1924. Jon Schwartz, the author of the Southwestern University sketches, tells of Dobie's tenure: "A self-styled 'outlaw of the campus,' Dobie was often at odds with the UT administration, but his course Life and Literature of the Southwest was known as the most popular one on campus. He was made a full professor in 1933, the first native Texan without a PhD degree to receive a full professorship in the university's English department."[7]

A number of often-repeated anecdotes about Dobie give a somewhat misleading impression of him. It is true that he never obtained a PhD and often had harsh words for pedantic scholarship, expressing his disdain of candidates for the doctorate who "merely transfer bones from one graveyard to another."[8] Even so, he was a committed teacher and spent his whole career with people who were interested in books and writing. His diatribe about the architecture of the university tower ("it looked like a toothpick in a pie and ought to be laid on its side and have galleries put around it"[9]) and his jibes about the sculptor Pompeo Coppini's fountain on the south end of the campus might suggest an out-and-out anti-intellectual who did not appreciate the finer things in life; such a characterization is simply not true. He was outspoken and opinionated but revered the glories of the English language. His years during World War II teaching at Cambridge were enormously meaningful to him. In his articles in National Geographic about those experiences, he expressed his love for the traditions and beauty of England and reaffirmed that Wordsworth was his favorite poet.

His stands against censorship were anything but a joke. He was "outraged and vociferous" about the firing of University of Texas President Homer P. Rainey during fierce debates on academic freedom, and there is more than a little suggestion that the refusal of the university to grant him an additional leave of absence for 1947 was politically motivated. He had frequently taken semesters off due to his terrible "cedar fever" allergies, but his last request was turned down and he left the university permanently.

As his longtime associate in the Texas Folklore Society Francis Abernathy wrote for the Handbook of Texas Online, Frank Dobie's "war against bragging Texans, political, social, and religious restraints on individual liberty, and the mechanized world's erosion of the human spirit was continual."[10]

A LOVE AFFAIR WITH THE LAND

Even though Dobie no longer taught at the university, he and Bertha continued to live in the house they had bought in 1923 right on the edge of the campus until his death in 1964 (she died in 1974). He did most of his writing there, and Bertha was his ever-helpful editor. When inscribing his books for friends, he usually wrote: "on Waller Creek." But they also shared a love for less-manicured land—for trees and water and bird and animal life.

At the first meeting of the Texas Institute of Letters in 1936, Dobie was the principal speaker at the evening dinner. His remarks were titled "The Earth Remembers," and he advocated that Texas authors write on Texas subjects: "Great literature transcends its native land, but there is none that I know of that ignores its own soil."[11]

Perhaps the hardest thing Dobie ever experienced was the sale of his family's ranch in 1951. He wrote to his sister,

"I feel that an end has come to something of a lifetime. I could not feel thus towards any other plot of ground, not at all towards these lots on Waller Creek where I have spent so many years. Something irreplaceable has passed from me. Perhaps I should have kept my part of the ranch and not have sold it, but I did not feel that I could keep up with the Houston millionaires, who no doubt will spend a deal of money on improvements. I know and like a great many people who do not mean so much to me as the ranch. It has been next to Mama in something to go to."[12]

CHERRY SPRINGS RANCH

While their home on Waller Creek in Austin was always their principal residence, in 1951 the Dobies bought a 746-acre ranch near Marble Falls in a purchase perhaps made possible by the sale of his father's ranch. The property was called Cherry Springs, and the Dobies enjoyed its uncultivated fields full of wildflowers and native grasses. Dobie wrote at the time, "No matter what improvements are put on ranch land, its essential worth consists of the grass it grows and nothing else."[13]

They would have continued to retreat to this haven of wild cherry trees and good water if Dobie's health hadn't begun to seriously deteriorate. In 1958 he suffered a severe heart attack at Cherry Springs. In 2000, Pauline Edwards Delaney, the next owner of the property, gave a talk for the Houston Literary Ladies Club in which she described what took place:

> He made it to the hall telephone, lifted the receiver and cranked the handle. The next thing he knew, he was in the hospital in Austin. Cranking the telephone for the operator not only rang the operator's bell, it also rang the telephones in every ranch house on the eight-party line. A late night ring of the telephone meant someone needed help. Everyone on the line, of course, jumped out of bed

and picked up his receiver. Not to listen in was bad manners. When no one responded to the operator's urgent plea, for "Number please," the neighbors, still on the line began asking each other if everyone was all right. When Dobie didn't respond, the nearest neighbor and his wife threw sweaters and jackets over their nightclothes, jumped in their truck, his wife rang the operator to let everyone know what was happening. They drove to the hospital in Johnson City, where the doctor did what he could, then sent Dobie by ambulance to Austin. "Always keep that telephone," Dobie said.[14]

Delaney kept Dobie's promise; she donated the telephone to Paisano. Although it is not a working phone, and Paisano is itself no longer on an eight-party line, its presence in the Paisano kitchen helps preserve that era for present-day residents.

Delaney and her then husband Mac Edwards weren't able to go out to Cherry Springs the first few years after they acquired the ranch, as Edwards's work was located in London for several years, but they kept in touch with the Dobies whenever they returned to Texas.

Delaney described one of their visits:

> The next August we came home on leave. The first thing we did, after checking in with family and friends in Houston, was go to Cherry Springs. On the drive from Houston to Austin we wondered if the Dobies might be interested in visiting. Their letters indicated that Frank's health was much improved and the tone of the letters was certainly friendly. We decided that the worst thing they could do was say, "Thanks, but no thanks." So we stopped in Austin, looked the number up in the telephone directory, and dialed.
>
> Bertha Dobie answered. She was delighted to

hear from us. And would they like to visit Cherry Springs? Indeed they would. How about lunch tomorrow? Edgar would drive them of course. (Bertha Dobie explained that Edgar Kinkaid was their nephew and had lived with them after his mother died many years ago. She identified him as a birdwatcher—"Quite a good one." Kinkaid was thought by many to be one of the leading authorities on Texas birds and in 1974 helped complete the two-volume *The Birds of Texas,* begun by Harry C. Oberholser many years earlier.)

Out at the ranch the next morning, about 10 o'clock, I was in the kitchen peeling potatoes for potato salad, frying chickens, stirring together ice cream makings when Mac, from the front porch, called into the house, "They're here!"

"They can't be," I protested. "It is two hours too soon. I'm not ready!"

I dashed to the porch, and sure enough, a car the color of a blue bird had just come through our front gate. Bertha later told us they bought the car because they had to. The model was the Lark (a small car, one of the last models made by Studebaker).

The front gate is about a mile from the ranch house. Most drivers make that final mile in maybe 15 or 20 minutes, depending on how many cows are in the middle of the road and what other obstacles have appeared during the night. My heart sank. I wanted to meet the Dobies, but I didn't want to meet them with lunch uncooked and my shirttail hanging out. Then I noticed the car was moving extremely slowly. Every so often it would stop, then inch forward then stop again.

At exactly 12 noon, the bluebird blue car pulled up to the yard gate and Frank and Bertha Dobie, their eyes shining, got out. They were followed by an angular young man swathed in a coat that flapped open like the wings of a flightless bird. All three of them had binoculars dangling from their necks.

"What a welcome," boomed Frank Dobie. "We saw a belted kingfisher, two orioles, a black chinned hummingbird, killdeer of course, a red tail..."

"Don't forget the painted bunting," Mrs. Dobie said.

Delaney and Edwards kept in touch with the Dobies until Frank Dobie's death and later made sure Bertha Dobie and her nephew Edgar Kinkaid were always welcome at the old ranch.[15]

PAISANO

The Dobies weren't without a retreat for long. After his heart attack, Dobie purchased a farm near Austin, but that place did not really suit him. In 1959, they purchased the property on Barton Creek only 10–15 miles from Austin that would become known as Paisano. In the 1970s, when invited out to the property by one of the fellows, John Henry Faulk recounted going with Dobie to look over the property before he purchased it and how much they both admired it from the outset.[16]

Dobie first thought of calling his place the Wild Gobbler Ranch, but decided on Paisano, a name of Spanish origin used in the Southwest to denote the roadrunner. He was also familiar with other regional meanings of the word— "compatriot," "native," and "rustic." The roadrunner image, the symbol of the Texas Folklore Society, became his personal symbol, and he used it on bookplates and elsewhere.[17]

As with the Cherry Springs property, he and Bertha considered Paisano a place for friends to gather and discuss life and literature. To Dobie, Paisano was "not an estate, not a ranch, not a farm, it is merely a place of some acres in the hills west of Austin, Barton Creek winding through it."[18]

FRANK DOBIE'S FRIENDS AND ASSOCIATES

A gregarious man, Dobie spent much of his time sharing

his thoughts with others. Despite his separation from the university, a stream of visitors continued to make their way to their comfortable backyard on Waller Creek or out to the wide stone gallery (porch) at Paisano.

Dobie's death on September 18, 1964, affected the Texas literary community deeply; the outpouring of praise and tribute when he died is evident in a special supplement to the book pages of the Austin American-Statesman that was published a short time later.[19] The Statesman had intended to review his most recent book, Cow People, copies of which reached him the very day of his death, but a much larger tribute was required.

Frank Wardlaw, who came to the university to establish University of Texas Press in 1950, had become a fast friend and companion of Dobie. The two had liked each other instantly. Wardlaw's decision to focus the press, in part, on regional publishing was influenced by Dobie, and Dobie advised him on many early manuscripts.

Wardlaw's eulogy at the funeral in Hogg Auditorium on the Austin campus was eloquent:

> On September 18, 1964, J. Frank Dobie died quietly in his sleep in his home on the banks of Waller Creek in Austin, nine days before his seventy-sixth birthday and two days before his forty-eighth wedding anniversary.
>
> It had been a good week for Frank Dobie. His wife Bertha had just returned from the White House where she had accepted on his behalf the Medal of Freedom together with a kiss, which was strictly for her, from the President of the United States (Lyndon Johnson). The morning mail had brought the first copies of his new book Cow People from Boston, this time encased in a jacket which he really liked. Rain had fallen on his beloved ranch Paisano, quickening the parched rocky hillsides with new life and sending Barton Creek surging down its long-dry bed.[20]

Wardlaw set the tone and atmosphere for honoring his and Texas's great friend. Other tributes followed: from Mody Boatright, who served as associate editor on the series Publications of the Texas Folklore Society, beginning in 1937; Harry Huntt Ransom, chancellor of the University of Texas, who had met Dobie when Ransom first came to the university thirty years earlier; F. Warren Roberts, director of the Humanities Research Center; Walker Stone, editor-in-chief of Scripps-Howard Newspapers, who had been a student of Dobie's when he taught at Oklahoma A&M; Dorman Winfrey, director and librarian of the Texas State Library; John Henry Faulk, who had been a student of Dobie's; Joe B. Frantz, a history professor at the University of Texas and close friend and student of Walter Prescott Webb; Lawrence Powell, dean of the School of Library Service (now the Department of Information Studies) at the University of California, Los Angeles; Wilson Hudson, also a UT Austin English professor and fellow folklorist; Edmund Heinsohn, the pastor emeritus of the University Methodist Church; Ned Bradford, editor-in-chief of Little, Brown, publisher of many of Dobie's books; and Henderson Shuffler, at that time curator of the Dobie Collection in the University Academic Center, now the Flawn Academic Center, at UT Austin.

More tributes from friends from over the state and nation followed. Over the years, biographical sketches appeared and eventually, his colleague Lon Tinkle brought out his meticulously researched biography in 1978.[21]

THE TEXAS INSTITUTE OF LETTERS

Tinkle and Wardlaw were among the friends of Dobie who actively pursued literary matters in Texas in an organization established in 1936—the Texas Institute of Letters. Inspired by various Texas Centennial activities and celebrations, a group of writers and teachers of literature met at the Hall of State on the grounds of the Centennial Exposition (the Texas state fairgrounds) to "promote interest in Texas literature and to recognize literary and cultural achievement."[22] TIL, as it is often called, continues its more than seventy-five-year tradition of recognizing Texas writers and their literary achievement with a wide range of prizes.

A full-scale history of the organization was written by William H. Vann, one of the founders, in 1966.[23] Lon Tinkle, another of the founders, credited Frank Dobie with much of the success of the early organization, though at first Dobie almost declined to become a member.[24]

In the preface to Vann's history, Tinkle writes:

> Surprisingly, it was that ferocious individualist J. Frank Dobie who most shaped and set the tone for the first quarter century of life of the Texas Institute of Letters. Dobie was the enemy of impersonal institutionalism in all its forms; he despised its worship of mere efficiency, its unconscious worship of power structures. Certainly he was a violent opponent of provincialism and of the phenomenon known as "Texas brags." But he was animated by a spirit of fraternity and by a belief in the fruitful and good and useful exchange of ideas between enlightened and civilized minds.

He adds that "without Dobie's staunch supervision, the Institute might very well have become what always threatens the institutionalizing of the arts, a back-slapping, herd-organization of stuffed shifts and their hangers-on." Tinkle was insistent that from the beginning, the regionalism that an organization like TIL implies must be interpreted broadly. "What Dobie and others in the Institute meant by 'regional writer' was not one who vaunted his little plot of earth above all others but one who lives in a daily environment of concrete objects (nature and architecture), of concrete fellow-citizens, of concrete values."[25]

Martin Shockley, professor of English at North Texas State University, succeeded Vann as secretary-treasurer. In his brief account of TIL based on Vann's more extensive history, Shockley, too, recognizes the importance of Dobie to the organization, writing "through the years, Mr. Dobie became, first, the Institute's most famous writer, later, its elder statesman, and, finally, its patron saint."[26]

Criticism was directed from time to time to the group for choosing the wrong books to recognize or for failing to include promising writers. Its very name sometimes drew ridicule as being pretentious. In 1936, however, the committee, knowing of no similar organizations in Texas, modeled it after the American Academy of Arts and Letters, but chose the term institute rather than academy.

The principal activity of TIL was to make awards for books either by a Texas author or on a Texas subject. The first non-Texan to get a TIL award was Paul Horgan, whose Great River was later to win a Pulitzer Prize.

While serious about the mission of the TIL, its members were noted for their conviviality. For some years, a group met the morning after the awards ceremony, calling themselves the Texas Institute of the Unlettered, to commiserate with those who did not win awards—at least those who had enough of a sense of humor not to take themselves seriously.

Frank Dobie won the award for the best Texas book of the year three times and served as president of TIL from 1953–1957. Though he was in many ways the heart and soul of the organization, there were many others—distinguished writers, teachers, and some publishers (such as Wardlaw at University of Texas Press and Allen Maxwell at Southern Methodist University Press)—who carried on the organization's work after his death.

HOW TO HONOR DOBIE

Someone as vital to an organization as Dobie was to the Texas Institute of Letters needed to be suitably remembered. According to Tinkle, Dobie's many friends started "dreaming up memorial ideas right away. One notion was to purchase by public subscription the famous old Ursuline Academy on the river in downtown San Antonio, a property then for sale, and convert it into a Western Museum named in Dobie's honor."[27] At a meeting of the Philosophical Society of Texas in Austin on December 5, 1964, Bertha Dobie and close friends Wardlaw and Tinkle discussed the possibility of using Paisano as a retreat for writers.

Bertha Dobie's health had never been strong. Although she enjoyed trips out to Paisano, and she and Dobie occasionally entertained friends out there, she felt it was primarily Frank's place to spend time with his friends, and she did not consider keeping the property after he was gone. She heartily endorsed the project.

WARDLAW HEADS THE DOBIE PAISANO PROJECT

Not long after that December meeting, Wardlaw took the lead in getting the project going. Though there were many other supporters, without Wardlaw's exhaustive efforts, a project of this character might never have come about.

He prepared two brochures, both of which included a reproduction of Tom Lea's defining portrait of Dobie.[28] The first brochure (July 1965) presented the details of the project in clear, simple terms. From the outset, the organizers envisioned raising money to buy the ranch from Dobie's estate and donating it to the university. The university would conduct it as a permanent memorial to J. Frank Dobie, and its use would be "restricted to purposes appropriate to this general principle." The primary use of Paisano would be to encourage creative artistic effort in all fields, particularly in writing. It was hoped that it would be a place where creative writers could go and work and where small groups could occasionally get together.

Paisano would be kept in its present (1965) more or less natural state. It would be a nature sanctuary with hunting perpetually prohibited. The ranch house itself would be kept in simple style "much as it was when Frank Dobie occupied it." Some of the furnishings would be kept there so the place would "always have an authentic Dobie flavor."

Wardlaw took all the proper steps to outline the details

of the gift to the regents of the university. By the time the first brochure was distributed, Wardlaw was able to assure contributors that the university would agree to accept the property on the terms mentioned above.

The brochure outlined preliminary plans for funding the fellowships and recommended the appointment of an advisory board. Wardlaw appointed a steering committee, all friends of Frank Dobie. This group of prominent business leaders, academic colleagues, and publishers included Dillon Anderson, Mody Boatright, Glen Evans, John Henry Faulk, O'Neil Ford, George Fuermann, Herbert Gambrell, Fred Gipson, John Graves, Wilson Hudson, Peter Hurd, Ralph Johnston, Tom Lea, Holland McCombs, Allen Maxwell, John Meaney, J. R. Parten, Walker Stone, Jay Taylor, Lon Tinkle, Frank E. Vandiver, and Wardlaw himself.

There was some urgency about purchase of the ranch because of the need to settle Dobie's estate. Ralph Johnston, a Houstonian who had become a friend and admirer of Dobie, bought Paisano outright to provide time for fundraising. He later contributed 10 percent of its purchase price of $76,200. This was only the beginning of the generosity of Johnston and his family. After his death in 1966, the Johnston Foundation continued to provide financial support for the writers' fellowships. It was — and remains — the only continuous financial support for the writers' fellowships. (A brief description of funding for the project through the years can be found in chapter 4.)

In 2000, Gladys Watford, Johnston's long time executive secretary and a longtime trustee of the Johnston Foundation, described Johnston's friendship with Dobie:

> Ralph Johnston first met Dobie through Walker (Red) Stone, a Scripps-Howard editor in Washington. Johnston and his brother Bill had been friends of Stone for many years and had given him hunting privileges on their Seco Ranch in Medina County. Each hunting season, Stone had the

privilege of inviting a group of his friends to hunt with the Johnstons on their ranch.

It was in the late fifties when Stone invited Dobie to join the group for a deer and turkey hunt. Stone had been in a class of Dobie's at Oklahoma A&M (later Oklahoma State University) in the 1920s, and they had stayed in touch.

Johnston and Dobie had an immediate rapport. They were kindred spirits and both had an inborn love of the land. Johnston loved Dobie's tales and became an ardent fan of his works. Evenings were spent in front of a roaring fire exchanging stories and listening to Dobie's tales of nature and wildlife. A real companionship developed among a very diverse group.

As long as his health permitted, Dobie joined the group at Seco Ranch. He wrote numerous articles about his experiences on these hunts. Although their friendship covered only the last few years of Dobie's life, Johnston had great admiration and affection for J. Frank Dobie.[29]

Dobie's last book, *Cow People*, had been dedicated to Ralph Johnston and Walker Stone.

THE GREAT ART AUCTION IN HOUSTON

The fundraiser to purchase Paisano and repay Johnston for holding the property off the market was a gala to be remembered. It combined a dinner and an art auction in the Crystal Ballroom of the Rice Hotel in Houston on May 11, 1966. It was designed to appeal to the philanthropy of prominent Texas oilmen, businessmen, ranchers, and of course, anyone who wanted to share in the memorial for Frank Dobie. The dinner and auction was not an official project of the Texas Institute of Letters, although most of those responsible for organizing the affair were TIL members.

Ralph Johnston was himself a prominent member of

Houston society, able to mount a lavish occasion. A scant two years after he died, Dobie continued to be a revered figure in Texas. Raising money in his honor was accomplished with no problems.

The second brochure, created for the occasion (May 11, 1966), again presented the precise details of the project. It mentioned that the first gift to the project had come from President and Mrs. Lyndon Johnson and named several individuals and foundations that had already promised funds.

A miniature version of the brochure was included in the actual dinner and auction invitation. Lloyd Gregory, an advertising executive from Houston, and Wardlaw cochaired the dinner; Stanley Marcus was the principal speaker.

Participants were invited to become sponsors or patrons. Sponsors who contributed $25 were entitled to one ticket for each $25 contributed; patrons contributing $200 could reserve a table for eight.

Separately, contributors could purchase a facsimile reproduction of Tom Lea's portrait of J. Frank Dobie—the same portrait featured on both brochures—for $35. Each reproduction was signed by Lea. The Meriden Gravure Company donated two hundred copies for the fundraising. Today, reproductions of the Lea portrait can be seen at the Dobie House on campus and out at Paisano Ranch.

The dinner honored Mrs. Dobie, Ralph Johnston, and the twenty Southwestern artists who donated their paintings for the art auction: Jerry Bywaters, Otis Dozier, Alexandre Hogue, Peter Hurd, William Lester, E. M. (Buck) Schiwetz, Olin Travis, John Biggers, Bill Bomar, Kelly Fearing, Michael Frary, John Guerin, Gillis King, Tom Lea, A. Kelly Pruitt, Everett Spruce, Bror Utter, Olaf Weighorst, Donald Weismann, and Ralph White. Many of the artists are still well known today. The auctioneer was Walter S. Britten, who had conducted the auction at the Houston Fat Stock Show shortly before the Paisano benefit.

The twenty paintings were reproduced in miniature in black-and-white in the brochure. Two, by Gillis King and

Donald Weismann, were of scenes at Paisano and two others, by William Lester and Ralph White, were of nearby landscapes. After their purchase at the auction, the Weismann, Lester, and White paintings were donated to Paisano, where they remain.

An article in Entre Nous Houston, a short-lived Houston society magazine that described itself as "The journal of vital people, elegant places, and interesting things"[30] is unsigned, but the tone and language indicates that the magazine had dispatched its best society reporter to the gala. He or she enthusiastically gushed:

> The glittering names gathered together for this evening were a rare blend of raw power, refinement, roughcut Westerners, education, philanthropy, and the golden tinkle of money in the air. In other words a polite and agreeable mixture which has made the Southwest the rugged force that it is, and Houston the metropolis of that awesome power.
>
> It was almost a show staged by what can be loosely referred to as the Stock Show Crowd, which insured its success right there. One of their philanthropic members, Ralph A. Johnston, an oil man and close friend of the late J. Frank Dobie, was on the hook for $76,000 and it was the prime mission of the dinner to get him off it, as well as do what can only be lauded as one of the finest contributions to the arts in the Southwest in many years.

The smallest details of the art purchases were noted, as were Stanley Marcus's beard and the "youthful beauty" of Oveta Culp Hobby, the publisher of the Houston Post, who was also well known as the first director of the Women's Army Corps during World War II.

The auction raised some $40,000, and other gifts totaled $25,000. Ralph Johnston was repaid but had already agreed to contribute 10 percent of the $76,200 purchase price for the 254 acres.

THE TRANSFER TO THE UNIVERSITY OF TEXAS

Wardlaw immediately set out to arrange for the transfer of the property to the university. University attorney Burnell Waldrep prepared a proposed deed for Mr. Johnston, and the board of regents accepted the gift at their meeting of July 8–9, 1966. The regents' agenda contained all the points made in the brochures Wardlaw had prepared for contributors. Chancellor Harry Ransom reiterated all items in a July 21, 1966, memorandum for the chancellor's file.[31]

On August 6, 1966, two days before Ralph Johnston's death, he signed the deed giving Paisano to the university. Few people had known about his terminal illness during the campaign to save Paisano.[32]

ENDNOTES

1 Lowell Mick White, *Mr. Texas: A Research Guide to the Work of J. Frank Dobie* (unpublished), 1. Copies in Southwestern Writers Collection, Texas State University, and Center for American History at the University of Texas at Austin.

2 Lon Tinkle, *An American Original: The Life of J. Frank Dobie* (New York: Little Brown, 1978), chapter 4.

3 George West Storyfest, November 4, 2011. http://www.georgeweststoryfest.org/events/2015/dobie-dichos.

4 Larry McMurtry, "Southwestern Literature?" in *In a Narrow Grave: Essays on Texas* (Austin: Encino Press, 1968); "Whatever Happened to Frank Dobie?" *Texas State Historical Association 2005*; "J. Frank Dobie — Mr. Texas" (symposium of the Southwestern Writers Collection, Alkek Library, Texas State University, San Marcos, TX, April 8, 2006); Don Graham, "J. Frank Dobie: A Reappraisal," *Southwestern Historical Quarterly* 42:1 (1988), 1–15. Reprinted in *The Texas Book* (Austin: University of Texas Press, 2006).

5 Steven L. Davis, *J. Frank Dobie: A Liberated Mind* (Austin: University of Texas Press, 2009).

6 Jon D. Swartz. *Historical sketches of J. Frank Dobie and Bertha McKee Dobie*, prepared for their induction into the Hall of Honor, Mood-Heritage Museum, Southwestern University, Georgetown, May 1, 1988, unpaged.

7 Ibid.

8 J. Frank Dobie, *Guide to Life and Literature of the Southwest with a Few Observations*, from chapter 1, A Declaration. https://www.gutenberg.org/files/314/314-h/314-h.htm. Accessed August 23, 2018.

9 *A Portrait of Pancho: The Life of a Great Texan, J. Frank Dobie* by Winston Bode (Austin: Pemberton Press, 1965).

10 "Dobie, James Frank," *The Handbook of Texas Online*. https://tshaonline.org/handbook/online/articles/fdo02. Accessed January 22, 2016.

11 William H. Vann, *The Texas Institute of Letters, 1936–1966* (Austin: Encino Press, 1967).

[12] Tinkle, *American Original,* 209.

[13] Ibid., 213.

[14] Pauline Edwards Delaney, "J. Frank Dobie's Home in the Hill Country," *Houston Chronicle Magazine,* June 9, 1996.

[15] Delaney, "Frank and Bertha Dobie," a talk for the Houston Ladies Literary Club, spring 2000.

[16] John Henry Faulk, personal communication, 1984.

[17] "Dobie, James Frank," *Handbook of Texas.*

[18] Dobie, J. Frank, *Rattlesnakes* (Austin: University of Texas Press, 1982), 91.

[19] "J. Frank Dobie," Special Supplement, *Austin American-Statesman,* October 25, 1964.

[20] Frank Wardlaw, *Statesman* Special Supplement.

[21] Tinkle, *An American Original.*

[22] John Edward Weems, "The Texas Institute of Letters," *Handbook of Texas Online.* https://tshaonline.org/handbook/online/articles/kqt01. Accessed January 22, 2016.

[23] Vann, *Texas Institute of Letters.*

[24] Betty Wiesepape, "Setting the Record Straight on 'Mr. TIL'," *Dallas Morning News,* August 7, 2005, Section G, 9.

[25] Vann, *Texas Institute of Letters,* x.

[26] Martin Shockley, *The Texas Institute of Letters,* unpaged, n.d. (probably 1970).

[27] "Writer to Get a Chance: Dallas Man to Use Dobie Scholarship," *Dallas Morning News,* July 11, 1970.

[28] *The Dobie-Paisano Project,* Austin, Texas, July 16, 1965.

[29] Gladys Watford, personal account, 2000.

[30] "Success of Paisano Project Now Assured," *Entre Nous, June* 1966, 53–63.

[31] Regents' Agenda, July 8, 9, 1966, Chancellor's File, July 21, 1966.

[32] "Paisano Ranch," *Handbook of Texas Online.* https://tshaonline.org/handbook/online/articles/app01. Accessed January 22, 2016.

The Ranch Property

Paisano speaks beyond the page…it promises the
eye, the ear, and the heart that nothing needs to
change and disappear, or if it changes it may not
have to change very much, and it can be for the
better.
— A. C. Greene, *Paisano*

A BIRD'S-EYE VIEW

The three things J. Frank Dobie claimed were all a person
needed for suitable habitat were grass, water, and trees;
judged by these criteria, Paisano's 253.96 acres are a place
where an individual can not only survive, but thrive. Dobie
himself, through the sort of deliberate, benign inattention that

works best to heal the wrung-out face of the Hill Country, began to turn hardscrabble back into native grass where he could. The decades the property has spent lying fallow since then continue that work. Paisano's acres now contain enough vegetation that approaching the house from the gravel road onto the property is like cleaving a green bowl from lip to lip. Spanish oaks, descendants of those whose acorns made the area hospitable to native populations thousands of years ago, sink their roots wherever there is water enough to support them. The wind still rustles the cottonwoods growing along Barton Creek's curves. Ashe juniper, the same shrubby evergreen locally known as cedar whose pollen made every January miserable for Dobie, has by now almost completely taken over the property. And water? For most of the year, Barton Creek still flows over the low-water crossing below the house, and the nameless boxed-in spring just west of it has enough depth to cool a six-pack of beer.

So *that* is Paisano, geographically speaking — grass, water, and trees, with plenty of rock thrown in for good measure; a superior habitat by Dobie's lights. The trees those early surveyors used to mark the property's boundaries have long since toppled or been felled by lightning. Barton Creek changes course infinitesimally with every flash flood that roars along it. Landmarks that fellowship holders describe matter-of-factly in the residency reports they make at the end of their stay become impossible to reach just six months later due to the growth of the cedar.

But in the largest sense, because it is no longer worked or cleared or grazed, Paisano is if not unchangeable at least changing only slowly. Increasing development between Austin and Bee Cave may make the sound of traffic from Highway 290 louder than it once was from the house, but a visitor who walks the property still sees much that visitors noticed thirty-some-odd years ago, when the Paisano project began; some of it, in fact, is now much wilder than it was then.

THE PROPERTY BOUNDARIES

The heart of Paisano—the portion of land on which the house itself is located and through which Barton Creek mostly flows—is a rectangle of 160 acres (a quarter section) on a north-south axis backing up toward what, when the property was first described in Travis County records, was not yet the community of Bee Cave.

Those early records locate the 160 acres, the original F. Kunze Survey, on Spring Creek, as Barton Creek was then called, about 11 miles west of Austin. Its boundary lines were drawn in *varas*, the unit used to survey Spanish land grants,[1] and were measured from cherry tree to stone mound to live oak to sycamore. In these records, arguably the first written account of the property, the use of natural features to delineate the boundaries illustrates how forcefully the landscape shapes discussion of Paisano and how deeply a sense of it as a place affects anyone who, for no matter how long or short a time, makes it home.

In 1891, thirty-one years after those original acres were recorded, S. B. Morgan of the adjacent Morgan Ranch sold Paisano's then-owner John D. Wende the final piece of land that now makes up the property: a rough triangle of 88.06 acres from the Hugh Frazier Survey and a strip of 5.9 acres from the Tyler Tap RR Co Survey that lay north of the Kunze tract.[2] Wende paid Morgan one hundred dollars for the land. In return, he received some of Paisano's most striking scenery: the section that contains the top of the S-bend Barton Creek makes through the property, the high limestone bluffs above the creek, and the swimming hole some Paisano fellowship holders have claimed is the property's finest.

PAISANO'S GENERAL LANDSCAPE

Paisano sits just to the west of the Balcones Escarpment, the geologic fault zone running from Del Rio to the Red River that separates the Edwards Plateau of Texas from the Coastal Plains. In its small way, the property reflects many of the larger topographical, geographical, and social forces the Balcones Escarpment exerts upon the face of this part of Texas.

"Dramatic changes in the landscape occur across this crustal discontinuity," write geologists C. M. Woodruff and Patrick L. Abbott in their preface to *The Balcones Escarpment*:

> On the west are plateau uplands and ruggedly dissected limestone hills. Soils are thin and stony, and the main agricultural use of the land is for range. The dominant native vegetation assemblage is juniper-live oak savannah, and groundwater is generally of good quality with ample quantities occurring at shallow depths from limestone aquifers.[3]

Reflecting this, Paisano consists mostly of rocky hills composed of Cretaceous-era limestone overlaid with inches of the shallow soil sometimes called Brackett soil. A few small pockets of deeper, slightly more fertile soil line the flat areas along Grape and Barton Creeks.[4]

Because Paisano has been left relatively untouched for over fifty years now, it can be difficult to remember that before Dobie purchased the property, the land was mostly cultivated or grazed. The landscape itself can be divided into four distinct topographies: the areas right around the house and yard, the cedar-studded areas that used to be pastures, the few sections of formerly cultivated fields along the creeks, and the creekbeds of Barton and Grape Creeks and the high cliffs that flank them. The property's previous occupants greatly shaped three of those four topographies — the landscape around the house, the former pastures, and the areas that used to be fields along the creeks.

Water shaped the fourth, most distinctive, topography, and in turn influenced the property's human occupation. Native tribes were drawn to the area by its abundance of water and game. The house itself was probably located on the flat, high land above the intersection of Barton and Grape

Creeks because of the proximity of fresh water (the house site is also just a few yards east of a boxed-in spring that served the house, as well as a wet-weather creek called Myrtle or Spring Branch). The Hartwig cabin, the only other dwelling still in existence on the property, sits just to the north of Thomas Springs Branch's curve across the eastern property line and back out again. Grape Creek wanders along the western property line until it joins forces with Barton Creek, creating more of a physical boundary between Paisano and the neighboring property than any fence line. Soil deposited by both Barton and Grape Creeks formed the property's few pockets of farmable land.

THE PROPERTY'S FLORA

The property is covered with Ashe juniper cedar, the much-maligned "brush" of the Hill Country. Commonly, cedar tends to shoulder out other plant species, but because Paisano has gone so many years ungrazed, the cedars on the property are intermixed with pockets of native grass— little bluestem, side oats, grama, tall dropseed, Indian grass and mesquitegrass, according to a survey of grasses Dobie requested during his lifetime—and with cedar elm, sycamore, and Spanish oak along the creek beds. The banks of Grape Creek are a tangle of the creek's namesake mustang grapevines; hints of the property's previous occupants can be found in the fig trees behind the house and in the little hard pears that fall from the trees along the western edge of the yard. Spring to midsummer, wildflowers—from Turk's cap to black-eyed Susan—grow in profusion on the flatter sections of the property. In late summer, Texas persimmons drop their fruit along the fence line around the house among the agarita and prickly pear cactus.

THE PROPERTY'S FAUNA

Writing about Paisano's animal life often becomes a way fellows try to articulate how it feels to spend time on the property. At the end of poet Todd Hearon's fellowship

(2003), he introduced his final report by saying, "Two days into my stay I wrote in my journal that I had yet to encounter the legendary Paisano wildlife. The next day, as if awaiting official record of my interest, the wildlife started to appear." Since the program's earliest days, fellows have recorded sightings of wildlife in their final reports, "animal watching," as fiction writer James Hannah put it in his, adding that he sometimes found himself rereading final reports he was especially fond of, "mostly the odd ones from city slickers who found the interplay of nature delightful and horrifying (as if lions hunted impala just over the fence under the junipers)."

The proximity of the Austin Zoo means that lions actually can be heard from the gallery of the house, particularly in the early mornings. In the program's earliest years, fellows mentioned the property's feral goats; more recently, longhorn from the adjacent Morgan Ranch have been visitors to the house. White-tail deer, lured by the feed some fellows scatter for them, visit the yard on a regular basis. At night, coyotes keep up a doleful chorus, and dogs belonging to fellows have tangled with porcupine, skunks, and in at least one instance, rattlesnakes. Fellows have written of spotting bobcats, foxes, raccoons, possums, rabbits, armadillos, and a variety of birds, lizards, insects, and snakes.

Even before Dobie's ownership, E. J. Rissmann, grandson of early owners John and Mary Wende, wrote in his unpublished recollection "Paisano and Periphery" that he remembered that when he was young "rattlesnakes came around the house for water...they liked to lie on window ledges, where they were often found at sunup, or stretched out on the edge of the gallery or on the grass."[5] In a 1964 tribute to Dobie, Frank Wardlaw reminisced about a visit to the ranch when not only did three deer run "lightly and without fear across the rock-strewn hillside above the house," but one of the men who earlier in the day that been setting out trees along the banks of Barton Creek saw "a large snake and, while he was looking for something to kill it with, encountered a bobcat, which caused him to forget all about the snake."[6]

THE APPROACH TO THE RANCH

Unlike any native populations that long ago lingered along the creeks and springs dotting Paisano, most modern visitors have lost the knack—if they ever possessed it—for getting their bearings by noting the subtle rise and fall of land or by scrutinizing cedar and oak trees. Instead, we tend to rely on what's most familiar to us to orient ourselves. At Paisano, this tends to be the main road. This dusty man-made connection between the outside world and the house takes up the lion's share of space in fellows' reports (particularly in musings over whether it can be safely used in times of flood).

As late as the 1910s, it took a half day to travel from Austin to Paisano. Now, the delays encountered along the route are more likely due to sprawl—Paisano being only a few miles as the crow flies from lattes, artisanal cheese, western-wear outlets, and an array of exurban big-box architecture. Once the main highway has been left behind, however, the commercial concerns become a local who occasionally sells jars of honey from the lowered tailgate of his pickup and a "private club" located cattycorner to a huddle of trailers. The county-maintained paved road becomes a road that has been oiled and graveled, and then, at the Paisano property, even those signs of progress are locked out: from here on, the road is just graded limestone.

For years, entering the property has required a stop at a gate emblazoned with an orange-painted *paisano* by some now-forgotten University of Texas welders. As one pauses there to unlock and then relock the gate, the property makes its forceful presence known. The air smells of the chalky limestone. Juniper cedars crowd close to the road, like inhabitants of some seldom-visited place who have come close to take stock of a stranger. At dusk, the shadows pooling below those cedars have a particular bluish cast, and the limestone shows up cool and white as bone. The wind soughs through the branches of the Spanish oak tree that extends over the road.

In 1966, E. J. Rissman described the road from the gate to the house:

> From the gate the road runs practically straight along a ridge to the left of Thomas Springs Branch, down to Barton, where it makes a sharp turn to the left, then crosses Barton at a tangent over a low-water bridge, and then up a sharp rise to the flat where sits the house.[7]

On a map, the graceful meander the road makes before it crosses the creek and climbs toward the house might be mistaken for one of the curves of Barton Creek. Today, a road crew would choose a more efficient way of getting from here to there, but back when the road was carved out, the path of least resistance seemed the best if not the only way to go, and no one since then has seen much reason to change things, though there are indications that the road may have once crossed Barton Creek at a different location (a change made most likely made due to the danger of high water at the first location).

The Property Lines and the Secondary Creeks

The Paisano gate is located on the property's southern boundary. As the road runs north to the house it follows a high ridge between two secondary creeks—Thomas Springs Branch and Grape Creek—that roughly define the ranch's eastern and western borders.

Thomas Springs Branch, the first of those secondary creeks, is reached by turning right (east) along the fence line at the gate, but only those hardy (or foolhardy) enough to brave the cedar thickets that choke this section of the property have the opportunity to see it. Like the cherry trees and rock mounds in the property's original survey, Thomas Springs Branch is useful mainly because it marks the ranch's eastern boundary.

Grape Creek, on the other hand, serves as more than just a reference point. Reached by turning left (west) at the gate and following an old track half a mile down the fence line past evidence of dry-stacked stone walls, Grape Creek's narrow course roughly follows the western property line. In wet years it lures walkers to its still pools and a miniature waterfall about five feet high. Even when the creek is dry, this area makes for interesting exploring because of the bluffs that line its right-hand (eastern) bank. These bluffs are topped by stacked walls. In his introduction to former fellow (1972–1973) Jim Bones's book of photographs of Paisano, *Texas Heartland,* John Graves hypothesizes that they were built to protect the small arable fields in the bottoms from the cattle that presumably grazed the higher land above the creek.[8] These fields, although obvious when Graves visited the ranch in the 1970s, now have been mostly reabsorbed back into Paisano's larger landscape of brush and trees. Only the walls and the disintegrating fence posts along the western bank of the creek give clues of the area's earlier cultivation.

BARTON CREEK

If the house itself is the heart of Paisano, Barton Creek is its backbone. The creek can be both a friendly introduction to life on the ranch and a reminder of the indifference the property sometimes shows those who reside in the house. Potential fellows receive a letter early in the application process from the current Texas Institute of Letters president that warns that rains sometimes flood the creek, making the low-water crossing from the house to the road impassable. If that letter isn't enough to make residents aware of water's forceful influence on the property, Barton Creek's changeability becomes clear the first time a new fellow fords the low-water crossing and sees the six-foot water gauges that stand on either side of it.

"At the house, stand at the cattle guard and look a mere ten feet ahead of you," wrote fellow Mylène Dressler (2002) in her final report, attempting to convey Barton Creek's power:

> During my stay, this is how high the water rose — in less than an hour. It was astounding to hear the sudden roar, then see water, water everywhere, all around the house, stretching to the opposite canyon, in all directions. And, once I got used to the idea that I no longer owned a Jeep Grand Cherokee, of course I was thrilled by the rage and rush of it.

As hard as it is to imagine during wet years when Barton Creek frustrates residents' attempts to get to — or away from — the ranch, the creek is a ghost of that powerful torrent in drier seasons. "Watching [the creek] has been like a time-lapse-photography lesson in geological change," wrote fellow Lisa Sandlin in her final report (1996):

> First there was water — not flowing really, not deep — but water — until month after month of blue and yellow weather sucked that — and the fishes grander than minnows — away. Then the white rock lay exposed, like the floor of a dry ocean. Then green shoots sprang up through the rocks, hardier and thicker daily. By the pieces of water that remained, a sprinkling of the tiniest yellow flowers on a seaweed stem so delicate as to be invisible; the yellow sprinkles surrounded the water and floated above it. If you stand far enough away in the late afternoon light, now in mid-July, you can see the transformation of these last wet areas almost complete: creek bottom gone to meadowland. When that has dried — a

white bone road. Like everyone else, I hope it
rains.

Although residents sometimes experience both drought
and flood during the same six months at the ranch, Barton
Creek is usually ankle- to knee-deep within Paisano's
boundaries, which makes the low-water crossing below the
house a perfect jumping-off point for exploration of the creek
and gives access to areas of the property that might otherwise
be difficult to reach.

Conversation Rock, the large flat rock rising from the
center of Barton Creek where Dobie is reputed to have
held court, is the first landmark upstream of the crossing.
At this point, the creek's left-hand (eastern) bank consists
of high bluffs that are difficult to access from the creek bed.
The easiest access to these bluffs is from the main road: just
opposite the wide, flat area where evidence of a gravel dig
can be seen, a walker can approach the top of these bluffs
and get a clear view of the house.

As the creek continues to curve to the southwest
upstream of Conversation Rock (the bottom of the S-curve
it makes through the property), the high bluffs gradually
diminish, disappearing into a tangle of grapevines and a
clay bank about 15 feet high just before Grape Creek meets
Barton. A flat area overgrown with cedar and grass lies at the
top of this bank. Still containing traces of the sort of humped
terraces used to combat erosion when sorghum or cotton was
farmed in the area, this field must have been one of Paisano's
pockets of "good" land.[9]

The opposite bank of Barton in this section is a beach-
like section of sand and scrubby debris. Cedar has taken hold
even in this rocky area, making it impossible to see how close
the house actually is to this section of the creek, but a faint
path leads the way from the bank up to the boxed-in spring
and the house.

Another flat section of the property lies a few hundred
yards further upstream. This extensive high, flat area on the

southern bank of the creek may have once served as pasture. It may also have been a home site, if the remnants of the stone walls that cross it are a clue. The eastern property line cuts just beyond this flat, wide, and shallow section of the creek.

If a walker stands at the low-water crossing and follows Barton Creek downstream instead of upstream, they trace the top of the S-curve it makes through the property. Several of Barton's choicest swimming holes lie along the creek here, including a "blue hole" visible from the crossing and a deep spot "about halfway between the low bridge and the eastern property line, near a shady elm tree."[10] Here, a meander in the creek has sliced the left-hand (western) bank into vertical, picturesque cliffs and worn the right-hand (eastern) bank into several sandy beaches often visited by raccoon, coyote, and deer and the last few Morgan longhorn, who have worn a path to the water.

The high cliffs that hew so tightly to the western bank are the main draw along this section of Barton Creek. "Here the canyon wren's tumbling, crystal song pours out in season," wrote the second fellow to reside at Paisano, A. C. Greene, "the chuck-will's-widow calls through the spring nights. Dripping springs, fern surrounded, chime from the rocks and on rare winter days, icicles form like beards off their ledges."[11]

Intrepid hikers approach these limestone bluffs by pushing through the dwarf palmetto and scrub along the western creek bank. The more cautious can access them by walking along the northern property line behind the house and turning to follow a southeasterly draining gully. In wet weather, these bluffs weep moisture and create moss-carpeted seeps that stain the limestone with mineral deposits; throughout the year, their ledges shelter Paisano's shyest wildlife (if the property has ever been home to a mountain lion, as has been occasionally rumored, it might survey its territory from here). Here also, the cliffs create Paisano's best overlook, a flat table rock that juts out over the ribbon of creek far below. According to the late Clay Williams of the Morgan

Ranch, one of his Morgan ancestors once worked his way along bluffs above the creek similar to these and discovered an ancient Indian bow and quiver placed carefully on a sheltered ledge.[12]

Paisano fellows are often seduced by Barton Creek's power and beauty, or healed by the "therapy of the creek," as resident Ewing Campbell (1992) describes it in his final report:

> Except for the echo of water falling from the *barranca* wall, sounding like the seep and drip of a grotto or cavern cathedral, all was silent along that run of the creek. I just stood there, watching the catfish in formation below me, one of them now and then turning in the current, flashing its silver belly. Such moments work miracles in a confused mind, and I am grateful to have had them.

"The creeks at Paisano are controlled by nature, not man..." A. C. Greene concludes. "[Barton Creek] curls and chatters among the rocks, and whispers into dark, tree hung places and pools where the imagination pictures both delights and dangers."[13]

The creek has damaged several cars and risen almost as high as the cattle guard on the road above the low-water crossing, but the house itself has never been flooded.

PAISANO'S MAN-MADE LANDSCAPE

As befits its status as lifeblood of Paisano, water—the vitality of every tiny wet-weather spring, the patina of limestone glimpsed at the bottom of each still clear pool, the vertical bulk of the cliffs above Barton Creek—touches residents profoundly. The beauty of Paisano's watercourses is apparent to even the most inattentive of visitors.

The pastures overrun with cedar cast a subtler spell. On these sections of the property, the emphasis is not on nature's work, but man's. We tend to honor this sort of landscape less but utilize it more. The corrugated metal shed and two-room studio just behind the house are two of the places fellows tend to explore first when they arrive at Paisano. The cement cistern, remainder of a chicken coop, and long, low shed for feeding livestock behind the shed give more evidence of the property's history, as does the barbed wire strung from cedar poles just beyond them to the north.

Here, in the shadows cast by tumbled-down stone walls and oak trees, a wet-weather spring creates a "stock tank" during wet seasons. Just beyond, at the northern edge of this pasture, a dump site full of rusty cans reveals that at one time inhabitants of Paisano must have eaten one flat tin container full of sardines for every sixty Pearl beer cans they church-keyed open and drained and tossed aside to rust, and that at one time the property must have been crisscrossed with dirt roads that made it navigable by pickup truck.

Only two of these "secondary" roads remain. The first, discussed in more detail below, leads to the Hartwig cabin, which sits on Thomas Springs Branch on the eastern property line. The second, which runs north behind the house along the western property line, was affectionately labeled Mockford Boulevard by 2001 resident Patricia Page in recognition of the neighboring landowners who came to her assistance during a particularly wet fall. This road, Paisano's "emergency exit," hugs the ravine of Spring Branch, a dry creek. Large areas of cedar, more former pasture, flank it to the east.

Cedar—or, more correctly, Ashe juniper—has always been scapegoated in the Hill Country. The possibly apocryphal story of the wealthy landowner who chopped down every cedar on his extensive property and was rewarded with the reappearance of water on the place (the idea being that cedars suck up so much water that the creeks no longer flow) is particularly widespread. But most people agree that cedar is more a symptom of how overworked this land has been than it is a cause.[14] Cedar has always existed in this area—just not to the extent that it does now. Cedar seeds much and grows quickly, which makes descriptions of Paisano's northwestern quadrant difficult. Deer paths, one of the only ways to orient oneself, disappear and reappear in response to the animal population. There are few landmarks.

"From behind the house, take 'Mockford Boulevard,'" wrote Page in her final report, describing a way to tackle this part of the property:

> And at the Mockford gate, walk roughly parallel to the fence line. Wonderful views of the hills, the creek, and the house (at certain points). Eventually go down a gulch and up for more bluff walking, sometimes fighting your way through some juniper (don't miss the oaks nearly obscured by them) to the boundary (a road belonging to a gated community is a sign that you've reached the boundary).

To describe this part of Paisano as anything other than "cedary" takes more than a passing acquaintance with Texas botany. But although few people admit to having much of a place in their hearts for the impenetrable barrier immature cedar makes, old-growth cedars provide important habitat for wildlife, including the endangered golden-cheeked warbler. Paisano now contains plenty of the type of mixed cedar and oak woodland, particularly in these ravine and canyon areas, that the golden-cheeked warbler requires for its nests.[15]

The Hartwig Cabin

The same description—cedar, limestone, grass, and sky—fits the area below the house and south of Barton Creek equally well. But while visitors orient themselves primarily by fence lines in the northern section of the property, south of the house the main road serves as the most obvious landmark for visitors. The Hartwig cabin, reached by following a secondary road that branches off the main road and leads to the eastern property line, comes in a close second.

The dilapidated cabin above Thomas Springs Branch is surmised to have been built by the earliest owners of the adjacent property — the Hartwigs — back when surveys were less accurate (the property boundary runs through the cabin itself). Thomas Springs Branch once may have been a reliable source of fresh water near the cabin, but the site lacks any evidence of the sort of outbuildings usually found around a house. And as John Graves points out in *Texas Heartland*, the soil around the cabin is not good.[16]

Although little information about the cabin's original purpose or owners can be deduced from it now, it is a single-pen cabin consisting of one log room about 16 feet square with side gables, a rear shed, and an exterior chimney centered in one gable wall.[17] The cabin has the sort of Louisiana hipped roof common to East and Central Texas, though the current tin roof and attic flooring (stamped "Calcasieu," the name of a long time Austin lumber yard) are probably later additions. The full dovetail notches in the cabin's corners require more skill than most styles of notching commonly found on Texas cabins and indicate that the builder must have known at least a little about he was doing, as does the sturdy masonry of the fireplace and the stone chinking between the logs.

The Hartwig cabin is one of Paisano's greatest evocations of the past; it tells the story of what might have been the fate of the main house a half-mile distant from it — what *would* have been its fate — under more normal circumstances: fallen out of fashion, falling prey to the depredations of time and the elements.

From the vantage of the porch of the Hartwig cabin, or what's left of it, it takes no great trick of the imagination to picture the sort of folktale Dobie recounts in his book *Rattlesnakes,* when the heat cast from a stone fireplace during winter weather is all it takes to hatch a nest of rattlesnakes beneath a cabin's wooden floorboards. Nor is it that difficult to feel kinship with E. J. Rissman's grandmother, who stood on the gallery of the Paisano house on the lookout for her husband who had spent the day in town, listening to the roar of the creek in flood and the sudden startling scream of a panther.[18]

Here, someone might once have waited for someone who never returned. These hills aren't far from the ones John Wesley Hardin and Ben Thompson lit out for in times of trouble; they are the same ones where Union sympathizers hid out during the Civil War, and where unreconstructed bushwhackers made camp afterward.

Paisano's greatest strength, its greatest seductiveness, lies to a tremendous degree in the way the past rubs shoulders with the present there, and in the elusive snippets of story—whether natural or historical—for which it is a repository. In many respects, Paisano, which can never be owned or returned to by those who reside there, becomes an imaginary country, an environment that sustains artists with its possibilities. As fellow Charles Behlen pointed out in his report in 1995,

> Annie Dillard says, "Appealing work-places are to be avoided. One wants a room with no view, so imagination can meet memory in the dark." That sounds true.... When I return to East Texas I will find my workplace less appealing and my view more restricted. Then my memory and imagination will meet Paisano in the dark.

ENDNOTES

[1] Surveyors used a varas chain of two varas, with a vara equal to 33 1/3 inches.

[2] E. J. Rissman, "Paisano and Periphery" (unpublished, housed in the Travis County Collection, Austin History Center of the Austin Public Library, 1966), 26.

[3] C. M. Woodruff and Patrick L. Abbott, preface to *The Balcones Escarpment*, a field-trip guidebook for the 1986 Annual Meeting of the Geological Society of America.

[4] David H. Riskind and David D. Diamond, "Plant Communities of the Edwards Plateau of Texas: An Overview Emphasizing the Balcones Escarpment Zone between San Antonio and Austin with Special Attention to Landscape Contrasts and Natural Diversity," *The Balcones Escarpment*, a field-trip guidebook for the 1986 Annual Meeting of the Geological Society of America, 20–32; also John Graves, introduction to *Texas Heartland: A Hill Country Year* (College Station: Texas A&M University Press, 1975).

[5] Rissman, "Paisano and Periphery," 9.

[6] Frank Wardlaw, *Texas Observer* (July 24, 1964), 30–31.

[7] Rissman, "Paisano and Periphery," 31.

[8] Graves, notes on the writing of *Texas Heartland* deposited in the Harry Ransom Center. (John Graves, Series 1, Folder 7, *Texas Heartland with Jim Bones*. Correspondence, research notes, drafts 74–75).

[9] See Graves, introduction to *Texas Heartland*, 21 and 27, for more information on farming in the area.

[10] Dagoberto Gilb, final report.

[11] A. C. Greene, *Paisano*, University of Texas at Austin, Office of Graduate Studies, Pamphlet.

[12] Clay Williams, caretaker at the Morgan Ranch until his death in 2000, interview with Katherine Hester.

[13] A. C. Greene, *Paisano*.

[14] "Untwisting the Cedar: Exploring and Uncovering Myths of the Ashe Juniper Tree," Elizabeth McGreevy Seiler.

http://designbuildlive.org/newsletters/2006Sept.PDF. Accessed January 22, 2016.

[15] Texas Parks and Wildlife Division website. http://tpwd.texas.gov/huntwild/wild/species/gcw/. Accessed January 22, 2016.

[16] Graves, notes on the writing of *Texas Heartland* deposited in the Harry Ransom Center. (John Graves, Series 1, Folder 7, *Texas Heartland with Jim Bones.* Correspondence, research notes, drafts 74–75).

[17] Terry G. Jordon, *Texas Log Building: A Folk Architecture* (Austin: University of Texas Press, 1978).

[18] Rissman, "Paisano and Periphery."

Settlers and the House

Men dwell softly on this land again, and it was time
for that.
— John Graves, *Texas Heartland*

BY THE EARLY 1970S, THE DOBIE PAISANO PROJECT WAS AN
established fact. Eleven fellows had already spent time at the
ranch. Frank Wardlaw, the friend of Dobie who had been
so instrumental in the creation of the program, was now the
founding editor of Texas A&M University Press. In 1972,
photographer Jim Bones spent his months at Paisano taking
pictures. Those images, as well as an introductory essay by
noted Texas writer John Graves, became one of the press's

earliest books, *Texas Heartland*.

In Graves' introduction to the book, which he wrote at the request of Wardlaw and Bill Wittliff, he suggested that the Texas Hill Country in general is the place "many Texans have come to revere as a kind of heartland."[1] His essay's aim was to convey "the special character of a particular region observed over time," just as Bones's photographs were intended to document a "Hill Country year." But their decision to focus on a specific piece of land — Paisano — also created a valuable examination of the property itself.

THE WENDES

In *Texas Heartland*, Graves introduces the Hill Country region by recounting a remark made by a friend many years earlier when a group spent a weekend at a place on the Balcones Escarpment "where a little river gushed out full-size from big springs and ran clear and strong for a few miles before merging with the Guadalupe." His companion declared: "This is where everybody would like to come from. There isn't a soul in Texas that wouldn't have been born here in these hills if he could have managed it."[2]

That reverence the Hill Country inspires in general is elicited as strongly by the land now called Paisano, the land that "during most of its history as a boundaried property …has been known locally as 'the Wende place,' after the family who owned it longest and got their living from what it produced."[3]

Descendants of the Wende family, such as the Dittmars, still populate this part of Texas, and the name appears throughout the area. The old Dittmar Road that ran to the family dairy farm in South Austin was upgraded in 2005. Wende descendants in other parts of the country have kept their interest in their pioneer forbears and can provide stories and letters and memoirs about them.

John Graves carefully researched the geological, historical, and agricultural aspects of the land for *Texas Heartland*. He also used a history of ownership of the property that Billy Porterfield, the first Paisano fellow, established through information found in Travis County records. Graves also knew the property well himself, having spent time out there with Frank Dobie and later with the Texas Institute of Letters members who established the fellowship project.

According to the research conducted by Graves and Porterfield, the first owner, James S. Burton, who acquired the property under a new state land law in 1860, never lived there. The second owners, Frederick and Lucy Kunze, acquired it in 1863. Graves speculates about why they did not keep the property for long, for it was sold to John Daniel Wende in 1865:

> About Kunze no significant wisps of information have come down, though it can be surmised that he was not strictly speculative in his aims, since he built a stout small house of hewn elm logs on the property, standing on a pleasant rise within a bend of Barton Creek among live oaks and cedar elms and facing southeast with its back to winter northers. Nor is it possible to keep from wondering futilely why, having established himself, he would have sold out to another German, John Daniel Wende, in 1865....Comanches, conceivably — they were active nearby in the 1860s.[4]

Graves also suggests that they could have left because of "political discord, or the bandit renegades known to have raided up along the Colorado out of Austin during the Civil War. Or bad health, or a discontented wife...Frederick Kunze's spouse Lucy could not write, and signed the deed to Wende with a forthright X."[5]

Before John Daniel Wende settled on the property he traveled quite a bit. A miller by trade, he was originally from Posen, in Poland. In 1849, he traveled to California during the gold rush. He returned to Posen in 1858, but after less than a year there, he traveled to Texas and settled near Austin, in the Cedar Valley settlement. Graves discovered that

> …like many of the Escarpment Germans, [Wende] joined the Confederate Army, and was sent to Brownsville on the Rio Grande as a saddlemaker…There he struck up friendship with another young German Confederate named Wuthrich, who while on furlough in Austin met and married a Wisconsin German girl born in West Prussia (who on her part had been visiting relatives in Austin and was stranded there by the war's turmoil). After a three-day honeymoon, the unlucky Wuthrich went back alone to duty at Brownsville, where he died of some sickness without ever seeing his bride again. Carrying the sad news to Austin, John Wende liked Mary Schemmel Wuthrich and was liked in return, and in July 1865, having been released from the defeated army and like most discharged soldiers ready to begin a settled life, married her.[6]

The Wende family lived at Paisano for nearly thirty years, and it remained the property of their son John Carl Wende for another thirty. Apparently, the elder Wendes moved into Austin in their later years, but the ranch remained a family retreat. Their daughter, Mary Christine, married Emil Rissmann (from nearby Cedar Valley) in 1889. After John Daniel Wende's death in 1897, Mary Wende moved to Cedar Valley to be with Mary Christine and Emil.

Although Ernest Rissmann (1897–1993), John and Mary Wende's grandson, did not grow up at the property that would come to be known as Paisano, he spent much of his young years on the Wende family's nearby ranch and took many excursions to the property, which was owned by his uncle John Carl Wende until the late 1920s.

A member of the Texas Folklore Society, Rissmann was known for his writing about the Southwest. Because of his association with J. Frank Dobie and other folklorists, such as Wilson Hudson at the University of Texas at Austin, he continued to visit the property after Dobie acquired it. Even after the university became its owner, he was given a key so he could go out there at will. At the urging of Professor Hudson, Rissmann wrote his recollections, "Paisano and Periphery," in 1966.

In "Paisano and Periphery," Rissmann described a day spent at the property:

> The place where we drove up that day was the spa, the Shangri-La, the vacation spot of all the family plus their associates. We three [his grandmother, his mother, and young Ernest] were to go there for a few days' vacation. My father was to follow later in the day, as was my brother [Walter Rissman] who was born at Paisano in 1890. . . . Paisano being untenanted, unoccupied, was the then current symbol to us of "getting away from things" and maybe in an emotional, physical and intellectual context it had a similar connotation, half a century more or less later, to Mr. and Mrs. J. Frank Dobie.[7]

Rissman's uncle John made his career in Austin rather than try to work the property. Rissmann related that "Uncle John ran on it a few cattle, or sold wood off it. But it was always somewhere to go, a country estate where my Uncle John said we could have recreation—he called it ree-creation."[8]

Willa Martin of Albuquerque, a great-granddaughter of the Wendes, remembers the stories of her Uncle Ernest. Descendants of Carl Wilhelm Wende, John Daniel Wende's elder brother, whose daughter Emelia married into the Dittmar family, also recall being told that Emelia spent much of her growing up years at Paisano. When a group from the

Dittmar family paid a visit to Paisano during a family reunion in 2002, several remembered playing at the old cabin.[9]

AFTER THE WENDES

John Charles Wende finally sold the property in 1928. From then until 1958, when the Dobies purchased the property, there were three owners, about whom we know relatively little: Antone and Minnie Holm (1928–1943); R. L. and Dicey W. Springfield (1943–1946); and George and Pearl Turney (1946–1958).

In "Paisano and Periphery," Rissmann remembered the Holms as being "two of the most inseparable elderly people I have ever known. Where one was seen was always the other, except when Mr. Holm occasionally worked at his trade as a cabinet maker in Austin." He said that "it was in later years, probably during the ownership of Mr. and Mrs. Turney, that Paisano began really to be cleared of brush."[10]

FRANK AND BERTHA DOBIE

The Dobie family's tenure at the ranch was not long — 1958–1964 — but in those few years they made it into a place that we now recognize as having major literary importance. One might even say the heart of Texas writing was located here.

The property itself benefited from the Dobie's ownership. By the time they arrived at the ranch, some of the cedar had been cleared. Graves relates that Dobie had some of the flatter parts cleared of cedar and sowed in new grass, noting that he "also continued the work of restoration on the place, conferring with government range specialists and often exulting over a reestablished patch of big bluestem or switchgrass."[11] Though more overgrown with cedar (Ashe juniper) than may be good for the land, Paisano now gives endangered species like the golden-cheeked warbler protected habitat.

THE HOUSE

The residents who followed — the long line of Dobie

Paisano fellows—found a comfortable, plain, but well-furnished house containing many items associated with the Dobies. These furnishings couldn't help but conjure up Dobie. In 1988, A. C. Greene wrote a short piece for *Southwestern Historical Quarterly* suggesting that Dobie's ghostly presence still occasionally graced the glider on the gallery that runs the length of the house.[12] James Whitaker (1980) wrote an essay published in *Texas Co-op Power* in which Frank Dobie was a ghost presiding over the house and property.[13]

An old photograph album Bertha Dobie acquired when she and Frank bought Paisano, now housed in the Southwestern Writers Collection at Texas State University,[14] shows that considerable alterations were made to the house over time. The log cabin the Kunzes had built was enclosed on all sides by the Wendes.

In a later refurbishing of the house, the old wallpaper was peeled off, exposing the original log wall. Fellows Ann Matlock (1975) and Paulina van Bavel Kearney (1978) persuaded the workers to build a window exposing the old log wall, and carpenters framed a 1×2 foot section in what is now the middle bedroom.

Rissmann recalled some features that have been changed: "The fence was close to the house, unlike today, and the fireplace in the east front room, not the west as now."[15]

A broad porch, or gallery as it is called in this part of the country, runs across the entire front of the house. Paved with large, flat stones, its roof supported by cedar posts, the gallery is nearly as important as the house's interior and has continued to be a gathering place for writers and their friends and families.

The house's interior consists of a good-sized living room with adjacent space for a dining table, an ample kitchen, and three rooms on the other side of the house—the back two used as bedrooms and the front room used mostly as a study.

When A. C. Greene, the second Paisano fellow, wrote a short brochure used for many years to inform applicants about the place and the fellowships, he described the house as "an informal, but comfortable spot for living, a backdoor sort of home." His description evokes the house much as it is today:

> Inside the house are flint pieces found or dug along the creek's campsites; there is Dobie's big handmade writing desk, bearing his date stamp of 1911—and paintings of Paisano and its wildlife abound. Country tools and old equipment decorate some walls, and in the slope-ceilinged kitchen a few square nails still offer to hold pots and pans.
>
> A huge fieldstone fireplace in the living room makes winter evenings cozy and was so beloved by Dobie that he had an air conditioner installed so he could bed down in that front room and to sleep by firelight even on summer nights. About the rest of the house, still in use, are dozens of things as Dobie left them, but living at Paisano is not living in a museum. Dobie was too free a spirit, too universal a man to have left this sort of legacy. Usefulness is a great contributor to both the charm and the peace of the old house. Its atmosphere of contentment is older than any one man's residency, and yet the rooms seem to retain some part of the wisdom of everyone who has shared them.[16]

Bertha Dobie used to tell friends that Paisano was primarily Frank's place, but she made sure it was comfortable and sent out a set of blue Mason ironstone dishes (a 1950s reproduction of a popular pattern, Bow Bells). When the Driskill Hotel in Austin was undergoing one of its many renovations, she purchased a handsome lobby chair with a large "D" carved in the back. Apparently, Dobie liked to sit out on the gallery overlooking the meadow, the creek, and the hills. Later, the chair was brought inside and Victor White (1970) undertook to refinish it, a project he recalled in a 1971 *Southwest Review* article. In describing his only partially successful efforts, he also describes the contents of the house. Paisano is fully recognizable from his account.[17]

A sampling of items associated with the Dobies and subsequent contributions from fellows and friends reveals some of the charm that adds to the fellows' experience there:

- A paisano carved of mesquite by Mody Boatright, friend and colleague of Dobie. Boatright, who helped found the Texas Folklore Society, donated his carvings to raise funds for the society, and gave one to the ranch.
- An antique, three-footed iron potholder that sits by the fireplace along with a cast-iron skillet with feet, a cover, and pothook.
- A punched tin fireplace screen (with a paisano design) made by Andre Jordan, husband of fellow Marcia Buffington (1996) and himself a runner-up for the fellowship.
- A deer-hoof rack, used for canes and walking sticks.
- An old saddle and bit and cavalry boots that were given to Dobie. These were not worn by Dobie, as some have thought.
- A clock made by previous owner Turney.
- Dobie's handmade writing desk and the Driskill chair.
- A crank telephone — the one that saved Dobie's life when he was at Cherry Springs ranch.

Several fellows worked on or created things for the ranch. A. C. Greene fixed up a long work table that has been used through the years as a primary place to write. Later, it was additionally braced by fellow Dagoberto Gilb (1988). Gilb also built a sturdy set of shelves for the kitchen.

Upgrades such as air-conditioning, along with gifts of furnishings from friends and from the Johnston Foundation and the Hart Foundation, made the house suitable for modern living. The house also has a washer and dryer.

PICTURES AND PHOTOGRAPHS

Paisano's collection of paintings, drawings, and photographs distinguishes it from any other country place. Some belonged to the Dobies; some were associated with people instrumental in creating the fellowship project; some were used to raise money to purchase the property.

These items hang throughout the house—not in any special way; they have been moved around from time to time, but nowadays they are carefully accounted for. The three paintings that were in the Houston art auction by then UT faculty members Donald Weismann, William Lester, and Ralph White are described in chapter 1. The print of the pen-and-ink portrait of Dobie made available to original donors is also mentioned in Chapter One.

The Dobies had some of the artwork that was given to them framed in local woods. *White Mustang Pacing*, a Tom Lea print, is framed in mesquite from Travis County, and a print signed by the Mexican artist F. Molina Campos is described on the back in Dobie's handwriting as "framed in red cedar grown across the street from us." Two prints probably brought back from England by Dobie are framed in madrona wood from Paisano. Dobie was amused by *A Playful Longhorn*, and *Grinning Sow*, a couple of wood-burned plaques that had been left at the house by the Turneys. Also preserved is a photograph of roadrunner tracks titled *Un Paisano Pasó por Aqui* that was presented by Edgar Kinkaid to his aunt and uncle.

José Cisneros (1969) did the beautiful calligraphy for a quotation from Bertha Dobie (see the epigraph of chapter 1).

Bill Wittliff's photographs of Frank and Bertha Dobie and Dobie's friend and biographer Lon Tinkle are in the dining area.

Works by regional artists in the front bedroom include *Chaparral and Cock*, a pen-and-ink drawing by artist C. M. Palmer; *Roping a Calf*, an etching by Henry Ziegler; *Heading North – Homeward Bound Cowboys*, a hand-tinted photo by Graves Peeler; and *Jack Rabbits*, a lithograph by Otis Dozier.

A large silkscreen of a vulture now has a prominent place in the hallway. Apparently, it had slipped in its mat by the time fellow and former English teacher Victor White got to the ranch in 1970, and he straightened it. He reported that Frank Wardlaw then called it "the well-adjusted vulture."[18]

One of the most interesting recent acquisitions is *Paisano, Full Moon*, a print of an original pastel by Glenn Whitehead. When the J. C. Penney Company relocated its headquarters to Texas, it commissioned a series of Texas scenes by Texas artists to be used for advertisements. The company gave the Texas Institute of Letters a sizable number of copies to use for fundraising for Paisano.

The house also contains an artist's proof of an etching of the approach to the house by Sylvan Furman, father of fellow Laura Furman (1981), particularly nice to have because it shows the wooden cross-piece over the road. The cross-piece finally deteriorated, and the metal pipe beside the cattle guard is not nearly as charming.

Ann Vliet, widow of Russell Vliet (1983), donated botanical specimens her husband had mounted very early in his career. Amy Adams (1999) contributed wildlife sketches made by her husband Bryan, a talented artist.

Through the various works of art and memorabilia, the personalities of the inhabitants permeate Paisano.

THE LIBRARY

Calling the books at Paisano a "library" makes it sound pretentious. But, as one would expect to find in a house for writers, there are books everywhere.

University of Texas Press provided the paperback editions of Frank Dobie's work. Books and articles about Dobie, such as Lon Tinkle's biography, *An American Original*,

Ronnie Dugger's *Three Men in Texas*, and accounts from the Austin paper at the time of Dobie's death in 1964 provide substantial information about Dobie and his close friends.

The library also contains a relatively complete collection of books by the fellows who contribute new work as they continue their careers. Bulletins, brochures, and books relating to the Hill Country also have been collected over the years, ranging from a checklist of the trees, shrubs, woody vines, flowering plants, and grasses on the nearby Mockford ranch by Phil Mockford to a collection of scientific papers, "The Balcones Escarpment," edited by Patrick Abbott and C. M. Woodruff Jr. (1986).

Many years ago Beverly Lowry contributed a number of paperback books by recent writers (and some classics), a collection that has grown as fellows have added good bedtime reading.

Paisano has been luckier than many of the surrounding properties. Having survived over-grazing and marginal farming in the nineteenth century, it fortunately passed through very few owners in the twentieth century — serving first as a retreat for the Wende family, and then falling into the hands of just a few, who did not do much with it until the late 1950s when the Dobies arrived. The Dobie Paisano fellowship project has occupied that piece of heartland, as Graves calls it, for more than forty years, facilitating an impressive amount of writing in that time.

ENDNOTES

[1] Graves, *Texas Heartland*, 11.

[2] Ibid.

[3] Ibid., 23.

[4] Ibid., 25.

[5] Ibid.

[6] Ibid., 25–26.

[7] Rissmann, "Paisano and Periphery."

[8] Ibid., 31.

[9] From correspondence with Willa Martin, the Wendes' great-granddaughter, March 9, 2013. John Daniel and Mary Christina Wende are buried in Oakwood Cemetery in Austin, TX. Carl Wilhelm Wende is buried in the Masonic Cemetery in Austin, TX.

[10] Rissmann, "Paisano and Periphery," 34–35.

[11] Graves, *Texas Heartland*, 28–30.

[12] A. C. Greene, "Frank Dobie Remembered," *Southwestern Historical Quarterly* 92 (July 1988–April 1989) 139–143.

[13] James Whitaker, "Mr. Dobie's Gift," *Texas Coop Power* (April 2003), 14–16.

[14] Southwestern Writers Collection, J. Frank Dobie Papers, Box 23, Folders 1 and 2.

[15] Rissmann, "Paisano and Periphery," 7.

[16] A. C. Greene, "Paisano," a brochure with pictures by Paul Bosner, n.d., but probably 1975.

[17] Victor White, "Paisano and a Chair," *Southwest Review* (1971), 188–196.

[18] Ibid., 190.

The Fellowships

The purpose of the Paisano program is to stimulate creative endeavor in the arts by making it possible for a person to work without distractions.
— Dobie Paisano Application, 1977

THE FRIENDS AND COLLEAGUES OF FRANK DOBIE KNEW WHAT THEY wanted when they selected writers to go out to Paisano. They wanted to support Texas writers or artists. They wanted to provide solitude and time, but it did not matter whether the fellows wrote about Texas. Although details of the competition were not spelled out in the original documents, Frank Wardlaw, who was then Director of University of

Texas Press, indicated that, with the advice of an advisory board, the management of the fellowships would be in the hands of the university.

The Advisory Board

The original advisory board included Bertha Dobie; Dobie friends and supporters Glen Evans, Mrs. Ralph Johnston, and Major J. R. Parten; Texas Institute of Letters members Martin Shockley and Lon Tinkle; and University of Texas at Austin professors Joe B. Frantz, Wilson Hudson, and Donald Weismann. Wardlaw served as chair. He and his assistant Iris Tillman Hill handled the applications. The Texas Institute of Letters Council gradually assumed the role of the advisory board, as members of the original board moved away or died. By 1974, the council had completely taken over this role. Reconstituting the advisory board was discussed both at the Texas Institute of Letters and at the university in 1987, but no action was taken because the need for another administrative group was not felt to be compelling. Thus, the Texas Institute of Letters Council has remained the advisory group to the fellowship administrator.

Wardlaw Leaves the University

When Wardlaw, who had established University of Texas Press in 1950, decided to leave UT Austin and become the director of Texas A&M University Press in 1974, he wanted to place the administration of Paisano in another university office. Wardlaw had overseen the Paisano project from its inception and supervised its operation from 1967 to 1974. He left guidelines for running the competition and information about the sources for the fellows' stipend.

He placed its supervision with then vice president and dean of graduate studies Gardner Lindzey. Dean Lindzey designated Audrey Slate, who was an assistant to the dean at that time, to take care of the details. Dr. Slate continued as director of the project until her retirement in 2007. Professor Michael Adams of the English department was appointed director in 2007. Since 1997, the project has been housed in the J. Frank Dobie House, the home of the Michener Center for Writers.

The fellowships are administered much as they were by Wardlaw, a tribute to his careful initial planning. However, the advent of the digital age has made the process more efficient. Guidelines and the application are online, as is information about former fellows and their publications. The website, www. utexas.edu/ogs/Paisano, was designed by and is maintained by Debbie Hirsch in the Office of Graduate Studies.

ELIGIBILITY

Beginning in January 1968, University News Service (now University Communications) would send out a general press release announcing the deadline in mid-March. From 1967 to 1974, fellows were chosen for a six-month residence. In the mid-1970s, the idea of offering the fellowship for a full year was proposed. Three fellows—Jim Bones, Claude Stanush, and C. W. Smith—each spent twelve months at the ranch. The council then revisited the idea of the yearlong residency—not because it hadn't proved productive for the fellows, but because giving the opportunity to more writers and artists seemed important. Beginning in 1975, the fellowships reverted to six months each, the system that continued until 2008.

The original eligibility statement read: "Applicants must be Texans or persons whose lives or work have been substantially identified with the state." The phrase "but there is no restriction on subject matter" was added in the early 1970s.

The question of eligibility eventually came under scrutiny as more writers from around the country began to hear about the fellowships and many writers and artists moved into the state. Applications were received that stated such things as "I was born in Montana, but was conceived in San Marcos." One year, an applicant explained that he was not from Texas but had spent every summer visiting his grandmother in Houston.

The Texas Institute of Letters Council adjusted the eligibility rules from time to time. When the question arose whether a non-Texan who simply stated that he or she would like to use Texas as the subject of his or her work would be eligible, in contrast to someone who had *published* work about Texas, the council decided on a firmer statement. Non-Texans would have to list *published* work with a Texas subject on their applications. The two-year residence requirement for Texans was changed to three years in 2004. Subsequent eligibility statements read: "at the time of application, you must meet one of the following requirements: (1) be a native Texan, (2) have resided in Texas at least three years at some time, or (3) have published work with a Texas subject."[1]

After 2008, the fellowships were split into a four-month fellowship that runs from September 1 to December 31 – the Ralph A. Johnston Memorial Fellowship, and a six-month fellowship that runs from February 1 to July 31 – the Jesse H. Jones Writing Fellowship. Requirements for each of the fellowships are given on the Paisano website.[2]

Artists and Writers

As originally proposed, the fellowships would be offered to visual artists as well as writers. Twenty artists had donated their work for the auction that raised money to purchase the ranch from Ralph Johnston, and it was understood that "artistic endeavor" might include more than writing.

The first artist selected was José Cisneros, whose career in El Paso had been launched by artist Tom Lea. Cisneros became the third fellow in 1969. Two years later, Ben Freestone, who had been a teaching assistant in studio art at the University of Texas at Austin, was the next artist-fellow.

Subsequently, the council decided the fellowship should go to artists every third year. There were artists in 1975–76 (Ann Matlock and John Christian) and in 1978–79 (Paulina van Bavel Kearney and Frank Armstrong). Christian and Armstrong are photographers; Matlock is a weaver; van

Bavel Kearney is a potter.

In the late 1970s, the council once again reconsidered the character of the fellowships and decided that although the artists used the fellowships well, support of writers should be the primary focus. The idea of offering the fellowships to artists every third year was abandoned, but the council decided not to drop artists entirely. Instead, a special application was created for visual artists, and the judging committee would consider these applications along with those of writers. The change was motivated in part because special equipment, such as a darkroom for photographers or a kiln for ceramicists, could not be provided at the ranch.

The Special Application

Beginning with the 1980–81 competition, a special application designed for visual artists asked many of the same questions as the regular application. But instead of a writing sample, it required submission of photographs, drawings, or slides. After this change, only one visual artist, photographer Alan Pogue (in 1983), was chosen for the fellowship. The special application was dropped in 1993; since then only writers have been eligible.

Criteria

From the beginning, quality of the work has been the most important factor for selecting fellows. Later, suitability for the fellowship and the fellow's work plan while in residence were also considered, and applicants were asked "Why do you feel that you would be a suitable Paisano fellow?" and to "describe the nature and extent of work you would expect to accomplish during a six-month (or four-month) residence at Paisano."

Because some applicants have been unfamiliar with the still-rustic setting of the ranch, in the mid-1980s the president of the Texas Institute of Letters began providing a letter that described both the beauties and the hazards of living in the country: "[Paisano is] not just a headquarters, but also a home for half a year. Writers who receive the fellowship must view it this way. It is their place to live, to think, and to write." The letter points out that each fellow becomes "part of a continuing tradition, a link with Texas's past and a promise of its future."[3] In general, the warning letter is taken seriously, although occasionally applicants feel they must wax eloquent about how much they love spiders and scorpions and all outdoors.

The same criteria have been used throughout the history of the fellowships: "Among criteria on which judges make the awards: quality of work, character of the proposed project, and suitability of the applicant to life at Paisano." Another sentence was added later: "The fellowship is designed as an opportunity for writers who can demonstrate exceptional writing ability and a clear idea of a project to be pursued within the time frame."[4] Amplification about criteria has been made from time to time. The Paisano website provides up-to-date application information.

FOR CREATIVE WRITERS

Neither the founders nor subsequent Texas Institute of Letters Councils have attempted to define "creative writing." Several of the early fellows were journalists, and while some ventured into fiction, they were primarily chosen for their excellence as nonfiction writers. When screenwriting came into prominence, it was accepted as suitable for submission as creative writing.

At one point, the idea of developing some kind of definition of what constitutes "creative writing" was tossed around. The term *belles-lettres* was considered, but ultimately that term was thought to be too narrow and not well understood today.

JUDGES

At the beginning, Paisano advisory board members chose the Paisano fellows. As the advisory board became less active, Frank Wardlaw started composing committees of four people, two of whom would be members of the Texas Institute of Letters and two of whom would be faculty members at UT Austin. The Texas Institute of Letters president and the chair of the advisory board initially served ex-officio. Eventually, the judging group became a six-person committee. Although Wardlaw asked some individuals to serve more than once, it was his practice to constitute an essentially different committee each year. At times, a member of the committee might be a member of both the UT Austin faculty and the Texas Institute of Letters. Wardlaw asked the president of the university to make the formal appointment of the university faculty members.

After Wardlaw left the university, the practice of asking a different committee to serve each year continued. By 2005, some 160 persons had helped select the fellows. The president of Texas Institute of Letters chairs the committee. Since the fellowship has been split, two separate six-member committees are now used. Each committee selects a winner and two runners-up. In recent years, the vice provost and dean of the graduate school has appointed the university-chosen committee members. Only in five cases have recipients had to turn down the fellowship, in which case it has been awarded to the first runner-up. Once a runner-up has moved into the fellow's spot, he or she becomes part of the permanent roster of fellows.

FUNDING

After several adjustments in the first two years of the project, in 1968 UT Austin assumed responsibility for the maintenance of the property and administration of the fellowship competition, and Texas Institute of Letters assumed responsibility for the fellowship stipends.

The stipend was set initially at $500 a month. The annual $6,000 came from contributions from the Ralph Johnston Foundation and the McDermott Foundation, along with smaller contributions from the Parten and Dickson Foundations and an annual amount from Texas Institute of

Letters members.

Wardlaw's remarks to Dean Lindzey in 1974 turned out to be prescient: "Despite the fact that most of this money comes from sources which can be counted on, I have usually had to write the donors and remind them when their contributions are due."

No serious difficulties with securing funds arose, however, until the early 1980s when three of the foundations ceased contributions for various reasons—primarily the death or departure of the key person who had arranged for the Paisano contribution. The Ralph Johnston Foundation, however, continued the support it had shown ever since Ralph Johnston made purchase of the ranch possible, increasing its donation every few years.

In the 1980s, a concerted effort was made to address the funding situation. John Graves wrote an eloquent letter to Texas Institute of Letters members in 1981 urging annual pledges, if possible. Members Marshall Terry, Eddie Weems, and many others answered his call. Later, members C. W. Smith and Laura Furman, both of whom had also been Paisano fellows, sought endowment funds. William S. Livingston, who by this time was vice president and dean of graduate studies, also wrote long, persuasive letters to the officers of several foundations about Paisano funding. Although no endowment funds were secured at that time, several of the foundations made one-time contributions.

Smith and Furman also applied to the Texas Commission on the Arts for funding and successfully obtained grants from 1980 to 1985. The commission's final award—$7,200—set the stage for increasing the stipend to $1,200 a month.

In 1986, when federal funding to the Texas Commission on the Arts began to diminish, Texas Institute of Letters member Leon Hale secured funding for one fellowship from the Houston Endowment. That funding, coupled with the steady contribution from the Johnston Foundation, ensured stability for the next ten years. The fellowships were formally designated the Ralph A. Johnston Memorial Fellowship and the Jesse H. Jones Writing Fellowship.

THE SUSAN VAUGHN FOUNDATION CHALLENGE GRANT

Although the Texas Institute of Letters was able to continue to raise the stipend for the fellows through the years, inevitably the amount needed to be increased. In 2000, Texas Institute of Letters received a $50,000 matching grant from the Susan Vaughn Foundation of Houston. A committee headed originally by Laura Furman and later by Texas Institute of Letters vice president Carolyn Osborn made extensive efforts to secure matching funds not only from Texas Institute of Letters members, but from former Paisano fellows, other Texas foundations, and other friends of Paisano. If met, the funds would be placed in an endowment fund to add to the Johnston Foundation and Houston Endowment yearly contributions.

Texas Institute of Letters had not actively worked on Paisano funding since the early 1980s. The fundraising challenge had to be met by April 2000. By early May, Texas Institute of Letters President Don Graham was able to report that $56,570 had been raised. A number of former fellows and Texas Institute of Letters members contributed and, with the generosity of several private foundations and individuals, the goal was reached. The stipend was raised for spring 2001 to $2,000 a month.

Other major donations during this period were received from the Clayton Foundation, the Burdine Foundation, the Stillwater Foundation, and the Louisa Stude Serafim Foundation.

In 2004, the Houston Endowment increased its donation for the Jesse Jones Writing Fellowship from $10,000 to $12,000. In 2006, having faithfully supported both that fellowship and Texas Institute of Letters's Jesse Jones Fiction Award for numerous years, the foundation endowed both awards, sending not only its yearly contribution for the Jones Fellowship ($12,000), but also $240,000 to endow the fellowship and $120,000 to endow the Jesse Jones Fiction Award.

Through the continuing generosity of the Johnston Foundation, the Houston Endowment, and various other supporters, the project has been able to increase the fellowship stipends over the years.

CHANGES

While the basic operation of the fellowships has not changed greatly, writing and writers have changed — both in Texas and elsewhere in the country.

Paisano's earliest fellows were primarily journalists like Billy Porterfield, A. C. Greene, and Gary Cartwright. Artists José Cisneros and Ben Freestone also held fellowships during the early days. Victor White was both a writer and a teacher. Later, many recipients had careers as creative writing teachers at universities and schools.

The development of academic programs for creative writers — usually master of fine arts degrees — gradually changed the applicant pool. Though MFA graduates do not dominate the pool, applying for writing opportunities like the Dobie Paisano fellowships has become a logical next step for writers in those programs. In addition to formal academic writing programs, many communities have begun to offer informal writers' workshops, increasing the opportunities for individuals to get practice and critical help with their writing.

While applicants for the Jones Fellowship are not required to have published work, a large percentage submit either published work or lists of work in print.

NUMBERS OF APPLICANTS

Thirty-four people applied for Paisano fellowships in 1974, the first year application records were kept. The number of applicants jumped to 91 in 1978. In the years since, there have been from 49 applicants (in 1981) to 136 (in 1999), the highest number of applications up to the time of this writing. Only twice between 1974 and 2008 were there more than one hundred applicants. After 1981, there were never less than fifty applicants a year.

The high number of applicants in 1999 may be attributable to the appearance of a feature story about fellow Lowell Mick White in both the Austin and Houston papers just before the application deadline. The annual announcement of the competition always draws a small, steady stream of applications up to the deadline date, but it has never had the effect of that one article.[5]

GENDER AND GENRE

The first thirteen fellows were men. Whether there were any female applicants before 1975 is unknown. In that year, Ann Matlock, a weaver, became the first woman to hold the fellowship.

In the fellowship's earliest years, the judges seriously questioned whether it was safe for a woman to live out at the ranch alone. Matlock had something of an edge because she had lived out there with her then-husband, Jim Bones, a few years earlier. However, she was chosen strictly due to her ability as an artist.

Between 1975 and 2008 the fellowships were awarded to twenty-eight women and fifty-one men.

Classifying the fellows by genre is difficult, if not impossible. Applicants are not required to submit work in only one genre, nor must they propose to write only in one genre during their residency. In several instances, the fellow has been inspired to go in new directions.

Fiction writers, however, dominate the list of fellows. At least fifty can be considered fiction writers. Eleven fellows are poets and ten classify themselves as nonfiction writers. Seven of the fellows, all from 1983 or earlier, have been visual artists.

Unlike many writing fellowships, the Dobie Paisano fellowships have never been earmarked for particular kinds of writing; that is, the judges do not set out to choose, say, a poet and a fiction writer or a nonfiction writer in any given year. The division of the fellowships has resolved the question of whether to choose a writer at the beginning of his or her career or one at more advanced levels.

While applicants are not asked about their ethnic identity, through 2008 seven fellows identified themselves as Hispanic and two as African American.

Forty years ago, virtually all the fellows were already living in Texas, and most of them were native Texans. Currently, some applicants are native Texans who have moved to other parts of the country; some are nonnative Texans who have spent the requisite number of years in Texas — perhaps as students at Texas universities and colleges — but now live elsewhere; and others are nonnatives who have moved to the state.

The program's flexibility allows for a diverse, talented group of writers who continue to contribute to the state's literary legacy.

ENDNOTES

[1] "Information for Applicants," http://www.utexas.edu/ogs/Paisano/info.html. Accessed January 22, 2016.

[2] Ibid.

[3] Letter from Dave Hamrick, President, the Texas Institute of Letters, included with the guidelines and application for 2005–2006. http://www.utexas.edu/ogs/Paisano/til/letters.pdf. Accessed January 22, 2016.

[4] "Information for Applicants."

[5] "Detour at Dobie," *Austin American-Statesman*, December 7, 1998, 1 and 8.

Part Two

The Fellows

Fellows 1967–1972

IT IS IMPOSSIBLE TO MAKE GENERALIZATIONS ABOUT THE WRITERS who have held the Paisano fellowships over the years. Some have pursued long writing-related careers. A few have turned in other directions altogether since their time at Paisano. All have expressed the feeling that their Paisano experience had an impact on their lives and careers.

After spending time at Paisano, some fellows began to receive honors and awards. Others continued the trajectory they were on before their fellowships and garnered even more recognition. But when fellows reflect on their time at Paisano—in the reports submitted at the conclusion of their fellowship, in passages in their writing, and in interviews and book reviews—they tend to focus most on the impact

Paisano had on their lives and the adventures they had while in residence.

Billy Porterfield

A. C. Greene

Eldon Branda

José Cisneros

Jack Canson

Robert Grant Burns

Victor White

Ben Freestone

Wynn Parks

Gary Cartwright

BILLY PORTERFIELD
June 1967

When the time came to choose the first fellow for Paisano, Frank Wardlaw and his committee (which included Bertha Dobie and Mrs. Ralph Johnston) made an auspicious choice — Billy Porterfield, a former *Houston Chronicle* reporter who had published a well-received nonfiction book, *LBJ Country* (Doubleday, 1965) two years before. A section of the book had won the Stanley Walker Memorial Award from the Texas Institute of Letters, and Porterfield's rising prominence in the newspaper world had led to a job with the *Detroit News*.

Porterfield had not been acquainted with Frank Dobie, but he had read everything Dobie wrote and had heard him speak at the 1960 Texas Institute of Letters banquet in Houston.[1] He moved out to Paisano in the summer of 1967 after Wardlaw, Wilson Hudson, and other friends of Dobie readied the house with new paint, some carpeting, and donations of furniture from various sources.

In a tribute that Porterfield wrote at the time of Wardlaw's death in 1989, he described being escorted by Wardlaw out to Paisano that summer: "He had keys, a great circle of skeletons to many doors, and that afternoon he inserted one into the door of Paisano and opened it for me. I have never been the same since."[2]

Porterfield began the first draft of his book *Diddy Waw Diddy* (1994) at Paisano. In the book's acknowledgments he notes, "It's been a long haul since Paisano — eight drafts over twenty-six years." Later he commented that the substance of the work didn't change much over the years, although from time to time, he found it necessary to give up fragments of it to "newspaper columns, magazines, and that plague of journalists, the collection of miscellanea." *Diddy-waw-diddy* is a term of multiple meanings. According to Porterfield, it was "used as a substitute for a word or name one does not want to use; hence the name of an imaginary place, often conceived of as fabulous and far-off."[3]

The entire Porterfield family moved out to the ranch. Porterfield's first wife, Mary Jo Reid Porterfield, was a writer herself and wrote her first book there. Billy drove their daughter to the old schoolhouse in Oak Hill, but their son was too young for school at that time.

During Porterfield's time at Paisano, he decided to purchase a mare and colt to bring out to the ranch. In his tribute to Wardlaw, he described his reasoning:

> At Paisano in the winter of '67 my tenure as a Dobie/Wardlaw apprentice, so auspicious in its beginning, was drawing to a depressing close, for I had nothing to show. No one was buying the novel and short stories I'd written there. I felt a failure. Wanting to leave something substantial and procreating, something in the spirit of Dobie, both profane and sacred, I went out and bought for the ranch a one-eyed little mare and her colt, dubbed Chapter and Verse. A. C. Greene was to succeed me as the writer-in-residence, and I'd envisioned A. C. writing and riding Chapter and Verse and then passing them on Pony Express–style to the riders and writers who would carry on Dobie's work at the ranch.
>
> When Frank Wardlaw came out and saw the ponies, he asked for a shot of whiskey. He sat and chomped on his fat cigar, shook his massive head, and said, "Billy, we can't have a loose herd of runty, half-blind horses of dubious disposition running around out here through perpetuity. You know how writers are nowadays. Dobie and you may be the last riding writers of the purple sage. Get rid of Chapter and Verse pronto."
>
> I said no prob, but this was as devastating a rejection as those from publishers.

Eleven years later, when Frank agreed
to publish a book of mine at Texas A&M
University Press — which he birthed in 1974 —
he insisted on naming the book himself. "Let's
call it 'A Loose Herd of runty, half-blind...'"
he said, pausing, watching my reaction. Then,
with a wink, he said, "No, 'A Loose Herd of
Texans.' How's that strike you?"
I asked for whiskey.[4]

After Porterfield's year at Paisano, Jim Lehrer and A. C.
Greene invited him to join *Newsroom*, an experimental news
show on Dallas' public television station, KERA. He became
the nightly news show commentator as well as a producer
and narrator of prize-winning documentaries. Porterfield
succeeded Lehrer as executive producer at KERA Radio and
hosted a morning show, the *Fife & Drum, Five & Dime, American Dream Hour*. Later he became a columnist for the *Dallas
Times Herald* and taught at Southern Methodist University.
In 1985, he joined the *Austin American-Statesman* staff.

Through the years, Porterfield's style brought delight to
his readers and reviewers. In a 1990 profile for the *Austin
Chronicle*, Brett Campbell wrote: "He picks characters who
let him make a larger point about their communities, and
somehow manages to find a touch of universal truth in the
most mundane people and places and events."[5]

When *Diddy Waw Diddy* was published in 1994,
Porterfield's longtime friend and colleague Dave McNeely,
who had also migrated to the *Austin American-Statesman*
as a columnist, wrote an affectionate review that followed
Porterfield's career from newspaper to newspaper (and also
TV station):

So Texas' rough-hewn poet, lover of
linking Greek fables to the lives of ordinary
people, found another forum [the Austin
paper] to relate the rhythms of life....I learned

where Billy got his love for the fables, and
those tongue-twisters that require a dictionary
to read his columns — which I lectured him not
to use. He hasn't listened, you may notice.[6]

After ten years back in Austin, Porterfield retired
to Topafossil, his hilltop home between Driftwood and
Wimberley, with his wife Diane and "began work on a
brace of novels, a wing of short stories, a poke of profiles, a
blindfold and a dare of adventure sagas, and a grab bag of
audacious essays and cogitations."[7]

A. C. GREENE
February 1968

A. C. Greene was already a well-established newspaper-
man when he was chosen for the Paisano fellowship. After
getting his start as a reporter on the *Abilene Reporter-News*, he
became a writer-editor for the *Dallas Times Herald* in 1960. He
resigned that position to accept the Paisano fellowship.

Greene and first fellow Billy Porterfield had a long
friendship, but Greene always teased Porterfield that Porterfield should have been number two rather than number one,
because "my credentials are much better than yours."[8]

Like Porterfield, Greene spent his time at the ranch
with his family — his wife Betty and their four children, all
of whom remember the place fondly, including occasional
visits by Mrs. Dobie.

The Paisano fellowship was a turning point in Greene's
career. In the afterword to *A Personal Country* written for a
new edition published in 1998, Greene says:

Thirty years have passed since those
months when I sat writing *A Personal Country*.
I completed the manuscript one stormy night
in April 1968, while I was a Fellow at Frank
Dobie's Paisano Ranch west of Austin. It was
a doubly momentous night. Our four children

were asleep in the two rear bedrooms of the rustic little farmhouse Dobie had used as his country retreat. Betty, my wife, was folding laundry in the large front bedroom we shared. (When you have four kids, you do laundry every day.)

I walked in, threw the manuscript on our bed, and as casually as I could manage, announced, "There it is...finished." Then, like Leigh Hunt's Jenny, "jumping from the chair she sat in," Betty kissed me. It was a kiss of affection, of course — we had been married for eighteen years — but it was more than affection and love, it was a salute, it was a sword-tap on the shoulder that knighted me into the nobility of the pen: I was an author.

I said it was doubly momentous, that night. As I had walked from the little tack room I used as a scriptorium back to the house, I heard the soft but terrible whisper of a large caliber bullet passing over my head. But not even this could intrude on my euphoria, and I didn't mention it to Betty until we had had two glasses of congratulatory wine on the stone-paved front veranda of the house. I called the local game warden and told him the sound put me in mind of a 30-0-6, and he agreed.

"But it wasn't anybody shootin' at you," he consoled me. "It was some ol' boy jack-lighting deer. I could probably go to the Circle Inn right now and put my hand on his shoulder. They'll deny it, but I'll warn 'em that if there's any more of it, I'm comin' after all of 'em." He paused and chuckled. "Your first book was damn near your last one, wasn't it?"

A Personal Country had been three years

in the making. It was started, you might say, by accident. As Book Editor of the *Dallas Times Herald* I had written a Sunday column about what I perceived as inevitable changes coming in Texas literature. The late Frank Dobie (I wrote) had been one of the worst things to happen to Texas writing, not because Dobie was a bad writer, but because his infectious style was so strong that an entire generation of Texas writers had tried to follow his lead and failed. It was something like the way Ernest Hemingway's style had done to writers in general.

Angus Cameron, Dobie's editor—first at Little, Brown, later with Alfred A. Knopf—had been the person who suggested that Greene write about his home territory: West Texas.

A Personal Country was my title, coming to me after praying over a couple of dozen others. At first Angus mused that everybody has a personal country, and I said, exactly, that's why I like it. He agreed, and wrote the dramatic jacket copy for the first edition. Artist Ancel Nunn did the illustrations and also painted the scene on the jacket of that first edition. The painting is of a lost school building in a sea of grass at Maryneal, a community south of Sweetwater. Knopf flopped the picture (reversed it) to fit the jacket. The original painting was owned by a retired banker at Plano who a few years later refused a handsome offer for it.

A Personal Country was published in September 1969. My first copy arrived when my family and I were living at San Cristobal, a beautiful layout several miles west of Austin. I found the book in my Route 6 mailbox, and had parked the van up off the road to look over my treasure. A deputy sheriff, thinking I was a hippie (because of the Volkswagen van) pulled off the highway, came over to where I was parked and asked, rather belligerently, "What do you think you're doin' here?"

"I'm reading this book," I said, displaying my shiny new treasure. "I wrote it."

Knowing that hippies were notorious writers of books, he wasn't persuaded. "You better move on. These people may not like you parkin' on their property."

I pointed to my house in the distance — a noticeable structure with three big stone arches — and stated (with quiet satisfaction), "That's my house," then to exact a bit more satisfaction, pointed and said, "And, incidentally, that's my mailbox."

In the years that have passed since *A Personal Country* appeared, I have written many other books of many kinds. I have even done the words for a set of operatic arias. But nothing will compare with my attachment, my "fatherhood," of that first book. As is often true of first books, I poured all my feelings and stories into it; consequently I have produced three other books, the germs of which are contained in *A Personal Country*. And, I trust, I am not through yet.

My own life has gone through significant changes in those same thirty years. Betty died a decade ago and I married Judy Dalton Hyland, a friend I met when she was visiting Betty after the house fire of 1967. I have undergone serious medical problems and drastic solutions including a heart transplant and prolonged radiology. When Judy and I moved to Bell County in 1992 I discovered I was kin to a whole raft of interesting people who had lived or were living there including my great-great grandmother, Revenny Sutton Craighead, a fabled beauty who died six decades before I was born. Also a few years back, I had Betty's body moved, with Bob and my son Eliot accompanying it, to the lovely family cemetery on Bob and Nancy Green's Shackelford County ranch. Judy and I will be buried there also, unless some unforeseen fate intervenes.

And I have great hopes that *A Personal Country*, having been readable for thirty years, will remain so for at least thirty more years.[9]

Greene had four more productive years with his wife in Salado. He published his first novel *They Are Ruining Ibiza* in 1998 and *Memory of Snow*, a book of poetry, in 2001. Not counting second editions, he wrote more than twenty-five books after his half-year at Paisano. He became known statewide not only for his books, but also for his long-running series of columns about places and events in Texas history in the *Dallas Morning News*. *The Fifty Best Books on Texas,* a list first published in *Texas Monthly* in 1981, and later, *The Fifty-Plus Best Books on Texas,* placed him at the center of a literary controversy over what Texas writing really is that has more or less died down over the last decade or two as more and more writers come into the state and many leave to establish careers elsewhere. He acquired a national audience when, for a short while, he presented Texas sketches on Jim Lehrer's *NewsHour* on PBS. By the time of his death in April 2002, he was frequently lauded as the "dean of Texas letters." He was one of the earliest winners of the Texas Book Festival's Bookend Award in 1998. At his memorial service in Salado, his colleagues, including Lehrer, spoke warmly of his work and his life.

Shortly after the Dobie Paisano fellowship was transferred to the Graduate School at the University of Texas at Austin, Greene wrote a brochure used to describe the Paisano program to applicants that concludes with a statement that might be a fitting epitaph for Greene himself: "[Paisano] promises that no man who gives to mankind, in the fullness of his talent and his art and his skill and his work, can ever die."

Greene is buried at Bob and Nancy Green's Shackelford County ranch.

ELDON BRANDA
August 1968

While Billy Porterfield and A. C. Greene had well-established careers as journalists, Eldon Branda was the first fellow to arrive at Paisano with academic training in creative writing. Ten years after he graduated from the University of Texas at Austin, he studied at the Iowa Writers Workshop, receiving an MFA degree in 1960. He then spent three years in Dublin at Trinity University. The Iowa workshop was among the first academic programs to offer creative writing degrees, and Branda was the first Paisano fellow to arrive with an MFA from there.

Branda's years in Dublin were the impetus for his best-known short story, "The Dark Days of Christmas," which appeared in a newly established University of Texas journal *Texas Quarterly* in 1966. The story was awarded an O. Henry Prize in 1968, along with stories from Eudora Welty, John Updike, and Joyce Carol Oates.[10]

The story is set in Dublin, but the characters are Texans — two elderly women and a student who has come to study at Trinity University. One of the women was born in Ireland but has lived most of her life on the Texas Gulf Coast. They have escaped well-meaning relatives who want to put one of them in a nursing home.

The women settle in a bleak suburb of Dublin, and the winter weather is dismal. But their lives are brightened by Billy, an American student, to whom they immediately begin to pay much attention. Though Billy fulfills his promise to spend Christmas dinner with them, he announces he is moving closer into the city — and their almost daily attentions to him will obviously cease.

After he leaves, they make tea:

> then sitting alone, Annie could see the ocean
> rising by the minute with all that rain. She saw
> the distant Texas shore about to be inundated,
> lost forever, and she heard the mournful horn.

> *Do not think you can escape them*
> *From night 'til early in the morn.*
> *The eyes of Texas are upon you*
> *Til Gabriel blows his horn*

> After a few more minutes in silence, one of
> them asks: "Do you think we might go home?"
> "I think we might just as well," said Annie.
> And they decide Billy can look after himself.[11]

How many readers of the O. Henry prize stories would have recognized the "The Eyes of Texas" is debatable, but Branda inserted an unmistakably nostalgic note in his poignant story.

Branda taught English at the University of Texas at Austin for a few years and wrote a major critical work on D. H. Lawrence, "Textual Changes in *Women in Love*," for a volume of *Texas Studies in Literature and Language* in 1964. However, his most significant achievement was yet to come. Joining the staff of the Texas State Historical Association in 1967, Branda took on a monumental assignment of preparing not just a revision but also a supplement to the *Handbook of Texas*.

The first two volumes of the *Handbook of Texas* were

published in 1952 under the editors Walter Prescott Webb and H. Bailey Carroll. The volumes were well received: the *London Times Literary Supplement* called the *Handbook* "the best systematic work of reference on any of the fifty United States…an invaluable tool for the scholar, the journalist, or anyone else." Along with a small staff, Branda was charged with the task of updating and expanding the work.

When the third volume, titled a supplement, was published in 1976, Joe B. Frantz, director of the Texas State Historical Association, noted in the foreword that Branda had spent most of nine years "gathering, authenticating, correcting, collating, proofing — in short editing. The first two volumes required twelve years of work. This third volume, a supplement rather than a revision, has taken another dozen years, in large part because of Branda's passion for perfection."[12]

Not surprisingly, Branda had a hand in writing many of the articles. His article on Paisano is a straightforward, detailed history of the property and the development of the fellowship program. Branda's love for Paisano is evident:

> One-hundred-foot limestone cliffs, the delight of free-roaming goats, drop down to Barton Creek, which flows near the front of the Paisano Ranch house. Plum and grape thickets grow near the creek along with pecan trees and sycamores; scrub oak, cedar, cedar elm, and redbud spread over the whole ranch, from a crumbling old log cabin which still stands secluded at one edge, up to and around the horse barn and meadows; umbrella-shaped China trees, elm and live oak, fig and pear trees surround Paisano's six-room main house, the back part of which has thick stone walls over one hundred years old. When cedar logs are lit in the massive stone fireplace in the living room, the ranch house can be kept warm in the coldest weather, a place for

company or contemplation.[13]

Eldon Branda died suddenly at his home in Austin on April 11, 2000.

JOSÉ CISNEROS
February 1969

Not often does a combination of talent and a series of unlikely but very fortuitous events result in a lifelong career of great distinction. But such was the case for José Cisneros, eminent artist and illustrator, who became the fourth resident and the first artist to hold the fellowship.

Cisneros was not a young man when he arrived at Paisano with his wife and daughters in the spring of 1969: he was fifty-nine. Born in Mexico in 1910, he had moved with his family to Juárez in 1925 and soon thereafter was sent to school at the Lydia Patterson Institute in El Paso, where he learned English. His few years at the institute were the extent of his formal education — he never had any formal training in art.

Instead, he went to work to support his parents and later his wife and family. For several years he worked as a window trimmer at a department store in El Paso, later moving his residence to El Paso. He always had a great interest in drawing, and several of his drawings were reproduced in magazines in Mexico.

John O. West, Cisneros's friend and biographer, writes in *José Cisneros: An Artist's Journey* that while working on window displays, Cisneros

> discovered a gold mine of material, a veritable treasure for one with limited funds: the showcards displayed in the windows were used on only one side, and the posterboard was then discarded. Cisneros asked for and received permission to keep the material, which he began to employ for his artistic

experiments. One technique he developed involved scratching the surface of the posterboard with his pen, an action, he recalls, that allowed the ink and any watercolors he used in his early years to spread in varying degrees of intensity, creating an unusual effect.[14]

While Cisneros received some modest recognition locally for his drawings, particularly in Juárez, in 1937

an event of great importance opened doors for him in El Paso, as well. Muralist and artist Tom Lea, a man of established reputation, was at work on a mural for the federal courthouse in El Paso. His subject was historical—the people who had come to the Pass of the North throughout its history. Interested in both the subject and the technique, Cisneros watched the creation take shape, and then took courage and came to see Lea with a portfolio of his own work.[15]

In a 2003 interview for an oral history by Adair Margo and Leanne Hedrick, Cisneros recalled that first meeting with Lea. Lea not only liked his work, he wrote a short note for Cisneros to take to Maude Sullivan, the librarian of the El Paso Public Library. Cisneros kept the note:

Mrs. Sullivan, this will introduce Senor Cisneros, who has just come into the lobby of the courthouse to show me his drawings, which I think, are EXCEPTIONAL. I thought you would like to see them and perhaps, exhibit them. This fellow has some stuff. Regards, Tom Lea[16]

Mrs. Sullivan went on to arrange an exhibit of forty of Cisneros's drawings at the library, and then the exhibit was sent to Juárez for display.

Lea also introduced Cisneros to printer and book designer Carl Hertzog. Frank Dobie admired Hertzog's work and, through him, came to know about Cisneros. In 1949, a book produced by the El Paso pair for Southern Methodist University Press was chosen as one of the American Institute of Graphic Arts Fifty Books of the Year. In Dobie's *Guide to Life and Literature of the Southwest* he comments:

> *The Journey of Fray Marcos de Niza* by Cleve Hallenbeck, with illustrations and decorations by José Cisneros, is one of the most beautiful books in format published in America. It was designed and printed by Carl Hertzog of El Paso, printer without peer between the Atlantic and the Pacific.[17]

At the onset of World War II, Cisneros took a course in aircraft metal work, thinking he would probably go to California to work in the aircraft industry. However, with a wife and children and widowed mother to support, he was prevailed upon to take a job with the El Paso City Lines (the bus company) in the painting department. The bus company was considered an essential industry because it provided transportation for soldiers at Fort Bliss and workers in industries vital to the war effort. In *José Cisneros: An Artist's Journey*, West recounts that

> Cisneros obtained a job with that organization, remaining there until his retirement and rising to the position of painting division foreman. An especial delight he recalls from those days involved the international streetcars that crossed the downtown bridges into Juárez. These he

decorated with the colorful flags of the states along the United States–Mexico border. He was thus able to express himself artistically in the daytime, and continue his studies and practicing at night.[18]

Lea and Herzog continued to encourage Cisneros and provide opportunities for him. Cisneros accompanied Hertzog to Paris, Texas, in 1948 to publicize a Hertzog publication, *The Red River Valley Then and Now*. Herzog and the book's author gave talks, and Cisneros brought some of his drawings to be exhibited at the library. Apparently, trips like this were permitted by his employers, for his mentors were very prominent and well-regarded citizens of El Paso. Cisneros himself had become a member of the Western History Association and various other historical organizations. The attention his work brought to El Paso had not gone unnoticed.

Lea and Hertzog were members—in fact very active ones—of the Texas Institute of Letters. Hertzog had also designed and published several works by Frank Dobie. Well aware of the newly established Paisano fellowships, they encouraged Cisneros to apply. Although he did not receive the fellowship the first time he applied, he was chosen for the spring of 1969.

Many years later he recalled that his immediate supervisor at the bus company was not happy about giving him a six-month leave of absence, but Cisneros told him "either you give me the leave of absence or I go by myself and you can do whatever you want about my job." Grudgingly, his supervisor permitted the time off.[19]

At Paisano, for the first time in his life, Cisneros was able to concentrate on his drawing. His time there resulted in a major outpouring of work that continued for decades. According to West, who titled the fourth chapter of his biography of Cisneros "Paisano Turning Point":

The change from the desert/mountain surroundings of northern Chihuahua and El Paso had a great impact upon Cisneros. He wrote Hertzog that "we saw a lot of turkeys this morning and deer jump over our front yard fence every day." . . . Hertzog had written to Cisneros before the move took place, urging him to take in the Institute of Texan Cultures in San Antonio, only sixty miles away, where he could see "Spanish armor, spurs with those long extensions and wide iron sides and many other items, connecting with your Big Project." Cisneros's ambition, his "Big Project," was one he had often discussed with Hertzog. They had described it as "Cortez to Cowboys," as the two traveled from Paris (Texas) to Austin back in 1948. His aim was to focus upon accurate, historically correct depictions of the horsemen of the Spanish Southwest. For years he had haunted museums when he was near them, and pored over illustrated books of horses and horsemen, learning about the riders' costumes, horse gear, the spurs, and equipment of some four hundred years of Southwestern history.

The Institute of Texan Cultures in San Antonio, where Cisneros did much of his research, not only provided an early exhibit of ninety-two of his horsemen, it also published a sampling of that exhibit, under the title *José Cisneros at Paisano, an Exhibit: Riders of the Spanish Borderlands*, with a biographical introduction by Al Lowman and a description of the Dobie Paisano project by Bertha McKee Dobie. [An example of Cisneros's beautiful calligraphy can be found at Paisano. He used the eloquent statement from Bertha Dobie's introduction to the exhibit.] The title "Riders of the Borderlands" in one form or another and the subject matter of that exhibit have been Cisneros's main concern ever since.[20]

Cisneros's drawings (112 of them) featured in a 1981 exhibition at the Centennial Museum at the University of Texas at El Paso. By 1984, a collection of one hundred drawings of horsemen were put on permanent display at the University of Texas at El Paso Library.[21]

For the next thirty years, Cisneros produced an endless stream of illustrations relating to Southwest history. Even in his later years, friends devised ways for him to continue to work. At a 2003 celebration of his work, West explained:

> When Father Time and macular degeneration removed his ability to do creative works, friends—including First Lady Laura Bush—acquired an enlarger for him by means of which he could project a sketch of older works he had kept in outline form. With the aid of the enlarging apparatus he could make his sketches bigger and fill them in with the cross hatched lines so familiar to those who know his previous work. He is delighted to be at work again, although he is not doing new work: his art—all his own—is back in the public eye thanks to the encouragement of his many friends and Adair Margo.[22]

New Mexico held a special day honoring José Cisneros in 2002, and El Paso held a day-long celebration in 2003. He was knighted by King Juan Carlos of Spain, awarded the Military Order of the Holy Sepulchre by the Vatican, inducted into the Cowboy Hall of Fame, and received the National Medal of Arts and Humanities from President George W. Bush. In 2005, he was awarded the Texas Medal of Arts.

Cisneros died in 2009 at age ninety-nine.

Jack Canson
August 1969

Jack Canson, a native of East Texas, had been a student at the University of Texas at Austin before the *Atlantic Monthly* published his story "The Surprise" in 1968 as an *Atlantic First*. Written in the first person, the story describes the UT campus in late summer:

> The university was a nice place to be in summertime then, a nice warm place that a lot of people might have thought was hot, but what to me was a good clean healthy feeling you could feel clear through your body when you walked across the street, or anywhere in the sun. The campus was where you could feel it best, where the sun seemed to fall with just the right amount of heat, just the right intensity. I always saw a lot of people in a strain walking from one building to another, but I knew what was wrong with them, you could see it on their faces. They were resisting the heat, that was it. Not me. I never was stupid. I knew about things like heat and resistance and friction. Friction was what you had to avoid, you see, because friction creates an unpleasant heat, the kind of heat you see people making ugly faces over.

In "The Surprise" Canson also describes the Uiniversity of Texas Tower:

> There were two windows in the room, and through the front one was an uninterrupted view of the university tower. I didn't have a shade on the top half of that window, and I could look out at it anytime and see the big round clockfaces on top of the tower. The window pulled down from the top, and I left

it open for a breeze and used it day and night anytime I wanted to tell time. From where I lived, the tower wasn't very far away, but because of the way the old house was situated, I was catercorners to it, and in order to tell the time sometimes, I had to read one hand off the part of the clockface I could see on the left and the other hand off the clockface I could see to the right. I had developed this ability to tell catercornered time over a period of several months, and I never knew anyone else who did it as a regular habit. A man without funds makes his way the best he can.

That tower was something to look at, even then. It was like looking up at a huge ugly bird staring down as you with two big bulging eyes that glowed in the dark. It was like an owl whose head and neck someone took and stretched until the eyes nearly popped out, and the way the corner of the observation deck jutted out, it made you think of a beak. You could tell time in that bird's eyes, I used to think, and then I would have confusing dreams of an owl perched on top of every building in town, going *whooo* every hour on the hour.[23]

"The Surprise" is a firsthand account of the Whitman shooting from that ominous-looking clock tower. The judges for the Paisano fellowship were impressed by Canson's debut and chose him to be the fifth recipient of the fellowship.

Writing from his home in Marshall in 2005, Canson recalled, "My greatest memories of Paisano involve the people I met and the friendships that were formed. A. C. Greene, Billy Porterfield, Frank Wardlaw, Don Weismann"

The last time I visited Paisano was for Frank

Wardlaw's wake. I flew in from Los Angeles and rode out there with Don Weismann. It was quite a party. I recall Gerald Manley retelling one of Frank's favorite stories, and it made me laugh and recall hearing Frank tell it one very special evening while I was living at Paisano. Frank wanted to bring Mody Boatright and John Graves out for some whiskey and spring water. Billy Porterfield came out and he and I dug a pit near the house and spent the day barbequing. We had a wonderful evening, it goes without saying. If you can imagine a better time than spending an evening under the live oak trees, listening to Frank, Dr. Boatright, and John Graves swap stories — well, that was a very good evening.

Canson spent a couple of extra months at the ranch because Robert Grant Burns, the sixth fellow, had to delay his arrival. Canson was delighted to stay a little longer:

When my time to leave did arrive, I didn't move far. Thanks to A. C. Greene, I moved on to what was then the Romberg property, which abuts Paisano to the north and goes all the way to Bee Caves Road. It had an incredible limestone house on a high cliff overlooking Barton Creek — 7-plus acres and miles of Barton Creek. I stayed there about two years.

It [Paisano] changed my life, no doubt, because when I applied I had been living in Mississippi working for a TV station that was very much involved in Civil Rights issues. I was stressed out and contemplating moving to a big city to make some money. Paisano changed my way of thinking about nearly everything.

Since his stay at the ranch, Canson's career has included a variety of writing, editing, and film production projects.

> After Paisano I opened a small advertising agency in Austin and for several years was involved mostly in political campaign work. Then I opened a film and video production company with a partner, Richard Kooris. [He later sold the company and moved to California.]

In Canson's Austin years, he was also "closely associated with Governor Dolph Briscoe, as his speechwriter and media consultant. I made a lot of TV commercials and public service announcements."

> I published a few stories in small periodicals like the *Texas Observer* and the *Southwest Review*. At some point, I became aware that all the longer form work I had been struggling with, beginning at Paisano, wasn't going anywhere. I had been working on a long novel set in East Texas, and as the years went by I began to realize how much unintentional racism it contained. That problem was later solved when in the midst of a nettlesome divorce a footlocker with my old manuscripts and family photos disappeared.

Later, Canson became involved in traffic safety education, work that eventually led to a large contract in California, where he relocated. "I created the first 'You Could Learn A Lot from a Dummy' seatbelt television campaign in California, and it ultimately became a very successful national campaign. Alas the only words I wrote after Paisano that were in any way on the public tongue were those."

His California contacts led to opportunities in the movie business and for a number of years he wrote screenplays and helped produce mostly low-budget movies. One of the sixteen movies he was involved with, *Nowhere to Run*, was based in East Texas. Ultimately, he found screenwriting unrewarding and moved back to Marshall in the early 1990s.

In June 2007, he reported that

> a few years ago I started writing again. I have been hard at work on *Mysteries of Caddo Lake*, a video documentary about the history of Caddo Lake, which is being narrated by East Texas native Don Henley of the Eagles....
>
> Although my literary output has been slight, I have spent all my time since Paisano — for good or for bad — making a living primarily on the back of the written word. I don't think I'd have had the confidence to do that had it not been for Paisano.[24]

ROBERT GRANT BURNS
February 1970

Robert Grant Burns was known as a musician as well as a poet when he became the sixth Paisano fellow. A contributor's note in the *American Literary Anthology* (Viking, 1970) lists him as "a pianist living in Austin, Texas. A frequent contributor to small magazines, he has published two books: *Nettie Petty's Recollections* (privately printed, Austin 1965), and *Quiet World* (Graficas Orion Press, Madrid, 1967)."

Burns's poem in the *American Literary Anthology*, "An Exhibit of Paintings by George Inness," was inspired, he said, by viewing a very large Inness exhibit held in Austin in 1966. His *Selected Poems* was published in 1993 (Waltonhof).

VICTOR WHITE
August 1970

Victor White was a well-known novelist in the 1940s and 1950s, having published four books of fiction. Born in Vienna in 1902 to a British father and Austrian mother, he immigrated to the United States at age seventeen and later studied at Rutgers, Yale, and the Sorbonne. He had a varied career as a writer, including stints as a reporter for *Life* and *Time*. In 1935, he became a permanent resident in Taos, where he met Frank Dobie in 1952. According to Lon Tinkle, who wrote a piece on White's Paisano fellowship for the *Dallas Morning News*, the Dobies had seriously considered buying a ranch in Taos, where many artists and writers had summer places.[25]

Tinkle knew White and in 1956 persuaded him to take a position at St. Mark's School in Dallas as resident author and master teacher. While at St. Mark's School, White continued his writing and reviewed books, along with Tinkle, for the *Dallas Morning News*. White won a Texas Institute of Letters short story award in 1965 and, following his decision to retire from teaching and devote himself entirely to freelance writing, he was chosen as the seventh Paisano fellow in the fall of 1970.

White was deeply affected by his six months at Paisano. The notes he left for future fellows include a description of how he dealt with the half-wild goats that kept getting into the yard.

I made a crude drag gate which fits over the cattle guard, for they [the goats] can come in over the cattle guard and that kept them out. They were, however, still hanging around outside the fence and occasionally one of the bucks — they have big horns and thick skulls — butted right through the wire. By firing a shotgun over their heads, I have pretty well discouraged them from coming around. Now

> when they try it about once every ten days,
> just yelling at them, and clapping my hands a
> couple of times is enough to make them beat it.
> *It pays to keep them away.* [Emphasis White's.]

He preferred the deer that ventured into the yard, which he fed liberally. In a piece published in *Southwest Review* in 1971, he noted that "a sturdy, unsentimental love of nature is what strikes one most in this living memorial to himself Frank Dobie left behind him, along with his books."[26]

The house and its contents most intrigued White. In the *Southwest Review* he declares

> But it's his [Dobie's] predilection for
> integrity in man-made things that I notice
> most. Everything in the house is sturdy,
> serviceable, plain—from the big, square
> rancher's desk with large pigeonholes and
> drawers, probably made by some not-quite-
> graduate cabinetmaker, not handsome but
> engaging by its honesty, to the massive sofa
> where, Bertha says, Frank used to like to sleep,
> rather than in any of the bedrooms, in order to
> watch the glowing logs in the fireplace as he
> went to sleep. . . .[27]

White had the advantage of knowing Bertha Dobie and clearly enjoyed asking her about items in the house. The one that intrigued him most was the large chair that the Dobies had bought from the Driskill Hotel when it was selling off furnishings. In the years since the Dobies had purchased the chair with a large *D* carved into the back, not only had it weathered but also someone had painted and varnished over the original wood.

In "Paisano and a Chair," another piece written for the *Southwest Review*, White tells about a team from the University of Texas furniture shop that came out to the ranch while

White was in residence to pick up the dining room chairs for mending. While there, "the foreman notices my chair and raves about its value as an antique. He says the wood is mahogany, bleached in order to give the parts of it coming from different trees the same tone." The carpenter suggested paint remover because White had a hard time removing all the grime and layers of varnish just with sandpaper and elbow grease.

When the furniture shop people return with the dining room chairs, the foreman brings "a cabinet-making buff from the accounting office" and

> ...he makes his friend admire the chair. The new expert joins in praising my prowess with the sandpaper, but he is of a different mind about the wood. It's magnolia, he says. Fine furniture in Louisiana and in this part of Texas, he asserts, was frequently made of magnolia, a wood that is naturally white and very hard. Always amusing, the differences between authorities. All I know is that it is a very stubborn wood and that I almost admire it for its stubbornness. And fired by the men's interest I return to my drawn-out chore until my thumb protests again and I go for a walk.[28]

Later in the piece, White spots some mistletoe in the trees and concludes: "Wax on the chair, and it is done! My tribute to you Frank, and to health and laughter and honesty and to our kinship with all that is green."

White did not complete the novel he undertook at Paisano. A number of unpublished manuscripts remain in the archives of St. Mark's School. He published widely in various quarterlies during the next decade.

Victor White died at his Taos home in 1981 at age 79.[29]

BEN FREESTONE
February 1971

A native of Vernal, Utah, (Lewis) Ben Freestone came to Texas after serving in the army. He received a bachelor of fine arts degree from the University of Texas at Austin in 1970 and then began to pursue a master of fine arts degree.

Freestone, who studied under Everett Spruce, Michael Frary, and Kenneth Fiske, was the second artist to receive the fellowship. UT Austin Department of Art and Art History faculty members Donald Weismann, Ralph White, and Ralph Lester had contributed paintings to the 1966 art auction that raised funds for Paisano. Because of the department's association with the Paisano program, art students naturally knew of the fellowship opportunity.

In 1972, Freestone's supervising committee approved and accepted a thesis that was not only completed at Paisano but also involved the physical property itself in its production.

The objective of both Freestone's Paisano fellowship and his thesis was "to develop a body of work and subsequent report based upon the Texas landscape." He completed nine acrylic paintings, the genesis of each one documented with slides included in his thesis.[30]

Abstract expressionism was one of the prevailing art movements of the period, and Freestone refers to Jackson Pollock's late work as not identical but perhaps related in technique to his. He points out that Pollock's work is "a product of studio techniques whereas those in this report are more directly related to nature."

In his thesis, Freestone describes how he went about creating the paintings. First, he photographed more than two hundred sites around Paisano. He then selected twenty-five for transfer to canvas. Nine of the twenty-five are discussed in the thesis.

Each canvas was placed directly on the earth's surface. "House painting rollers and brushes, loaded with pigment, were then applied to the canvas to produce a *frottage* of the surface beneath."[31] *Frottage*, "the technique of making an impression of the texture of wood, stone, fabric, etc.; also the impression itself...is an adaptation by the Surrealists of the traditional method of making a rubbing."[32]

Freestone experimented with various methods of applying the paint to the surface of the canvasses. For instance, *Site 22* represents "a synthesis of the various techniques and compositional elements of the series. It retains the visual imprint of nature by direct development from the earth's surface, while at the same time it permits the fullest exploitation of studio techniques."[33]

Freestone writes that the series of paintings he produced "represent a body of work that utilizes nature to bring about an unexpected variety of new-found effects onto the surface of the canvas...It was found that many of the effects extracted from nature could be duplicated in the studio where they could be more effectively manipulated and controlled."[34]

After Freestone's time at Paisano, he had a long career as an interior and landscape designer, primarily in Los Angeles. He then returned to Vernal, Utah. A 2004 article in the *Vernal Express* summarizes his work:

> Freestone interiors and landscapes have frequently been featured in *House and Garden*, *Veranda* and *Women's Wear Daily* magazines.
>
> His work has received awards from the Los Angeles County Museum of Art for landscape design and from the Los Angeles chapter of the American Society of Public Landscape Designers. He has received several American Society of Interior Designers awards and the Los Angeles chapter of the American Society of Public Landscape Designers.
>
> His architecture, floral and interior designs, stained glass works and landscaping for Southern California's Brentwood, Rodeo district and Beverly Hills is matched by his

interiors and landscapes commissioned in Hawaii and Italy.

Distinctive Freestone homes are also found in Chicago and Palm Beach. He has continued to design for Vernal homes and businesses.

In 2004, Freestone recalled that one of the Paisano landscapes described in his thesis was purchased by a Houston auto dealer and he that saw the painting in one of the dealer's commercials shortly after.[35]

Freestone died in 2007.

WYNN PARKS
AUGUST 1971

Soon after Wynn Parks completed his MFA degree from the Iowa Writers' Workshop, he became the ninth Paisano fellow. Then Parks embarked upon a long career in many parts of the world that embraced not only writing but art and geology as well. In 2002, he won the *Austin Chronicle's* Eleventh Annual Short Story contest. His prize-winning story was published in the January 31, 2003 issue. His writing has appeared in a number of magazines and journals since his Paisano residency.

Of his thirty-year odyssey as writer and geologist, Parks says:

After Paisano, I needed money to go abroad to write. Falling back on my experience as a coal exploration geologist, I took my family and went to Alaska to work for six months. My wife and daughter stayed in Anchorage, while I was flown into the bush. As a drilling supervisor in an isolated winter bush camp, I often felt like I was living in some latter-day Jack London tale. Though my original "abroad" plans were to return to Turkey where I'd lived as a boy, in Alaska I saw an article in the *National Geographic* (August 1972) about the Greek Cycladic Islands. From that I learned about the Aegean School of Fine Arts, on the island of Paros. After corresponding with the school's founder, Brett Taylor, an expatriate American painter, I ended up going there to teach creative writing to a grab-bag of international students and wandering freelance artists. Over the next thirteen or fourteen years I was on and off Paros. Between bouts of teaching, I forayed out as far east as Mashad, in eastern Iran, and parts in between. There were trips into Italy, Germany, England, and Morocco.

Meanwhile the stays in Greece were financed by periodic ventures back into exploration geology. That took me to the Philippines...The early eighties were rough years. [He describes his return to the United States and subsequent divorce.]

Two years later, I was back in Paros, licking my wounds, when Brett Taylor died. We'd become tight friends over the years, and suddenly I found myself wearing the ASFA director's mantle. I did a short, intense stint in that capacity, as well as writing/printmaking instructor. Three or four months after my friend died, I paddled out onto the Aegean with my friend's widow and helped her put Brett's ashes into the sea. After my time as director, I served on the school's board, once as president.

In late '83, I came back to the states to recover from a mysterious case of hepatitis. I'd hit the road again the next spring, back to Greece, but when the bachelor's life began to interfere with my writing, I retreated to

Cornwall in England, where I rented a room
from a writer-friend I'd met while on Paros

In Cornwall, I began a collection of short
stories (one of which won the *Austin Chronicle*
prize) about life, and expats, in the Greek
islands. That is when I met my present wife,
Jacqueline, who was in British theater and a
classically trained singer.

Parks moved to Florida with his wife and her son Joseph,
whom he described as growing "from a small English
school boy to an American dude." In 2007, Parks reported
that his newest fiction was being readied for publication
and that there was a website for Brett Taylor's paintings
(www.bretttayloraegean.com). In 2007, he was working to
establish a memorial for his stepson, who had been killed in
an accident in 2004.[36]

GARY CARTWRIGHT
FEBRUARY 1972

Gary Cartwright, like Porterfield and Greene before
him, had a background in journalism when he became the
tenth Paisano fellow. He had received a BA in journalism
and government from Texas Christian University in 1957
and covered police news for the *Fort Worth Star-Telegram*
and sports at the *Fort Worth Press*. In 1960, he became a
sportswriter at the *Dallas Times-Herald*; three years later, he
moved to the *Dallas Morning News* as a sports columnist. His
first book, *The Hundred Yard War*, was published in 1967, at
which point he left newspaper work and became a freelance
writer.

In the years since Cartwright's Paisano fellowship, he
has been, as he put it in 2005

...[an] author, screenwriter, journalist
and senior editor at *Texas Monthly*. He joined
the *Monthly* staff in 1981 but has written for

the magazine since its inception in 1973. His work has also appeared in numerous other magazines including *Harper's*, *Esquire*, *Rolling Stone*, *GQ*, *Reader's Digest*, *National Geographic Traveler*, *Sports Illustrated*, and the *New York Times*. He has written three screenplays and published eight books, including *Blood Will Tell: The Murder Trials of T. Cullen Davis*, originally published in 1979, and *Galveston: A History of the Island*, originally published in 1991.[37]

By 1970, Cartwright formed part of a cadre of young, talented, and rowdy Texas writers who were calling themselves Mad Dog Inc. Less interested in Texas's rural past than they were in the political and social changes transforming the state, Cartwright and Bud Shrake, Billy Lee Brammer, Larry L. King, Dan Jenkins, and Peter Gent, are the focus of Steven L. Davis's 2004 book *Texas Literary Outlaws: Six Writers in the Sixties and Beyond*.

In *Texas Literary Outlaws*, Davis, long time assistant curator of the Southwest Writers Collection at Texas State University, says Bill Wittliff encouraged Cartwright to apply for the Paisano fellowship:

> In his application for the fellowship, Cartwright called himself "a serious, sworn, full-time starving writer, born in Texas, living in Texas, and writing about Texas. I have published one novel, one screenplay and numerous magazine articles, and my shelves sag with other manuscripts—including a finished novel—, which haven't been published because they are not good enough. I have known some success and a lot of failure, and I am blithely ignorant of other forms of work. I am at the moment embarrassingly

destitute, in great need of the physical and spiritual benefits of this fellowship. I need to lean against Dobie's rock." Cartwright suggested that he would use his time at the ranch to do a "Villains of the Southwest" book, a series of character studies in the New Journalism style. He concluded, "Maybe I will discover something about the nature of villains, maybe not. But I ask you to consider my case. Otherwise, I may have to rob a bank, thus becoming the subject rather than the author of this concept."[38]

In 2006, Cartwright wrote of his experiences at Paisano:

The time that I was at Paisano in the early '70s was one of turbulence across the country and across my field of vision as well. War was raging in Vietnam. Blacks were rioting and burning cities across America. It was the era of Mad Dog Inc., drugs, rebellion, repression, and public craziness. I had just returned from three months in Durango, Mex., where a screenplay written by my pal Bud Shrake was filming later released under the title *Kid Blue*. Shrake and I were working on another screenplay in Durango that had been optioned by *Kid Blue*'s producer, Marvin Schwartz. Marvin was a true Mad Dog himself and he gave Shrake and me and other Mad Dogs whatever we needed in Mexico to make our lives (and progress of the film at hand) workable if not altogether sane. Coming back to Texas and moving into Frank Dobie's hallowed digs at Paisano was a way to catch my breath.

Or so I thought. As it happened several members of the cast followed me back to

Texas as my guests at Paisano, including actors Peter Boyle, Howard Hesseman and, for a short time, Dennis Hopper. Marvin Schwartz joined the group, and so did former Dallas Cowboy football player Pete Gent and his wife Jodi. They had shared a house with us in Durango where Pete had started work on his first novel, *North Dallas 40*. My first few weeks at Paisano were a continuation of the long, wild, frequently out-of-hand party that had been Durango. Work took second and sometimes third or fourth place. By the time all the guests had gone home four or five weeks later, I needed a vacation. Paisano, of course, was the perfect place to take one. The serenity and openness of the ranch allowed me time to think and regroup, without the pressure of publishing or worrying about a paycheck. I don't remember another time in my fifty-year career when I enjoyed that luxury, which might be interpreted to mean that luxury and writing are mutually exclusive.

At this point, I had already published my first novel, *The Hundred Year War*, and had a contract with Doubleday to write a second novel, tentatively titled *Call Clyde to Supper*, a political novel meant to support my belief that freedom was being repressed in America by a runaway political establishment, abetted by lapdog press; in particular, newspapers like the two where I'd worked in Dallas, the *Morning News* and the *Times-Herald*. My protagonist was a hard-drinking crime reporter, not unlike my own self. The advance on the second novel, however, had been spent on a previous sojourn to Mexico, this time in the fishing village of Zihuatanejo. Over the four hot months in Z I had managed to write not one word, a lapse that I characteristically blamed on my lack of foresight in bringing an electric typewriter to a village where the power failed at least eight times a day. The Paisano fellowship, therefore, came at a perfect time in my life. The proposal I submitted to the fellowship project was the same book I was under contract to write — *Call Clyde to Supper*. As I recall, I did write maybe one hundred pages at Paisano but I couldn't keep my mind on the book, which was ultimately a disaster and never got published. After a while, I put the book aside and wrote a ten-thousand-word essay on my experiences in Durango, which was later published in two parts by *Ripoff Review*, a San Francisco-based magazine started by some of the crazies I'd known in Austin in the late '60s, including the cartoonist Gilbert Sullivan.

In retrospect, Paisano was a growing experience, no doubt necessary to my future development. Thirty years later I'm writing the novel I couldn't write back then, or something close to it — a novel in which a Dallas crime reporter watches and discovers the heart of a beast of a city (Dallas) for which I've always had a love-hate relationship. The subtext, however, is no longer a sense of repression and future peril, but a rearview look at Dallas in the '30s when Bonnie and Clyde were rampaging, Benny Binion was running the rackets and gambling and vice were wide open in Texas. Oh, and the screenplay that Shrake and I were writing back in Durango? It finally got filmed, in a highly altered form, in 1991, in an ABC Television movie called *A Pair of Aces*, with Willie Nelson, Kris Kristofferson, and Rip Torn. In the writing game, everything is grist for the mill, or at least that has been my experience.[39]

Cartwright was a senior editor at *Texas Monthly* until his retirement in 2010 at age seventy-six. He died in 2017.

ENDNOTES

1 Billy Porterfield, interview by author, April 12, 2005.
2 Billy Porterfield, "Wardlaw Recalled as Mentor at
     Paisano," *Austin American-Statesman*, June, 1967.
3 Billy Porterfield, *Diddy Waw Diddy* (New York: Harper
     Collins, 1994), acknowledgments.
4 Porterfield, "Wardlaw Recalled."
5 Brett Campbell, "Billy Porterfield: Storyteller," *Austin
     Chronicle*, February 2, 1990.
6 Dave McNeely, "Keeping up with Billy Porterfield,"
     Austin American-Statesman, February 5, 1994.
7 Billy Porterfield author biography given to Audrey Slate,
     April 12, 2005.
8 Porterfield, interview, April 12, 2005.
9 A. C. Greene, "Afterword," *A Personal Country* (Denton:
     University of North Texas Press, 1998), 329–334.
10 William Abrahams, editor, *Prize Stories 1968: The O. Henry
     Awards* (New York: Doubleday, 1968).
11 Ibid., 257.
12 The Texas State Historical Association, *The Handbook of
     Texas, a Supplement*, Volume III, 1976.
13 "Paisano Ranch," *The Handbook of Texas, a Supplement*,
     1976, 687–688.
14 John O. West, *José Cisneros – An Artist's Journey* (El Paso:
     Texas Western Press, 1993), 21–23.
15 Ibid., 23.
16 José Cisneros, interviewed by Adair Margo and Leanne
     Hedrick, 2003.
17 Allen Maxwell, "Remembered: Dobie, Webb," *Dallas
     Morning News*, February 23, 1969.
18 West, *José Cisneros*, 29.
19 Cisneros, interviewed by Margo and Hedrick, 2003.
20 West, *José Cisneros*, 109–110.
21 Ibid., 112.
22 John West, "Cisneros Reborn," an exhibit, Adair Margo
     Gallery, El Paso, Texas, 2003.

23 Jack Canson, "The Surprise," *Atlantic Monthly* 222 no. 2 (August 1968), 74.

24 Jack Canson, e-mail to author, June 27, 2005.

25 Lon Tinkle, "Writer to get Chance: Dallas Man to Use Dobie Scholarship," *Dallas Morning News*, July 11, 1970.

26 Victor White, "Paisano and a Chair," *Southwest Review*, Spring 1971.

27 Ibid.

28 Ibid.

29 "White, Victor Francis," *The Handbook of Texas Online*.

30 Lewis Ben Freestone, "Paintings from Paisano," MFA thesis, University of Texas at Austin, August 1972.

31 Freestone, "Paintings from Paisano."

32 "Frottage," *Harper Collins Dictionary of Art Terms*, 2nd edition, 1991, 166.

33 Freestone, "Paintings from Paisano."

34 Freestone, "Paintings from Paisano."

35 *Vernal Express*, November 17, 2004.

36 Wynn Parks, personal communications, September 1, 2005, and July 9, 2007.

37 Gary Cartwright, personal communication, August 9, 2005.

38 Steven Davis, *Texas Literary Outlaws* (Fort Worth: Texas Christian University Press, 2004), 253–254.

39 Cartwright, personal communication, August 9, 2005.

Fellows 1972-1979

THE DIVERSITY OF BACKGROUND, AGES, AND EXPERIENCE THAT characterized the first group of fellows continued in the 1970s. Because of the original decision by the Texas Institute of Letters to consider applications from visual artists, the group included photographers Jim Bones, John Christian, and Frank Armstrong; weaver Ann Matlock; and potter Paulina van Bavel Kearney. The awards to artists, given every third year, were discontinued in 1980.

Two of the six writers awarded fellowships during this period, Kathryn Taylor Marshall and Allen Hannay, were graduates of creative writing programs (University of California, Irvine, and University of Iowa). C. W. Smith had an MA in English. Jan Reid and Stephen Harrigan had recently embarked on careers as journalists and freelance writers and would become prominent writers for *Texas Monthly* and other publications. Claude Stanush already had an international journalism career when he returned to his San Antonio roots in 1962. Bones, Stanush, and Smith held fellowships lasting a full year (the last yearlong fellowship was Smith's, in 1974–75).

Jim Bones

Claude Stanush

C. W. Smith

Ann Matlock

John Christian

Kathryn Taylor Marshall

Jan Reid

Stephen Harrigan

David Ohle

Paulina van Bavel Kearney

Frank Armstrong

Allen Hannay

Jim Bones
August 1972

Photographs, like everything else we see, are fugitive illusions derived from light. It causes mist to rise, wind to blow, and rain to water the land. Scattering, sunlight makes the sky blue, and striking chlorophyll, it makes green plants grow. Animals harvest its energy as blades and stems and seeds. Gas, oil, coal, plastics, minerals and metals, all are vibrating atoms of light. The atmosphere, the oceans, the very rocks of the planet are the distillate dross of our star.
Texas Heartland

With a long, steady focus, photographer Jim Bones has devoted more than three decades to recording, studying, and interpreting the natural world. From 1972 to 1973, he turned that thoughtful eye on the cycle of the seasons at Paisano. A year later Texas A&M University Press, under the direction of Frank Wardlaw, published those photographs along with essays by Bones and Texas writer John Graves as *Texas Heartland: A Hill Country Year*. *Texas Heartland* remains, until publication of this volume, the only published book completely devoted to Paisano.

From 1962 to 1967, Bones attended the University of Texas at Austin, where he concentrated on geology and biology, as well as English and art. He served as a teaching assistant to renowned photographer and professor Russell Lee. Subsequent to his Paisano fellowship (from 1975 to 1978), Bones would work in Santa Fe, New Mexico, as a printing assistant to Eliot Porter, whose work as a nature photographer became known worldwide.

Bones has produced more than twenty-five portfolios of photographs—the earliest in 1969 for *The Creative Eye* by Kelly Fearing. In 2005, a portfolio of Bones's digital fine art prints was published in Santa Fe.

As a photographer, writer, teacher, and guide, Bones has long been an advocate for environmental causes. Along with his work as photographer and nature guide, he has been a consultant to the seed-ball movement, traveling to Japan to learn the techniques of seed-ball propagation. A concept by Japanese agriculturist Masanobu Fukuoka, seed balls are "a new tool for revegetation." Hillary Loring and Dee Ford Perkins of the Adobe Seed Ball Consortium explain:

> In arid areas, germination of seeds is often quite difficult. The wind blows seed away from the site, rain washes seed into arroyos, the desert heat diminished the viability of the seed embryos. Rodents, birds and insects consume much of the exposed seeds.
>
> Seed balls take care of all these problems. Appropriate seed mixtures are encased in a ball of red clay and soil humus. The clay protects the seeds from the drying sun, rodents, birds and insects until sufficient rains come. The rains melt the clay, allowing seeds to sprout protected within a mini environment of the nutrients and beneficial soil microbes found in the humus and clay. Although not all seedlings with a seed ball will survive to maturity, the appropriate species for each micro location will be there to survive.[1]

Bones moved to Alpine, Texas, in July 2005. Although he has experienced serious problems with his eyesight, he continues to photograph and work on other visual projects with the aid of digital technology. He has even "been able to restore most of my old faded transparencies with the new digital technology. I am at work saving much of the Paisano work now."[2]

Bones's yearlong residency at Paisano has echoed

throughout his life and work. The plea he makes for conservation at the conclusion of *Texas Heartland* rings true four decades later.

> Paradoxically, in wild pursuit of life we leave
> the greatest mark in what we leave untouched.
> So save for the children's sake a little unspoiled
> land and love and grace and green leaves may
> in time heal the wounded earth.

CLAUDE STANUSH
August 1973

Claude Stanush got his journalistic start as a cub reporter for the *San Antonio Light*, but he was determined to go to New York. He became a staff writer for *Life* in 1944. During his thirteen-year career at *Life*, he was assigned first to the Hollywood–Los Angeles bureau and then based in New York, "where I wrote party, nature, science and religion stories; and finally, as chief of correspondents for the Washington, DC, bureau, I covered the government and national and international issues."[3] His "Religions of the World" articles were a greatly admired series in *Life*.

After Stanush left *Life*, he spent the next four years in New York working at a publishing company. He also spent a great deal of his own time reading literature and philosophy. He read Anton Chekhov for the first time "and was so moved by his compassion and his intuitive insights into the lives of his characters that I was moved myself to want to write fiction."[4]

Stanush wrote and published dozens of short stories and a novel. Two volumes of his collected stories have been published. *Sometimes It's New York* (2007) was published with editorial assistance by his daughter Michele Stanush, also a writer.

Stanush, heralded by the *San Antonio Express-News* as "a writer of profound grace and astonishing agility,"[5] is also known as the only Paisano fellow to ever bring bank robbers to the ranch.

In the summer of 1973, a rancher friend of Stanush's who lived in Uvalde told him about the remaining members of the so-called Newton Boys, who from 1919 to 1924 robbed eighty banks and six trains and were credited with carrying off "more loot than Jesse and Frank James, the Dalton Boys, Butch Cassidy and all the other famous outlaw gangs put together."[6] The gang had originally consisted of all four Newton brothers and a fifth member, but one brother had died and another was mentally unstable. Joe and Willis, the remaining brothers, were living in retirement outside Uvalde. Stanush's friend said the old men had fabulous stories to tell and urged Stanush to record their exploits before it was too late. Although much had been written about the gang, a lot of it was wrong.

According to Michele, her father invited Joe, who was seventy-two, and Willis, eighty-four, to Paisano, where he began recording their stories. He thought they would be there for an afternoon, but they ended up staying several days.

Because Stanush wanted to do a more professional job than his old tape recorder allowed, he later got in touch with Professor David Middleton of Trinity University and the two of them did more interviews with Willis at Trinity. Altogether they recorded some thirty-five interviews, starting with those that took place at Paisano.[7]

Although Stanush's original intention had been to compile an oral history, Joe and Willis Newton were amenable from the start to a documentary film about their exploits (and later capture, incarceration, and return to life in Uvalde). With a grant from the Texas Commission on the Arts and help from the film department at Trinity, Stanush and Middleton produced *The Newton Boys: Portrait of an Outlaw Gang*, a 16 mm film which premiered at Trinity in 1976. The film won several prizes and was shown widely around Texas. The oral history was published in 1994.[8]

In 1998, Austin filmmaker Richard Linklater made *The Newton Boys*, a 20th Century Fox film cowritten by Stanush, Linklater, and Clark Lee Walker. In 2003, Stanush and

Michele, who had been thirteen at the time the Stanushes lived at Paisano, began to work on a biographical novel based on the life of Willis Newton, published as *All Honest Men*.

In a section of Stanush's 2007 collection *Sometimes It's New York,* the narrator encounters a snake in an environment similar to Paisano.

> The thing I was after lay at the edge of a stream-bed. It was unmistakable, stretched out full-length on some chalky-white stones — long and black and fat and stub-tailed.
>
> I could feel my heart beating at my chest. I was in the kind of mood that, like flood water, overasserts itself until it finds its own level. Nervously, I began to look for the right kind of rock. Heavy enough to crush the skull. The locus of life. The vulnerable part.
>
> There were plenty of rocks around; the creek bottom next to where the thing was sunning was nearly dry, except for one deep pocket of water. In May, when my family and I had come down from the city to spend our summer in the country, spring rain had filled the gravelly channel. The water moved slowly along, picking up speed where the land dropped away, until it plunged over the boulders with a frothy roar. But now, after a long summer's drought, there was only a trickle, barely enough to keep the stream alive — except for occasional pools.
>
> The pocket of water in front of me was small, though likely the largest for a stretch of several miles. Which is precisely why *it* was here. A snake, too, has to eat.

Later in the story, the narrator decides he has to get rid of the snake because it poses a danger to his young children.

In the late afternoon, as the shadows were lengthening, I went down to the pool, armed with my rock. I had wanted to take the boy with me, he was old enough now to know, and being a boy might understand without a lot of explanations. But I decided against it. He really wouldn't understand, and it would be too complicated to explain. He'd think it was just another snake. One more, one less, what difference would it make?

The big fat cottonmouth was here, lying on the rocky bank, undisputed lord of his domain, and at my approach, as usual, he reared up and opened wide his white jaws.... Did I say, Undisputed Lord of His Domain? Well, I should have said, Undisputed except for me. Anyway, whatever was happening inside of him (adrenaline to the nervous system, venom squirting into the fangs), the adrenaline was certainly gushing inside of me, for my heart was beating wildly....

Except now I knew why it was!...

And there was no way out. I had to take the risk!

I came within a few feet of the thing, so frightened I could scarcely move, and it, sensing that the issue was no longer make-believe, no longer feinting and lunging and camouflage, but life or death, reared up to almost a third the length of its big body. It had power too!

Poison from those little sacs that sit right at the hinges of the snake's jaws, injected through the curved, hollow fangs into a main artery....

But then...having reared up one fraction higher than the complicated laws of gravity permit—that is, one fraction beyond that invisible point where force and counter-force produce stability—it fell forward.

It landed flat, the mouth closed, the head exposed on the sunbleached sacrificial stone...

I hurled the rock—with all the power and fury I could summon.

It landed squarely.

The body twisted and writhed. It rolled over and over on the ground, as if the coils were all in a knot and it was trying to untie itself.

But it was only the reflexes playing themselves out. The vital center, the locus of life, had been destroyed.

With a splash it convoluted into the water

Immediately, in the crystal clear liquid, I could see the long, contorted form surrounded by pinkish perch, yellow-bellied bass, whiskered catfish, hundreds of tiny silver-flashing minnows, the entire congregation of the pool, all pressing their noses against the black flesh tipped by the blood-red head which now was beginning to color the water.[9]

Claude Stanush died at home in San Antonio in 2011. He was ninety-two.

C. W. SMITH
August 1974

Stanush would be neither the first nor the last Paisano fellow to pay attention to the property's snakes. In 2005, C. W. Smith, the fellow after Stanush, related:

I think my most salient memory was the day I decided I was going to crawl along that bluff over the creek that's downstream from the house and there looked to be deer trails along about 50 feet up from the creek and it looked like deer or goats had been going back in there so I started crawling along and I couldn't stand. I had to crawl along the path and I was sort of coming around a boulder and I came face-to-face with a very big rattlesnake. I was on my hands and knees and he was right there and what instantly came to my mind was if I get struck, I'm too far from anything to get out of this and I'm just a goner so I just sat there and eventually he just backed up and that was all right. I remember I wasn't really afraid of snakes but the day I arrived Claude Stanush met me in the yard wearing Vietnam army snake guards on his shins and he said he never went outside without them. Then Ann Matlock told me there was a coral snake in the front yard every now and then at night but that they were really shy and you didn't have to worry about them. But I had a lot of encounters with the water moccasins in the creek that were a little more scary because they don't give you any warning and they're very aggressive.[10]

A few years after Smith's fellowship, he wrote an article for the *Dallas Times Herald* about Paisano and Stephen Harrigan, the 1978 fellow. While the article centered on the Paisano fellowship, its history, and some of the prevailing ideas about what the program's focus should be, Smith also related an encounter Harrigan had had with a coral snake while living on the property, using the anecdote as a springboard to explore Harrigan's writing and attitudes toward the natural world.[11]

The opportunities Paisano gave fellows to experience the natural world turned out to be, Smith felt, the single most important part of his time there. "I think mostly my memory is distinctly of the natural world, of walking around the lands, and swimming in the creek, and all my snake encounters."

Smith was fortunate to have Jim and Ann Matlock Bones as frequent visitors at Paisano during his fellowship. Bones was a fellow in 1972; Ann, a fellow in 1975.

> He and Ann would come out and they would take me on walks. They both knew a lot about the flora and fauna. So I learned a lot about native plants and animals that I already knew something about because I had grown up in West Texas and New Mexico, but I hadn't ever really had that kind of saturation exposure to Texas flora and fauna…I read a lot of Bedichek [the naturalist and close friend of Dobie's] and I remember Dobie's nephew, Edgar Kinkaid. Kinkaid had worked with Suzanne Winkler on bird books, so I learned about the birds of the area and I read about the area's natural history. So my memories of Paisano are of a natural retreat and a place where I learned a lot.

He also read all Dobie's books.

> So it was the kind of place where it was more educational for me than anything else rather than being the sort of place where I was going to get a lot of writing done. It was a place where I was going to get to learn much and that has probably stayed with me.

Smith found that absorbing the nature around him had a strong influence on his writing.

> When you have the names of things in your head, then when your characters walk around

in that world you know those things pop up,
as being part of the fixtures of their lives. The
characters might stand under a chinaberry
tree whereas before my Paisano experience
they were just standing under a tree. My
sense of the world having nomenclature was
greatly heightened by that and that shows up
all the time in what I write now because I have
continued to learn and continued those things
I started learning then.

Smith is both a writer of fiction and a teacher of creative
writing. He is the author of nine novels, a collection of short
stories, and one autobiographical book. Seven of his novels
were written subsequent to his Paisano fellowship. His novel
Purple Hearts, set in Beaumont in the 1940s, was published by
Texas Christian University Press in 2008.

Smith began teaching creative writing at Southern
Methodist University in 1980 and has been chair of its
creative writing program for several terms during the past
twenty-five years. In 2005, he said of his students:

I have really enjoyed working particularly
with undergraduates. I think they're talented
and they're good students — they are serious
and earnest. I find they are still interested in
writing fiction. Sometimes I wonder where
they read it and when they read it because I
don't get the sense that a lot of them are very
big readers. But it seems they just want to
write to express themselves.[12]

Ann Matlock
August 1975

J. Frank Dobie reportedly described a good morning of
writing as "I've been in a weaving way." He probably meant
that he had been weaving words together.[13] At Paisano, artist

Ann Matlock was literally weaving, for the stated purpose of her fellowship was to "produce weavings based on the colors, textures, patterns, and moods of Paisano and the Hill Country."

Matlock was the only weaver to receive a Paisano fellowship. She had spent a year at the ranch in 1973 with her then-husband Jim Bones. Two years later, she herself applied. Initially, the judges did not seriously consider her because she had already spent some time out at the ranch and, more importantly, they had serious questions about whether it was appropriate for a woman to live alone in Paisano's isolated environment. Records on the gender of applicants were not kept in the fellowship's early days, but apparently no women had even applied before Matlock. The judges overcame their concerns and awarded her the fellowship because of her interesting project and her unquestionable artistic skill.

Matlock had had the opportunity to become acquainted with Bertha Dobie during Jim Bones's earlier fellowship. Her memories of the ranch include an anecdote Mrs. Dobie related to her then about bringing Ralph Johnston, the program's primary benefactor, to Paisano during the period when funds were being raised to purchase it. The two had hoped to see wild turkeys and when they got up to the gate, a huge flock came across. Mrs. Dobie said "it just went on forever; there was the biggest flock of wild turkeys she had ever seen." Clearly Mrs. Dobie felt the trip out had influenced Johnston in his philanthropic efforts.[14]

Matlock also had her snake stories. In 2006, she remembered a

> ...really large coach whip snake that lived under the house. There was a little crack in the masonry underneath the porch glider. So if you'd have friends out, everybody would be sitting on the porch, several on the glider. One day the snake had obviously been sitting there looking out past the feet of the people sitting on the glider

and to the front yard. The snake finally spotted a little field mouse that it wanted and shot out just like a bullet. I mean it must have shot out from under that glider and out into the yard. The people on the glider just levitated. I told that story to some former fellows and they had had similar experiences. That was a very long-lived and infamous snake.[15]

Also during Matlock's fellowship, she unexpectedly hosted a group of Navajo women weavers at the ranch. The group had come to Austin to show and sell their work at an upcoming auction at the invitation of several local weavers; they were also scheduled to give weaving demonstrations to publicize the upcoming event. Matlock had arranged their schedule. The weavers did not feel comfortable in town and decided to return to the reservation the night they arrived. Matlock invited them to spend the night at Paisano instead, and they fell in love with the property. The two weavers who gave weaving demonstrations stayed all week with Matlock and her husband; the others, eleven in all, stayed at the ranch on the auction weekend.

The women taught Matlock how to spin Navajo-style, and she taught one of them how to use her spinning wheel, which they thought was a hilarious tool. She also showed them her natural plant dyes. "I gave them some of the ones they liked because some of the plants don't grow on the reservation." They took almost everything she offered except cochineal, the red dye produced from the dried bodies of scale insects that feed on prickly pear cactus, because they didn't want to use products that required killing something.

In 2006, Matlock described their visit to the ranch:

So with some fourteen guests sacked out all over the rooms [and the hostess and her friend, the Navajo reservation VISTA volunteer, having to sleep on the rug in front of the fireplace], they were awakened on Sunday morning when knocking on the front door came two Jehovah's Witnesses who had climbed over the gate [never left unlocked], forded Barton Creek, and hiked all the way up to the front door in their Sunday clothes to save us. They looked in and there was just this house full of Indians and then these two Anglos that were flopped out on the rug. They offered their literature and I thanked them and told them to go right back out the way they came. They left a few last pieces of literature in the front gate, but I thought: what did they think? What an insane houseful we had that day.

Matlock has been an artist and weaver for the past four decades. Formerly on the faculty at Ohio University, since 1991 she has headed the fibers and art education programs at Lamar University in Beaumont. She maintains a house and studio in Johnson City.

Matlock now includes silk yarns among her weaving materials, though she still uses mohair and wool. Her earlier pieces were primarily wearable items. Most of her work now is intended for wall display. A 2005 article about an Austin exhibition of her work described her as a "tapestry weaver." Although still partial to plant forms, she said

I have also worked from sky, clouds, and landscapes, as well as some architectural forms. I have made watercolors of plants, rocks, water, and natural landscape forms for many years. This has been my way of being focused and learning from the natural world. The colors and gestures of natural forms are an endless source of interest for me — expressive but also abstract.[16]

In 2005 and 2006, Matlock began to work with Moroccan women who have organized textile cooperatives. She has taught the women natural dyeing to revive that art, once highly developed in Morocco. A video based on her teaching has been made by the University of Ifane in Morocco.

JOHN CHRISTIAN
February 1976

John Christian's lifework — photographic documentation of the Huichol people of the Sierra Madre of western Mexico — began about six years before he became a fellow. His absorption of Mexican culture and rural Mexican life began much earlier. Though he was born in Texas, Mexico City was home for the first sixteen years of his life. His father, a mining engineer, took the family to visit mines, introducing Christian to rural Mexico — especially La Huasteca, the gulf lowlands on the east coast, and Zacatecas in the west. Spanish, which Christian learned mostly from two Tlaxcalan women, was his first language. In the provinces he first heard the indigenous languages and began to develop a fascination with native cultures. When he was about nine, he set foot for the first time in Viri-cuta (or Wirikuta), the magic cactus land of the Huichol high in the mountains of central Mexico, to which he would return twenty-two years later on a trek to the east with Huichol *hikulai-tame* (peyoteros).[17]

Christian's interest in photography began in the mid-sixties when he discovered Edward Weston's *Daybook*. He developed his photographic skills through contacts with friends, reading, and experience. In 1970, he began fieldwork in the Sierra de los Huicholes. While his work has concentrated largely on the Huichol people, he documented their nonnative neighbors as well. The Huichol attracted Christian primarily because of their isolation, which has allowed their culture to remain relatively unaffected by modern influences.

At Paisano, Christian set up a darkroom in the outbuilding behind the house for printing the photographs he had taken in Mexico, often hauling water from the store at the intersection of Circle Drive and Thomas Springs Road known as "the Circleville grocery" or collecting rainwater to wash his prints.

Christian usually spends about three weeks of every year in Mexico in regular trips to the region that have continued for nearly forty years. In recent years, he has been writing text to go with his photographs. He plans to put his photographs, ethnographic information, and perhaps some personal observations—he has some fifteen volumes of journals to draw on—into book form.

Over the years there have been many exhibits of Christian's works, including *A Sacred Place*, 1981 (Texas Memorial Museum); *A Sacred Place: A Journey into the Huichol Sierra*, 1984 (Nettie Lee Benson Latin American Collection); and *From the Red River to the Rio Grande — Texas Photographs*, 1991 (Center for American History—then the Barker Texas History Center); as well as numerous exhibits in Mexico. *A Journey to Uxata* traveled in northern Mexico for three years.

In 2006, Christian said of the crucial time he spent at Paisano: "It's like a Guggenheim, but with a ranch."[18]

KATHRYN TAYLOR MARSHALL
August 1976

Kathryn Marshall was familiar with the rumor that at least one early fellow was so spooked about living out in the wilds of Paisano that he left before the fellowship ended, and she wasn't afraid to admit she was scared when she arrived at the ranch. She had been living in Southern California for several years before her fellowship and, though she was excited about moving to the property,

> I got out there and I was scared to death. It was fall and the creeks rose and the lower-water crossing got covered; all the rattlesnakes came to nest on the front porch. I was pretty much a Southern California city girl when I came

back to Texas. Some bikers came through the property, and my daddy brought me a rifle so I could shoot the bikers, or whatever. But fall was so beautiful. I spent a lot of time just walking around the property, just walking and walking and walking and I relaxed into it eventually.[19]

By the time Marshall arrived at Paisano, a number of previous fellows had written a few words on the wall over the desk in the front bedroom. Artist José Cisneros had started the tradition with a sketch of a conquistador. Although Marshall knew some of the fellows were quite well-known Texas writers, she was unimpressed. Thinking the writing just looked like a bunch of graffiti by a bunch of older guys, she decided, "I am not going to sit here for six months and look at this stuff." She went out and bought a bucket of yellow paint and painted over the writing, never thinking she was covering Texas history. "I thought it was ugly and I got rather upset about it."[20]

When Marshall's paint job was discovered by some of the "older guys," one would have thought someone had painted over the Sistine Chapel ceiling. The incident created a buzz for several years afterward at Texas Institute of Letters meetings, but the furor died down as it was realized that, though the first few jottings were charming and certainly Cisneros's sketch was a loss, it was unlikely the practice would have continued for the next thirty-five to forty years.

Marshall finished her second novel, *Desert Places*, at Paisano. After her fellowship, she spent over twenty years out of Texas as a teacher of creative writing at Tufts, Harvard, Mount Holyoke College, and Clark University and worked as a journalist with credits at publications such as the *Boston Globe*, *Washington Post*, *Los Angeles Times*, *Commonweal*, and the *Discovery Channel* magazine. Her stints as a magazine editor included one as health and fitness editor of *Cooking Light*.

While women characters were central to Marshall's

novels, her interest in writing about women also led her to compile and edit the oral histories of twenty women who served in Vietnam for *In the Combat Zone: An Oral History of American Women in Vietnam, 1966–1975*. In a 2005 interview, she said, "I didn't really know why I was so drawn to writing about women in traumatic situations but I was."

In the late 1990s, Marshall returned to Dallas, where she had grown up, and "in a moment of complete insanity decided to go to nursing school." Though she was not a practicing nurse for long, she went on to be a manager of Agape, a nonprofit medical clinic serving the indigent in East Dallas.

Jan Reid
February 1977

When Jan Reid moved to central Texas in the early 1970s and was looking for writing assignments, he was directed to the editor of a new magazine, *Texas Monthly*. His first article, about a robbery and car chase in San Antonio, appeared in the fourth issue of the magazine in May 1973; he has been connected to *Texas Monthly* ever since.

In 1977, when Reid completed his Paisano fellowship, he told the University of Texas publication *On Campus*, "I'm mainly just concerned with storytelling." Of his writing, he said, "Ever since I first wanted to write, my principal ambition has been to write novels."[21] Before Reid's fellowship, he had written nonfiction for magazines and published his first book, *The Improbable Rise of Redneck Rock*, an examination of Austin's music scene in the 1960s and 1970s.[22] His Paisano fellowship resulted in a novel, *Deerinwater*, published in 1985.

On April 20, 1998, Reid was the victim of a crime that would reverberate through his life and writing. A hobbyist boxer himself, Reid had recently published an article about Jesús Chávez, a young Mexican-born, Chicago-reared boxer who had gained considerable attention in the United States but had been deported from his adopted home of Austin and was struggling to keep his top world ranking.

In later writing about the event, Reid related that in April 1998, the recently deported Chávez was scheduled to participate in a fight in Mexico City, and that Reid's *Texas Monthly* colleagues Michael Hall and John Spong

> ...had fallen into the thrall of the character and the story. Along with one of John's friends, David Courtney, they had cooked up the idea of going down there to watch the fight. By the time the idea got to me they had cheap airfare and a borrowed apartment in a nice part of town. Why not? We were unaware that the same month the United States Department of State added Mexico City to its list of most dangerous foreign destinations.

The day after the fight the four spent the day and evening in Mexico City, ending at the Plaza Garibaldi, a popular place for beer and mariachi music. The driver of the taxi they hailed at the evening's end delivered them into the hands of two *pistoleros* with .38 revolvers who robbed them of money and watches. Reid, who took a swing at one of the robbers, was shot. A bullet went through his wrist and abdomen and lodged in his spine.

He received excellent care at a Mexico City hospital, though at first his prognosis was paralysis. Through friends at *Texas Monthly* and in the Texas state government, Reid was moved quickly to Houston, where he was treated by the famous trauma physician Dr. Red Duke. (Duke was a well-known figure in the state, partly because he had a popular TV program for a few years in the 1990s.)

A few weeks after the shooting, as Reid was recovering in a Houston rehabilitation hospital, friends from all over the state gathered for a tribute and fundraiser to help with his medical expenses. Among those who turned out in support of Reid and his wife Dorothy Browne were Molly Ivins, John Graves, Kinky Friedman, Gary Cartwright, and Larry L.

King. The *Austin American-Statesman* reprinted the remarks delivered at the event by former Texas governor Ann Richards, who promoted the idea to publish the collection of Reid's articles that would become *Close Calls*.

Reid's recovery was slow and painful, but as soon as he was able, he resumed writing. He wrote extensively of his experience: in "Left for Dead," a long article in *GQ*, and in the final chapter of *Close Calls: Jan Reid's Texas*. A book-length account of the event, *The Bullet Meant for Me*, was published in 2002.[23]

Although Reid had not been known particularly as a political writer, he had long experience working with people in Texas state government and had been a speechwriter. In the 2000s, he teamed up with Lou Dubose, a former editor of the *Texas Observer*, to write about two notable politicians from Texas, Karl Rove and Tom DeLay. University of Texas Press reissued *The Improbable Rise of Redneck Rock* in 2004; in July 2007, Reid finished *None of My Own*, one of the novels he had begun years before. Another novel, *Comanche Sundown*, was published in 2010.

Reid continues his busy writing schedule. His most recent book, *Let the People In: The Life and Times of Ann Richards*, is a tribute to the late Ann Richards, who spoke so eloquently of his talents when he lay gravely wounded.[24]

Stephen Harrigan
August 1977

Steve Harrigan completed his first novel, *Aransas*, at the ranch. Since then he has produced a steady stream of articles and books of nonfiction. Many touch on the natural world, such as his books of essays, *Natural State* and *Water and Light*, and his long essay accompanying *Contemporary Texas*, a photographic portrait of the state. His early novels, *Aransas* and *Jacob's Well*, were followed some years later by the large-scale works of fiction *The Gates of the Alamo*, *Challenger Park*, *Remember Ben Clayton*, and *A Friend of Mr. Lincoln*.

Harrigan is also a screenwriter, with credits for *The Last of His Tribe* for HBO, *The O. J. Simpson Story* for Fox-TV, and *King of Texas* for TNT. He is also an adjunct professor in the MFA program in writing at the Michener Center for Writers at the University of Texas at Austin.

In *Conversations with Texas Writers*, Harrigan addresses being both a writer of nonfiction/journalism and novels.

> For me, journalism and various sorts of nonfiction writing have always been a means to an end. I've always thought of myself essentially as a novelist. And frankly, journalism is the way I made my living for a good part of the time that I tried to position myself as a novelist. But what I discovered along the way is that I could not have been a halfway decent novelist if it had not been for the demands of journalism. I learned how to shape a story from writing magazine articles. I learned how to gather information. I learned how not to be awed by the process of writing, just to get the thing done. It helped me a great deal in discovering the writer I wanted to be.
>
> In many ways nonfiction and fiction are very similar. You still have to deal with a certain database of information and experience. You have to shape that knowledge into a compelling narrative story — or at least in the kind of writing I do, that is the case. There are, of course, profound differences. A novel is fundamentally a work of the imagination. A magazine article or a nonfiction book is a work of fact. And you have to give yourself permission when you're writing a novel to depart, as you need to from that information base. You have to rein your imagination in sometimes when you're writing nonfiction.[25]

When Harrigan took the fall of the Alamo in 1836 for a subject, he had plenty of opportunity to use everything he knew and believed about writing nonfiction and fiction. He spent eight years gathering and sifting through the Alamo stories. In an interview with the *Austin Chronicle* in 2000, he noted, "I knew there was no point in telling the story unless you told it in a kind of global perspective. The purely Anglo version of it has been told long enough, *ad nauseum*." He also remarked:

> At this level of ambition, everybody is complex. Everybody has mixed motives. Everybody has feet of clay. And that's what's exciting to me as a novelist, is to depict people who are flawed and three-dimensional. I don't think there are any heroes in this book.[26]

In January 2001, a year after *The Gates of the Alamo* was published, Harrigan and four other writers participated in *Laura Bush Celebrates America's Authors* as part of George W. Bush's inauguration.[27]

Harrigan's next novel tackled NASA, the space agency located near Houston. Exploring the relationships among astronauts and their families a few years before the Columbia tragedy, *Challenger Park* received considerable acclaim.[28] His novel *Remember Ben Clayton* received the James Fenimore Cooper Prize, given by the Society of American Historians for the best work of historical fiction.

Harrigan has taken on far-ranging subject matter for over thirty years, but his essential nature might be glimpsed in a poem he wrote at Paisano:

KITCHEN
You were not yet six months old
that morning I saw the deer outside
the kitchen window, poised there
by the propane tank, poised

in the frosted acreage
between the house and the spring.
You were asleep beneath the swan decals
on the headboard on your crib
dreaming something you would not remember
or recognize, some old imageless dream
that would be with you all your life.
You did not see the deer. Still I choose
to remember holding you up to the window,
both of us leaning over the sink
staring at the down on the frozen lawn.
I remember how she came to the window
and stared back at us, wanting in,
tired of so much sorrow and grace.
This is the dream I have invented for us both.
It took place one early morning
while you were sleeping
and I was at the kitchen window
looking out at the deer
who stood in the frost,
in that place beyond memory,
wanting in.[29]

David Ohle
February 1978

While he was at the ranch, David Ohle kept what he called a "sporadic logbook." One of the first entries was about a pair of old boots that sat in the front room. Visitors would ask him if the boots in the corner were Dobie's. Ohle wrote, "I was informed by Wilson Hudson, a friend of Dobie's, that they were not, that Dobie's feet were of such a peculiarly pigeoned and gnarled persuasion that his boots were custom made by a well-known bootmaker in San Antonio."

Elsewhere in the journal, he wrote:

> ...saw a shriveled, dead bat hanging from
> a cedar by fishing line. Through binoculars

I could see the hook in the lip just like a mudcat. Surmised that someone fly-fishing there on Barton Creek had entangled the line in the tree, cut and abandoned it. The bat, that night, thinking it a tasty bug, took a snap at it, was hooked out of flight forever, presumably starving to death. When I looked at the bat's face I thought of the mummified remnants of dead saints. At another angle it seemed the embodiment of evil. Going back to the house I noticed for the first time a poem by Steve Harrigan on the wall, which was apparently inspired in part by the sight of the hanging bat. [Obviously a less benign poem than the one quoted earlier.] The poem, however, claimed the bat was hanging from a sycamore. Had some agency moved it? Not likely. I was certain it had been a cedar. Nevertheless the poem was a good one and I read it several times.[30]

In the early seventies, when Ohle had been a graduate student at the University of Kansas and writing a novel for his master's thesis, he sent the first portion to Gordon Lish, the legendary editor at *Esquire*, where it was accepted and published as a novel excerpt. That led to the publication of *Motorman* by Knopf in 1972.

Interviewed at Paisano a few years later, Ohle described his work as "fabulism and social science fiction." His writing has been described as "visionary literature." Whatever the labels, Ohle has what one reviewer calls "a small underground of ardent fans."

In 2008, Benjamin Strong, an editor at *Fanzine*, wrote in *The Believer*:

When *Motorman* (1972), David Ohle's surpassingly weird first novel, was brought

back into print four years ago to coincide
with a long-awaited sequel, *The Age of Sinatra*,
acolytes appeared from the blue, professing
devotion ("awesomely carving deep, black
holes into the edifice of the English language"
was how Ben Marcus described the book) as
if they'd been waiting all their lives to testify.
Because, as another author/fan, Gabe Hudson,
remarked, it wasn't a cult Ohle had generated;
it was a sleeper cell.[31]

In 2006, Ohle recounted his personal acquaintance with
one of the more prominent members of the beat generation,
William S. Burroughs:

I met Bill in the late 70s when I was
teaching at the University of Texas in Austin.
He was invited there for a reading and I hosted
him a few days, along with his assistant, James
Grauerholz. It was actually Grauerholz who
asked me to transcribe certain Burroughs
manuscripts into electronic form for further
editing. Grauerholz had read *Motorman*. I
don't know whether Bill had or not.[32]

After a few years in the English department at the
University of Texas, Ohle moved to Lawrence, Kansas, where
he has taught fiction and screenwriting at the University of
Kansas. It was in Lawrence that Burroughs, who lived there
from 1981 until his death in 1997, asked Ohle to edit his late
son's unfinished novel.

I knew William Sr. for the last ten years of
his life here in Lawrence. Saw him at least
once a week, was a pallbearer at his funeral.
I also know his assistant, James Grauerholz.
Burroughs Sr. and James both knew I was a

dependable researcher, editor and writer. I had done preliminary editing and transcriptions of three of Bill Sr.'s own works *Queer, Western Lands*, and *The Cat Inside*. Two other people had tried and given up on doing Billy's "book." So Burroughs hired me for a fee to "edit" Billy's last novel, *Prakriti Junction*. But when I got to Ohio State, where the filed boxes were stored, there was no novel to speak of, so I conceived the idea of doing a memoir, a compilation of his writings, his letters and testimonials about him. This is all explained in the Introduction to *Cursed from Birth*.[33]

Ohle teaches part-time at the University of Kansas. His third novel, *The Pisstown Chaos*, was published in 2008.

PAULINA VAN BAVEL KEARNEY
August 1978

One of the two artists selected for the 1978–79 residencies, Paulina van Bavel Kearney was the only sculptor and potter to hold the fellowship. A University of Texas fine arts graduate, she specialized in ceramics and had taught in the Austin area for several years before arriving at Paisano with her husband and four-month-old daughter.

In her application she explained:

> In 1975 I developed a unique method of finishing and firing my shapes that combines some of the ancient techniques of the Southwest Indian cultures with modern industrial technology. The marriage of these two different traditions has produced a very unusual and appealing style of pottery, which I have concentrated on refining for the last three-and-a-half years.

She felt her work had created "a renewed respect for the simple but laborious techniques of the ancient Southwestern Indians."[34]

Over the past three decades, van Bavel Kearney has become a well-known artist and craftsman in the region. She still uses the techniques she began using at Paisano. Her work has been featured in numerous exhibits in galleries and museums, including yearly appearances at the Winedale Spring Festival, where she has won many awards.

An artist's statement she wrote in 2004 resembles her earlier remarks about her work, but reflects years of continued contemplation.

> I have worked over the last twenty-five years to perfect an innovative combination of techniques and forms. I use both modern and ancient techniques achieved through research, trial and error. I use a terra sigilata finish which is polished by hand and I fire the clay in the presence of sawdust.
>
> I believe that some of the most expressive objects in ceramics today are those which reveal the natural qualities unique to the material and emphasize the powerful effects of the passage through fire. By exploiting these traits, clay artists offer a unique and vital contribution to the world of art, particularly when the objects relate to the vessel form. Since pottery has been an essential utilitarian item for thousands of years, it has a universal identity and an instinctive appeal to all people. Therein lies its power as a symbol.
>
> I use the vessel form as symbol of mankind's Presence. I have constructed abstractions of the vessel with only vestiges of the container identity remaining. Flattened, with emphasis on an asymmetrical silhouette,

they give form to a gestural drawing of a classical vase shape. With these forms I hope to achieve a metaphor for mankind and its dependent relationship with nature.

I also create classical vase forms that are fired with the same terra sigilata finish with sawdust. The highly polished surface and the control I have been able to achieve over the colors in the firings are unique and a signature style that I will continue to produce in infinite variations. Each of my pieces since 1976 has been dated and signed on the base.[35]

FRANK ARMSTRONG
February 1979

When Frank Armstrong was chosen as a Paisano fellow, he had a good day job as a photographer for the University of Texas at Austin News and Information Service, employment that occupied him five days a week and some evenings and weekends. He welcomed the opportunity Paisano gave him to delve more deeply into what photography meant to him.

In an interview that took place while he was at the ranch, he explained:

> Photography is a found art. You find it in all the purity of form that exists in nature and it is a matter of isolating it.[36]
>
> In my work I depict the "social landscape." By this term I mean a view of the land, both urban and rural, and those objects that man has chosen, either intentionally or not, to place on the land as symbols of himself. I try to record, but not to interpret, what Walker Evans called "modern cultural artifacts." I explore those "artifacts" in the landscapes in which they are set and the relationships that exist between the objects, the land and time. In

> my search for man-symbols, I also find a need
> to explore the pure landscape so that one can
> serve as a foil for the other.[37]

A social landscape, in his view, has no people in it, but it is a landscape that is impacted by man.

As his philosophy of photography evolved, Armstrong found that the 35 mm camera did not continue to satisfy the demand of the kind of images he wanted to make, and he made a "rather joyful leap to large format." He explained, "While throughout my career I have continued to exhibit these social landscape images, it was during this move to the large format that I began my interest in the more classically pure landscape." He made his first trip to Big Bend National Park, Texas, in 1975 and in 1976 made his first large-format black-and-white image.

Over the years Armstrong returned to Big Bend with his large-format camera. "I go to let its quietness quiet me, its power energize me, its solitude rest me. In some ways, the pictures are unimportant, merely the excuse."[38] In 2004, he marked twenty-nine years of photographing that landscape.

In 2001, Armstrong's Big Bend photographs were published to great effect in *Rock, River & Thorn: The Big Bend of the Rio Grande*, a monograph published by Scotia-Waterous, Canada.[39] With introductions by former Paisano fellow Jan Reid and Roy Flukinger, former long time curator at the Ransom Humanities Center at the University of Texas, the book displays the Big Bend region in all seasons and in all times of day. In the artist's statement Armstrong included in *Rock, River & Thorn*, he affirms:

> In the simplest terms, I photograph because it
> is a way that I can openly relate to my private
> world. I don't always understand this private
> side, but through photography I can at least
> get it out in the open and examine it from
> a visual standpoint. I want to understand

how my reality relates to the physical world I move through every day. My photographs are the tangible evidence that I did exist in a particular space at a specific time, and that I did experience the relationship of the objects as defined by the light that appear in my photographs. For me, photography is a process of things seen becoming things known.

Landscape has held its popularity for so many artists because of the universal truths it represents. One thing we can all agree on is that there is an earth. And there is general agreement on what is beautiful about this earth. Photographs that deal with universal truths are the most successful. The private truths are just that, private. My photographs reaffirm my presence and allow me to bear witness to the beauty of the earth.

The Big Bend country is a unique and unaltered landscape. There is evidence that man has lived in the area for more than 10,000 years. The mountains remained unchanged throughout the ages. Every morning that I view the new sun raking across the landscape, I feel as if the land has been reborn and myself along with it. It is my hope that through my photographs I will be able to share with others some measure of my feeling for this remarkable place.[40]

Armstrong has now turned to digital cameras.

Since purchasing my first serious digital camera in December 2002, I have not shot another roll or sheet of color film. This does in no way mean I have forsaken film—far from it. About 70% of all I shoot is B&W film. All formats from 8 × 10 down through 35 mm are still part of my equipment. Thus said, I must admit to favoring my Pentax 67 system over all formats for B&W work.[41]

In the summer of 2007, Armstrong made a long road trip photographing cemetery gates upon which the name of the cemetery was posted as a sign for everyone to see. Armstrong explained, "I am only interested in those cemeteries that have unusual, ironic, whimsical, dark, or just plain funny names." After the trip, he resumed teaching photography at Clark University in Worcester, Massachusetts and to his photographic work.[42]

ALLEN HANNAY

August 1979

When Allen (Chip) Hannay finished his fellowship in early 1980, he left detailed notes for his successor, including descriptions of the neighbors and the adjoining ranches. The neighbor who lived to the south of Paisano was an elderly rancher named Morgan, whose father had come to Oak Hill a century earlier in a wagon train. Hannay was one of the last fellows to have a chance to visit with Morgan, who died in 1981. A great storyteller, Morgan told Hannay about an event that allegedly occurred on the property to the west of Paisano:

> Back at the turn of the century, a couple named Levi settled there and ranched in near seclusion. On the day Mr. Levi died, his wife walked four miles up Grape Creek to Mr. Morgan's house, and her first comment on arriving was, "This is the first time I've been off in thirty years." That night she went back home, and several days later the house burned under suspicious circumstances. The hired man was seen walking to town. A week or so

passed before a fisherman found Mrs. Levi's body, weighed down with stones in the creek. The hired man said he knew nothing about it, but a year later he threw himself in front of the San Antonio bound train.[43]

Ernest Rissman also recounts this story in his memoir "Paisano and Periphery," although in his version the wife's body had been weighed down with an anvil.[44]

For some years after Hannay's fellowship, he and his family lived on a small ranch near Dripping Springs, but in 2000 they bought a small farm on the Guadalupe River in Comfort, and Hannay began teaching at St. Philip's College in San Antonio. When they bought the place, it housed thirty-eight cats and eighteen dogs. According to Hannay, "it took us all summer to fix the place up—the kids remember it as the summer they lived in a tent—but it all came out fine."[45]

ENDNOTES

1 Hillary Loring and Dee Ford Perkins, "Seed Balls: A New Tool for Revegetation," a presentation of the Adobe Seed Ball Consortium.

2 Jim Bones, personal communication, January 22, 2006.

3 Claude Stanush, *Sometimes It's New York* (San Antonio, Texas: Wings Press, 2007), 213.

4 Ibid.

5 Steve Bennett, "Author Wrote for Life, Express-News," *San Antonio Express-News*, March 28, 2011.

6 Willis Newton and Joe Newton, as told to Claude Stanush and David Middleton, *The Newton Boys: Portrait of an Outlaw Gang* (Buffalo Gap, Texas: State House Press, 1994), prologue.

7 Michele Stanush, personal communication, July 18, 2007.

8 Newton et al., *Newton Boys*, xvi.

9 Stanush, "Live and Let Live," in *Sometimes It's New York*, 165 and 172–73.

10 C. W. Smith, interview with Audrey Slate, November 22, 2005.

11 C. W. Smith, "The Pleasures of Paisano: They're Not for Everyone," *Sunday Magazine, Dallas Times Herald*, February 12, 1978.

12 Smith, Slate interview, 2005.

13 "Weaver at Paisano," *On Campus*, February 5, 1976.

14 Ann Matlock, interview with Audrey Slate, February 3, 2006.

15 Ibid.

16 Jean Scheidnes, "Ann Matlock: Tapestry Weaver," *Austin American-Statesman*, June 2, 2005, E10.

17 Introduction, "A Sacred Place," Texas Memorial Museum, 1982.

18 John Christian, interview with Audrey Slate, April 12, 2006.

19 Kathryn Taylor Marshall, interview with Audrey Slate, November 22, 2006.

20 Ibid.

21 Jan Reid interview at Paisano, *On Campus*, August 1977, 16.

22 *The Improbable Rise of Redneck Rock* (Heidelberg Publishers, 1974; Austin: University of Texas Press, 2004).

23 *Close Calls: Jan Reid's Texas* (College Station: Texas A&M University Press, 2000), 234; Jan Reid, *The Bullet Meant for Me* (New York: Broadway Books, 2002).

24 Jan Reid, *Let the People In: The Life and Times of Ann Richards* (Austin: University of Texas Press, 2012).

25 Frances Leonard and Ramona Cearley, eds., *Conversations with Texas Writers* (Austin: University of Texas Press), 2005, 140–141.

26 *Austin Chronicle*, March 24, 2000, 46 and 48.

27 *Austin American-Statesman*, January 20, 2001.

28 Thomas Mallon, "Satellite of Love," *New York Times Book Review*, April 9, 2006, 7.

29 Stephen Harrigan, "Kitchen," *Sleepyhead* (New York: Calliope Press) 1980, 29.

30 David Ohle, Paisano logbook, February 1 and 2, 1978.

31 Benjamin Strong, "The Pisstown Chaos," *The Believer*, October 2008, http://www.believermag.com/issues/200810/?read=review_ohle. Accessed January 22, 2016.

32 Savannah Schroll-Guz, "Motorman Meets the Son of Naked Lunch," *Hobart*, September 2006.

33 Ibid.

34 Pauline van Bavel Kearney, Paisano application, 1978–79.

35 Pauline van Bavel Kearney, Artist's Statement, 2004 for Art of the Pot Studio Tour.

36 "Photography at Paisano," *On Campus,* August 15, 1979.

37 Frank Armstrong, Paisano application, 1978–79.

38 Frank Armstrong, biographical sketch, March 2008.

39 *Rock, River & Thorn* (Calgary, Canada: Waterous & Co., 2001).

40 Armstrong, biographical sketch.

41 Frank Armstrong, personal communication, July 20, 2007.

[42] Allen Hannay, final report, 1981.

[43] Rissman, "Paisano and Periphery," 34.

[44] Allen Hannay, personal communication, July 30, 2007.

[45] Allen Hannay, personal communication, July 30, 2007.

Fellows 1980–1988

IN THE PAISANO PROJECT'S FIRST THIRTEEN YEARS, THE FELLOWSHIPS
often were awarded to writers pursuing careers in short- or
long-form journalism. In the 1980s, however, writers who
considered themselves primarily fiction writers or poets were
the norm. Almost a third already held or planned to begin
teaching careers. More than half were women—a marked
difference from the previous decade, when only three had
been selected as recipients. During the 1980s, three Latino
or Hispanic writers and one African American writer spent
time at Paisano.

William Martin

James Whitaker

Laura Furman

Harryette Mullen

John Davidson

Sandra Lynn

R. G. Vliet

Alan Pogue

Cheryl Ann Cessna

Terry Galloway

Lisa Fahrenthold

Sandra Cisneros

Rosemary Catacalos

Pat Ellis Taylor (LittleDog)

Tim Hatcher

Catherine Agrella

Dagoberto Gilb

William Ripley

WILLIAM MARTIN
February 1980

One of the lasting effects of William Martin's Paisano fellowship was a desire to find a place in the Hill Country. Over thirty years after his fellowship, he and his wife spend about half their time in Wimberley. The rest they spend in Houston, where Martin is now an emeritus professor of religion and public policy and a senior fellow for religion and public policy in the James Baker III Institute for Public Policy at Rice University.

The direction of Martin's career, both as a writer and as a teacher, began early: After his college work at Abilene Christian University, he went on to Harvard Divinity School and Harvard University, where he obtained both the BD and PhD degrees. A chapter of his doctoral dissertation was published in *Atlantic Monthly* — the beginning of a long career as a writer on religion and social issues.

When Martin became a Paisano fellow, he was already an associate professor at Rice University and had begun writing a monthly column of church reviews for *Texas Monthly* that drew the attention of a *60 Minutes* segment.

His expanding interests are described in a Rice University faculty biography:

> During the 1970s and 1980s, Professor Martin concentrated mainly on religious broadcasters and was one of the first academicians to give serious attention to what came to be known as the Electronic Church. At the end of the 1970s this led naturally to increased attention to fundamentalist involvement in politics and the rise of the movement known as the Religious Right. This work culminated, after dozens of articles, in his writing *With God on Our Side: The Rise of the Religious Right in America* (Broadway Books, 1996), the companion volume to the PBS mini-series of the same name and for

which he served as chief consultant.[1]

Martin has also written a biography of Billy Graham — *A Prophet with Honor: The Billy Graham Story* — and has provided an eighty-page addition to the revised edition.

At the Baker Institute he works on issues of religious and public policy and also on drug policy issues. A summer 2007 project included

> working with Ambassador Edward Djerejian, Executive Director of the Baker Institute, on a book about American policy with respect to the Middle East, with particular attention to Islamic countries, drawing heavily on his experiences as US Ambassador to both Syria and Israel, as well as decades of additional experience in the region.[2]

While Martin enjoys his time at his Hill Country retreat, he nevertheless has remained heavily engaged in the areas that he began pursuing much earlier — religion and society.

James Whitaker
August 1980

Jim Whitaker's first book of poetry, *From Hell to Breakfast*, was published by Lucille Press in 1977. He completed his second book of poems at Paisano and, at the close of his residence, remarked: "You learn to be quiet and watch for nature rather than tuning out, like you do in the city." During his fellowship, his daily routine was one of long walks, reading, and then writing at night.[3] While Whitaker returned to life in Austin and his work as a librarian after his fellowship, he did not lose his close feelings for the ranch. Almost twenty-five years after his stay, he wrote a short article about Paisano that concluded with an imaginary encounter with J. Frank Dobie.

One night the risen moon through Mr.

Dobie's bedroom window wakes me. Bare feet on worn linoleum, through narrow halls I follow an intuition—like smoke trailing an updraft—past the 1850s fireplace, to the front door. There a man wearing a hat is visible through the screen, seated at the redwood table on the flagstones. I wander through the pinging screen door and sit on a crude wooden chair. Mr. Dobie turns toward me. "What do you have to drink?" he asked, tilting his head with the same ironic smile my father used. I tell him about the Austex tamales and bad drinking water. We talk in the moonlight. "It's got to where I don't want to go into town much anymore," Dobie tells me. "No, I'd rather set out here and listen to the wild turkey cluck. Have a talk with you crazy young kids once in a while, watch the night sky. . . . Has the old rancher in the beat-up Dodge pickup been around?" I nod. "He's a ghost I think. He thinks a Comanche haunts him, and makes them both come back here," he tells me. "They both maybe killed their first deer up on that hill—and way before the first world war."

"I was reading one of your books today," I say, "the one about the longhorns."

"Ha!" he slaps his knee. "Now, see, that's one where I don't care what you or anyone else thinks about—it's my only book I'd care to live by. Thank you for mentioning it to me tonight. And thank you for coming out. You're welcome to stay in my house."

Bare feet back up the hall to bed. Those flagstones must have been on the river bottom once, I thought. They feel better than linoleum on the soles of your feet. I lay staring at the ceiling, trying to see the mysterious island water stain that had been above my bed, back home on the range.

I work at dawn and tiptoed to the living room again. By moving with stealth, I was able to peer out the window and see the doe and fawn behind a gently moving hedge of mist, grazing with great wary delicacy upon Mr. Dobie's lawn.[4]

Whitaker retired from the Harry Ransom Center at the University of Texas at Austin in 2003. He continues to write poetry.

LAURA FURMAN
February 1981

Laura Furman had already been writing and publishing short stories in her native New York when she seized the opportunity to move to Houston as senior editor of *Houston City Magazine* in 1978. Some three years later she was awarded a Paisano fellowship.

By the time she left Paisano, she had completed the four-hundred-page manuscript for *The Shadow Line*, a novel set in Houston. She also finished a short story for the *New Yorker* that was published shortly thereafter and brought home some fig preserves that she had put up with fruit from one of the large fig bushes at the ranch.[5] Since then she has pursued a multifaceted career in writing, teaching, and editing.

Before settling in Austin in 1980, Furman taught creative writing at the University of Houston and Southern Methodist University. After a year as a Guggenheim fellow, she became a member of the English Department at the University of Texas at Austin, teaching in the MA and MFA programs in writing. She was the founding editor of *American Short Fiction*, a University of Texas–affiliated literary journal three times nominated for a National Magazine Award.

In 2002, Furman became the series editor of the annual *O. Henry Prize Stories* anthology. Austinites know O. Henry as an early resident whose small cottage is now a museum in downtown Austin. In a 2005 interview in *Beatrice,* Furman said, "The writer of the Gift of the Magi is commemorated in Austin and elsewhere, but his most important monument may not be his stories, which many readers still love, but the *O Henry Prize Stories,* founded in 1918 by his friends to honor him and to 'strengthen the art of the short story.' Rather than being relegated to literary history, O. Henry will always be associated with the current masters and promising talent in contemporary writing."[6] She described the editorship of the series as a formidable, yearlong job of choosing the prize stories for each year's volume from entries from many sources.[7]

Furman is the author of four collections of short stories, *The Glass House* (1981), *Watch Time Fly* (1983), *Drinking with the Cook* (2001), and *The Mother Who Stayed* (2011); two novels, *The Shadow Line* (1982) and *Tuxedo Park* (1986); and a memoir, *Ordinary Paradise* (1998). With Elinor Standard, she coedited *Bookworms,* an anthology of writing about reading.

HARRYETTE MULLEN
August 1981

Although poet Harryette Mullen's mother and her grandmother, who were visiting her from Fort Worth, couldn't understand how she could survive "alone in the wilderness" (particularly without an automobile), she managed very well at Paisano with some help from her sister and brother-in-law, who was an economics professor at the University of Texas at Austin. Her sister picked her up about once a week to go grocery shopping and she had the pleasure of getting to see her very young nephew.[8] After her fellowship, Mullen stayed in Austin a few years through the Visiting Writer, Artists in the Schools Program of the Texas Commission on the Arts before moving on to graduate work at the University of California, Santa Cruz, where she wrote a dissertation on slave narratives that was later published by Cambridge University Press.

As an English department faculty member, first at Cornell

University and since 1995 at the University of California, Los
Angeles, Mullen has pursued her scholarly interests, poetry,
and other writing ever since. She has written extensively on
African American poetry, African and African American
folklore, literature by writers of color, and feminism, as well
as the aforementioned slave narratives.

Her early poems, *Blues Baby*, were reprinted in 2002.
When she was interviewed at the end of her stay at Paisano
in 1982, she had completed the poems and discussed writing
them with the reporter from *On Campus*: "I'm not afraid to
look inside myself. I'm not afraid of what I'm going to find
there."[9] She offered this poem for the article:

MAGIC BLUES
>I burned fourteen feathers in a china bowl,
>knotted the ashes in a pink handkerchief
>to keep under my pillow,
>but one morning I woke up
>and love had flew out the window.
>
>I sprinkled blue powder
>in that left and right shoes
>and tied the laces in a bow,
>but one morning I woke up
>and love had tiptoed on out the door.
>
>I wrote "stay put" in red ink on white paper,
>folded the paper into a square,
>and buried it under a stone,
>but one morning I woke up
>and love had packed its bags and gone.
>
>Blues is stronger than magic
>It's like they say in the song:
>soon as you get used to love
>it's done up and gone.[10]

Reviewing Mullen's fifth volume of poetry, *Sleeping with the Dictionary*, Mary Parks suggests, "wordplay can be serious business." She explains that the book incorporates anagrams, acrostics, homophones, and puns, Tom Swifties, and rhymes. It also uses techniques from the French literary group OuLiPo (Ouvroir de Littérature Potentielle).[11] The volume was a finalist for the National Book Award and several other national prizes. One example (there's at least one entry for each letter of the alphabet):

> I beg to dicker with my silver-tongued companion, whose lips are ready to read my shining gloss. A versatile partner, conversant and well versed in the verbal art, the dictionary is not averse to the solitary habits of the curiously wide-awake reader. In the dark night's insomnia, the book is a stimulating sedative, awakening my tired imagination to the hypnagogic trance of language. Retiring to the canopy of the bedroom, turning on the bedside light, taking the big dictionary to bed, clutching the unabridged bulk, heavy with the weight of all the meanings between these covers, smoothing the thin sheets, thick with accented syllables — all are exercises in the conscious regimen of dreamers, who toss words on their tongues while turning illuminated pages. To go through all these motions and procedures, groping in the dark for an alluring word, is the poet's nocturnal mission. Aroused by myriad possibilities, we try out the most perverse positions in the practice of our nightly act, the penetration of the denotative body of the work. Any exit from the logic of language might be an entry in a symptomatic dictionary. The alphabetical order of this ample block of knowledge might

render a dense lexicon of lucid hallucinations.
Beside the bed, a pad lies open to record the
meandering of migratory words. In the rapid
eye movement of the poet's night vision, this
dictum can be decoded, like the secret acrostic
of a lover's name.

Asked what effect her Paisano fellowship may have had
on her writing career, Mullen replied: "It was probably the
most peaceful and inspiring six months of my life."[12]

John Davidson
February 1982

Before John Davidson became a Paisano fellow, his
nonfiction narrative, *The Long Road Home: The Story of a
Mexican Worker's Perilous Crossing into the United States*, was
awarded the 1979 Texas Institute of Letters Most Significant
Contribution to Knowledge prize.

While Davidson worked on a novel and a short story
during his residency, he has pursued a career as a freelance
journalist ever since. Davidson held senior editorial positions
at the *Atlanta Journal Constitution*, *Texas Monthly*, *Vanity Fair*,
and the *San Antonio Express-News*. He edited *Texas Architect*
and writes frequently about culture, society, and politics.

As a freelance writer, he has contributed to *GQ*, *Fortune*,
Mirabella, *Elle*, *House & Garden*, *Preservation*, and *Mexico
Business*. One of his articles for *Mirabella* included a vivid
account of filming at Willie Nelson's property west of
Austin.[13] He's also written interviews with famed filmmaker
Ismail Merchant, the director Simon Callow, and actress
Vanessa Redgrave.

Sandra Lynn
August 1982

You go south from Fort Davis
until you come to the place

where rainbows wait for rain,
and the big river is kept in a stone box,
and water runs uphill.
And the mountains float in the air,
except at night when they go away to play
with other mountains.

That is not a poem by Sandra Lynn, but rather a saying attributed to an old cowboy whose name is forgotten. Lynn used it as the epigraph to her poems about the Big Bend country.

In 1973, when Lynn first visited Big Bend, she was "surprised by the strength of my initial response to that remote, strange, and beautiful region. Extinct volcanoes, the Rio Grande and its canyons, the Chihuahuan desert, and relict alpine woods—all gathered into a corner of the *Desplobado*." [The term means "unpopulated," and was the name given to the Big Bend country by Spanish explorers.][14] She began writing poems about the Big Bend at that time. Not long afterward, one was reprinted in a magazine of the Sierra Club with a photograph taken by Richard Fenker Jr., then a professor at Texas Christian University. Fenker then asked her if she would like to join him in working on a collection of poems and photographs of the region. A published version of their collaboration would appear several years later.

Another unplanned development was her collaboration with her then husband, composer Richard Brown, who wrote music for French horn and piano to accompany her first poems. He later orchestrated and wrote more music for a small chamber ensemble to accompany the later poems as well. The logical next step, Lynn thought, would be a reading and exhibit of the photographs, accompanied by the music.

The world premiere performance of *Where Rainbows Wait for Rain* was held at Gallery 104 in Austin on September 2, 1983, with poems read by Lynn, photographs by Fenker, and a chamber ensemble conducted by Brown. The photographs remained on view for six weeks.[15] This was the first—and

167

possibly only — time that poetry, photography, and music combined could be attributed, in part, to a Paisano fellowship.

Where Rainbows Wait for Rain was published by Tangram Press in 1989 — a permanent record of the Lynn-Fenker collaboration. In 2007 two poems were reprinted in *What Wildness Is This*, an anthology of Texas writing.

Brown wrote other music while Lynn was a fellow at the ranch. He completed a score for a ballet, "Ballabile," that was performed by the Austin Ballet Theatre in February 1983. Both he and Lynn sent in final reports after the fellowship; he was correct in stating that "this was the first musical work to be written at Paisano."[16]

In 1999 Lynn wrote *Windows on the Past: Historic Lodgings of New Mexico*, the first book on New Mexico's historic hotels, inns, and guest ranches.

R. G. VLIET
February 1983

At the end of Russ Vliet's residency, he left these notes:

A DAB OF PHILOSOPHY

"Rolled round in earth's diurnal course," I lie in the hammock, in shade and a stiff, cool breeze, and have upon me again so strongly the sense that there cannot be the lived life without a conscious relationship with "rocks and stones and trees" — with cicadas and bluffs, the nearly fleshlike substances of water and air, and live oaks and cedar elms and prickly poppies, my contemporaries. This consciousness is one of the stipends that comes with Paisano.

A PRACTICAL MATTER

The house, though it has its history, isn't burdened with it: the rooms are plain, the furnishings simple, and right away the house is our own. I have sat down at Dobie's desk, where I am writing this now, and made it my own.

ENSALADA DE NOPAL

All about the ranchhouse are patches of prickly pear, the new, tender leaves abundant through June and July. We make a fine Mexican salad with them. The best leaves are those that have fleshy, spur-like spines growing on them. Cut the leaves from the mother plant. Using a board to hold the leaves, los nopales, so as not to get a handful of prickers, scrape the leaves with a knife on both sides. Be sure to get rid of the tiny, mole-like knobs out of which the prickers grow, and trim off the edges of the leaves. Wash the leaves, cut in quarter-inch slices and simmer with salt and a clove of garlic until tender, twenty to forty minutes. Drain and rinse and put in the refrigerator to cool. Slice onions and tomatoes and chopped cilantro and add these to the chilled nopalitos, salt to taste, add diced chiles, if desired, toss and serve. The cooked nopal leaves have a texture somewhat like okra.

THREE PENNIES

There is a saying that if you see only one black vulture soaring it's a sign of bad luck. Not to worry: you will seldom look up and see less than four.

The progressive chords of wildflowers this spring has been like music.

If only the figs would get ripe before we leave.[17]

While virtually all Vliet's novels and poems have Texas

settings, Vliet and his wife Ann, an English professor, lived in different parts of the country after their college years in San Marcos. They had returned to Texas often to visit, but Vliet believed that he "needed distance to give perspective to his vision of Texas as a narrative setting."[18] Vliet devoted full time to writing, producing two novels and three books of poetry over a period of eighteen years. His writing, though critically well received — Malcolm Cowley described his work as close to being a national treasure[19] — was not widely known. He was recognized for his poetry in 1966 and 1970 and for his fiction in 1977 by the Texas Institute of Letters.

When he received the Paisano fellowship he felt that he was ready to return to Texas permanently. Sadly, cancer, which he had a decade earlier, recurred shortly before his Paisano stay. Despite having to undergo chemotherapy, Vliet kept at work steadily on his fourth novel, *Scorpio Rising*. After his Paisano stay, he and Ann returned to Massachusetts where Ann was completing a teaching commitment. After that year they had plans to return to a little house in Kyle.

That fall he wrote from North Adams, Massachusetts: "It's lovely here, all the trees — whole mountainsides of them — are changing and in full color. One moves through a burning world. But how we miss Texas. We will be down there next summer, and in 1986 we will come back to stay permanently."[20]

Vliet finished *Scorpio Rising* five days before his death but never had the chance to return to Texas.

ALAN POGUE
August 1983

Photographer Alan Pogue left these words for the next resident: "Becoming the Culligan Man was not my goal at Paisano. My commitment was to print my portfolio at J. Frank Dobie's ranch and I had to clean up the water in order to do that. The improvements cost me $3000 and a lot of time. I could not afford either. I would not do it again, so think kind thoughts of me when you take a shower."[21]

Times have changed, of course, and shortly after Pogue's stay, the University of Texas at Austin replaced the water system. However, Pogue's determination to make some fourteen hundred prints of photographs of farm workers led to the successful completion of a portfolio, *Agricultural Workers of the Rio Grande and Rio Bravo Valleys*, published by the Center for Mexican American Studies at the University of Texas at Austin. The portfolio led famed photographer Russell Lee to praise Pogue as a "top photographer of the social and political scene in the Southwest."[22]

One has to go further back into Pogue's life to learn where his intense and passionate interest in social justice comes from. After serving as a medic in the Vietnam War, he returned with a deep desire "to use photography to look into society's wounds for the possibility of cultural healing. On a battlefield, a medic has to be able to see clearly, honestly and to be strong in the love and mercy required for the work of healing."[23]

The documentation of Texas farmworkers was just the beginning. His involvement with several prison reform groups led to extensive work on Texas prison conditions. In 1999, a nationwide show on prison conditions was exhibited at the Washington Center for Photography.

Outside Texas, he has made many trips to Iraq on behalf of Veterans for Peace and in 2007 he went to Pakistan on behalf of a Japanese peace group.

In Austin, he founded the Texas Center for Documentary Photography and has been the photographer for the *Texas Observer* since 1972. He published a major collection of his documentary photography, *Witness to Justice*, in 2007. University of Texas Press describes the range of his work:

> This book opens with images of social protests
> of the 1960s and early 1970s, along with the
> countercultural scene around Austin, Texas,
> and prominent cultural and political figures,
> from William Burroughs and Allen Ginsberg to

Ann Richards and George W. Bush. Following these are suites of images that record the often-harsh conditions of farm workers, immigrants, and prisoners—groups for whom Pogue has long felt deep empathy. Reflecting the progression of Pogue's career beyond Texas and the Southwest, the concluding suites of images capture social conditions in several Latin American and Caribbean countries (El Salvador, Nicaragua, Cuba, Puerto Rico, Mexico, and Haiti), the effects of the Israeli-Palestinian conflict on ordinary people, and the lives and privations of Iraqis between the two recent wars.[24]

From his early work, produced under less-than-ideal conditions at Paisano with earlier photographic techniques, to his present-day use of digital methods, Pogue has hewed to his original vision: portraying the poor and oppressed in all parts of the world.

Cheryl Cessna
February 1984

About a dozen years after she had been a Paisano fellow, Cheryl Cessna sent the Paisano director what she called "some stream-of-conscious thoughts about my time at Paisano—a time I still feel as almost sacred." She had the unusual opportunity to become acquainted with John Henry Faulk, the noted folklorist, raconteur, and friend of J. Frank Dobie. Faulk had originally interested Frank Dobie in Paisano and the two of them scouted the property prior to Dobie's purchase of the ranch in 1956.

J. H. F., as she designated Faulk, hadn't been out to Paisano in many years when he visited with her three or four times in 1984.

He called me Sweet Pea and said, "You're

living out here all by yourself?" Our love of characterizations and folklore dovetailed beautifully.

J. F. Dobie was his mentor, and the sense of his history of the place tying in with my sense of history was astounding: my love of folklore from an early age—listening to my elders' stories and recording them on tape for posterity.

Pear Orchard, Texas, his fictional city, and Uphill, Texas, mine...such a meeting of minds.

McCarthy Era and blacklisting ruined his career and finances, colored his entire life, and our conversations were peppered with talk of the First Amendment. He could quote it verbatim, and I came away with a new understanding and respect for it.

The reverberations from one life to another and the connections that endure; these I treasure.

Again, I love folklore and its importance in understanding ourselves and others and our shared history.

I cherish people. Everyone has a wonderful story to tell, and I would love to hear them all.

There are many disparate elements here. I've tried to put them all together and to make spiritual meaning out of it all. I hope it's conveyed the sense of magic and wonder that Paisano meant (and still means) to me.[25]

TERRY GALLOWAY
August 1984

The only writer/performance artist to hold a Paisano fellowship is Terry Galloway. From time to time she has disavowed the term "performance artist," saying it sounds like someone who "sets her hair on fire," but regardless of what the combination of writing and performance is called, it has been the heart of Galloway's work. Galloway is the central actor in all her writing, and it is almost always autobiographical. Also significant is the fact that she is a deaf artist. Defying the problems attendant upon profound deafness, which she has dealt with since childhood, she has performed not only in Austin but also in several venues in New York, around the country, and in Mexico City, Toronto, London, and Edinburgh.

The formative background for Galloway's work took place when, as an undergraduate, she spent summers at the University of Texas at Austin's Winedale Shakespeare program. She played many roles in the performances, and some still remember her Falstaff. A few years later she became a founding member of the improvisational troupe in Austin, Esther's Follies.

She has written and acted in some half-dozen plays and monologues, many of which she has revised several times. A viewer who saw *Out All Night and Lost My Shoes* in the mid-1980s would have seen a different show five or ten years later. Galloway moved between Austin and New York several times. After a reading or performance on a New York stage, or after one of her tours with Performance Space 122's Field Trips, she oftentimes would return to Austin for a short run of the work at an Austin theater. In 2001, The Rude Mechanicals helped her develop one of her longer plays, *In the House of the Moles*, which was subsequently workshopped at the Mark Taper Forum in Los Angeles.

Her publications are as eclectic as her performances. A chapter of her memoir *Mean Little Deaf Queer* (Beacon Press, 2010) has been anthologized, alongside work by David Sedaris and Margaret Atwood, in *Sleepaway: Writings on Summer Camp*.

Her interest in and compassion for people with disabilities — not just deafness, but disabilities of all sorts — is evident in her work. In the early 2000s she directed a series of summer workshops for the Actual Lives Performance Project. The project is described as making "theatre out of the raw material of real life, with a focus on the lived experience of disability." Galloway declared, "In one short week we've produced enough in funny, angry, edgy, silly, provocative work to keep you bolted to your seat."[26]

Since the early 1990s Galloway has lived most of the time in Tallahassee, Florida, where her partner and oftentimes collaborator Donna Nudd was on the faculty of Florida State University. Together they founded the Mickee Faust Club, a self-described "community theater for the weird community," which includes a Florida branch of Actual Lives. Each year this mixed ability company writes and produces a variety of cabarets, radio shows, and video shorts. Their video shorts have been featured in over two hundred film festivals

While her performances have been well received in New York and abroad over the years, she has been particularly warmly embraced in Austin. On returning to the city to present short runs of her work, she was featured on the cover of the *Austin Chronicle* in 1993 and 2002 with accompanying interviews and discussion of her work.[27]

She has received recognition for her wide-ranging work, such as the National Communication Association's Lifetime Award, but Galloway insists that "Paisano remains most dear to my heart."

LISA FAHRENTHOLD
February 1985

While Lisa Fahrenthold worked on a collection of short stories while she was at Paisano, she had already published a nonfiction work, *Admissions: The Extraordinary History of Brackenridge Hospital*, with her coauthor Sara Rider in 1984.

SANDRA CISNEROS
August 1985

In 1991, concerned that she was not able to make a living as a writer in Austin (and before several signal honors and awards would come to her), Sandra Cisneros was interviewed by a reporter from the *Daily Texan* about her experience at Paisano. She said she was grateful for the time to write and for having the financial burden lifted with the stipend. She declared:

> I have to say that Dobie Paisano is what made me decide to stay in Texas. I am very glad I did, because what happened after Dobie Paisano is that I started to write a few Texas pieces. My new book (*Woman Hollering Creek*) is practically all Texas stories. I didn't write them at Dobie Paisano, but Dobie Paisano is what altered my destiny, what allowed me to decide not to march out of the state.[28]

While recognition was slow in coming, it finally came with a vengeance to Cisneros. Her first important work, *The House on Mango Street*, began to be placed on the reading lists of schools and colleges attempting to include voices of women—particularly Latina and Chicana women. Ramon Saldivar, then (1986) professor of English at the University of Texas at Austin, explained: "She writes about issues that male Chicanos have not addressed, like what it means to be young, female and talented in an urban society."[29]

In the mid-90s, Cisneros's earlier work was reprinted by Vintage Books, a division of Random House; she received several National Endowment for the Arts awards; and, drawing the most attention, she was named a MacArthur fellow in 1995. She was featured at the first Texas Book Festival in 1996 and went on to receive one of the festival's Bookend awards for distinguished achievement in Texas letters. In 1997 she received the Texas Medal of Arts.

Even back in the lean days, she was very generous with her time with other writers, particularly women writers. In post-Paisano days she led a group from the Women's Peace Center in Austin. Later in the 1990s in San Antonio, a city she made her principal residence and embraced for its combination of cultures, she began devoting her attention to a workshop for Latina/o writers. Originally held in her own home, the workshop brought together writers of diverse talents but with a shared sense of community. She named the workshop Macondo, after the small town in Gabriel García Márquez's book *One Hundred Years of Solitude*. Its faculty and alumni include several MacArthur fellows and more than twenty-five published authors. During the seventeen years that Cisneros ran the workshop, over two hundred poets, novelists, translators, journalists, scholars, children's book authors, and anthropologists participated. In 2012, Cisneros passed the Macondo Workshop on to the Guadalupe Cultural Arts Center in San Antonio after she decided to relocate to San Miguel de Allende, Mexico.

In its first years the workshop was held by invitation one week in August in San Antonio. In 2006, Cisneros incorporated the workshop into the Macondo Foundation. According to its organizational history, the Macondo Foundation is

> ...committed to bringing together a diversity of writers crossing borders of all kinds. As an association of socially engaged writers united to advance creativity, foster generosity, and honor community, the Macondo Foundation attracts generous and compassionate writers who view their works and talents as part of a larger task of community-building and non-violent social change.

The Foundation holds events at several sites in San Antonio, and Our Lady of the Lake University has hosted the Macondo Workshop, providing space for workshops, seminars, and performances as well as housing at no cost for workshop participants. Cisneros has been joined in support of and participation in the venture by many writers not only in Texas but internationally.[30]

Cisneros has also founded the Alfredo Cisneros Del Moral Foundation in honor of her father, an upholsterer. When Cisneros was at Paisano, a friend donated money to purchase a new sofa for the ranch. Cisneros, citing lessons learned from her father, accompanied the director and the donor to a store to ensure that the sofa was of suitable quality and its construction was sound.

Texas writers have received more than $75,000 since 2000 from the Alfredo Cisneros Del Moral Foundation.

With major accomplishments in her own writing (a novel, *Caramelo*, nine years in the making, was published in 2002; *A House of My Own: Stories from My Life* was published in 2015), and important contributions to Latino writers, artists, and others via the Macondo and Alfredo Cisneros Del Moral Foundations, Cisneros can still look back at her peaceful time at Paisano. Just after she finished her fellowship, she wrote: "Walking home over a route we've learned by heart, under a night sky so familiar we wear it on our shoulders like a cloak, the little Paisano house gleams in the distance like a lantern, so much home we wish we never had to let it go."[31]

ROSEMARY CATACALOS
February 1986

When Rosemary Catacalos became the director in 2003 of Gemini Ink, a thriving San Antonio literary center founded by Nan Cuba, she was already well known as a poet, writer, teacher, and as a literary arts administrator. A San Antonio native of Mexican and Greek descent, Catacalos had been a poet in the San Antonio schools from the late 1970s to 1984. She also worked as a television producer of young people's programs. Her book of poetry, *Again for the First Time*, won the Texas Institute of Letters poetry prize in 1985.

In 1986 she became the spring Paisano fellow, following poet Sandra Cisneros, who had come to San Antonio to work with the literature program of the Guadalupe Cultural Arts Center. That was the only year two poets were chosen.

Catacalos was a Stegner Creative Writing Fellow in

Poetry at Stanford University from 1989–1991, the first of several Paisano fellows to hold Stegner fellowships. (Other Stegner fellows include Thomas McNeely, Chris Wiman, and Marcia Buffington.) After her fellowship, she extended her work in arts administration as executive director of the Poetry Center and American Poetry Archives at San Francisco State University. She was also an affiliated scholar at the Institute for Research on Women and Gender at Stanford University. In 2013, she was named poet laureate of the State of Texas.

Throughout, she has continued to write poetry and has been published in a wide variety of national journals. A chapbook, *Begin Here*, was published in 2013 by Wings Press, which also issued a thirtieth-anniversary edition of *Again for the First Time* in 2014.

At the conclusion of her fellowship, Catacalos wrote:

> Often, I think, those of us who must make time for our writing while maintaining a full-time job, don't easily take the risks associated with new directions. Instead, because time is so limited, we tend to do what we already know we can do. The freedom to question and even to fail is one of the greatest gifts Paisano has to offer us as writers.[32]

PAT LITTLEDOG (formerly Pat Ellis Taylor)
August 1986

Both Pat LittleDog, or Pat Ellis Taylor if you go back to the late 1980s, and her work are hard to describe. The writer Carolyn See, reviewing *In Search of the Holy Mother of Jobs*, wrote: "If Charles Lamb was a woman and a Texan, and wrote about drugs, sex, rock 'n'roll, reptiles and unemployment, he'd be Pat LittleDog! This fearless being gives new and wonderful meaning to the phrase: 'familiar essay.'"[33] Pat LittleDog's flamboyant personality and unconventional lifestyle — such as living in a tent in the Barton Creek greenbelt or sharing the basement of bookstore Paperbacks Plus with a husband (now ex)—are reflected in her poetry and in her stories.

As Anne Morris related in an interview in 1990, "When the Atlantic Monthly Press brought out an edition of *Afoot in a Field of Men*, national reviewers singled out Pat Ellis Taylor as a name to watch among writers of fiction." But a divorce changed all that, LittleDog told Morris. "'It's my real name,' she said flatly, perhaps a little tired of explaining the change. I assumed it when I got divorced in April. Taylor was my ex-husband's name. She says dog names are common to many Indian tribes. Hers is Cheyenne."[34] Her subsequent stories and poetry are published under LittleDog.

Paisano was perhaps the ideal place for LittleDog. Her description of the ranch's effect not only on her work but on her personal feelings as well tell a great deal about this writer.

The ranch was unusually dry in the fall of 1986:

> I have always been sensitive to weather, and that drought on the land seemed to reflect the personal drought that I was suffering, too, when I came. But hot and dry as the land was, it seemed to welcome me, so that even in the height of the temperatures I stayed outside, lying nude on the big rock by the creek, casting my own fate in with the land's—a basic optimism that the drought would break and we would both get better. And that is the way it happened—the winds came, then the rains, the creek rose, the waters came rushing, subsided, rushed again, while the mud grabbed me and the wet leaves tangled in my hair and my clothes. And just as the limestone allowed the water to course through itself freely, the stories began to come out of me. At first a torrent of words, almost incoherent, seeming like babble. When the flood subsided

I was amazed—pieces of stories were scattered
all over the room like the debris cluttered
in high branches as well as piled up at the
roots, nesting materials for snakes as well as
blue herons. So I began work then in the fall
of sorting and sifting what had come to be
in that great torrent, trying to make sound
houses from my own words for my thoughts.
In the past two weeks the sun has come out
and stayed out, the temperatures have become
heavenly, the creek water illuminated with
brilliant dancing lights. And just as the clouds
have lifted out of the valley, they have lifted
off of me, so that I have been able to see what I
am doing and what direction I now need to go
with the work I have done here.[35]

Living at Paisano and subsequently her outdoor living
on Barton Creek (though quite brief) convinced LittleDog
she wanted to live in the country. By the late 1990s, LittleDog
was able to buy ten acres in Caldwell County, where she has
continued to live. At first she and a friend had only a tent
out there—no electricity or running water—but she now
has a mobile home with septic system and electricity: all the
luxuries of life.

In 2002 LittleDog suffered a stroke that left her with
some impairment. However, she has been able to continue
writing poetry. When asked about the transforming effect
Paisano had on her, LittleDog resurrected a poem she began
while at Paisano about the wedding at the ranch of one of her
sons. She completed it twenty years later. The final stanzas of
"ending/beginning":

And I
will always remember
til death ever after
the record of marriage

that remains in
the rock cliffs
and swims in the air

that could have been anywhere
but was
specifically here
(while dobie continues
to ramble on and on)

TIM HATCHER
February 1987

While high water at the ranch presented problems to a number of fellows, only two—Tim Hatcher and Mylène Dressler—saw their cars swallowed by Barton Creek.

Hatcher recalled:

> For several days the creek waters had been too high for me to drive across in my Honda Civic, so I had been parking at the creek and wading across to get to the house. On the night of Thursday, June 11, there was an intense thunderstorm and when it ended I walked down the driveway to the creek to check on my car. During the storm, the creek had risen several feet, and so I reached the water's edge about fifty feet earlier than I had expected to. I had to wade into the creek until the water was up to my chest just to get an unobstructed view of the opposite bank. When I shined my flashlight beam across the creek—as debris was rushing past me, all I could see in the darkness was the backside of the interior rearview mirror. The water had completely surrounded the car and flooded it up to about the radio. At that time the water level was 5 feet 6 inches at the crossing. The

crest of the flood did not arrive until Saturday, June 13, when the waters reached 9.5 to 10 feet. That morning water depth had only been 2 feet 6 inches. The day before I had arranged to have my car towed to higher ground, but the high waters on Saturday reached the car a second time.

Needless to say, the car was totaled.[36]

Tim Hatcher had been writing plays and film treatments as well as doing some freelance technical writing and working with several theater groups in the Dallas–Fort Worth area when he took up residence at Paisano. His plan was to complete a play called *The Death of Floyd Collins*, a dramatization of an actual incident that unfolded in February of 1925 in rural Kentucky. Floyd Collins was a small-time entrepreneur who, along with his father, owned and operated a tourist attraction called Crystal Cave. Coerced by his father, he began exploring another, unused cave, only to become trapped by a cave-in. Floyd remained imprisoned for almost two weeks, pinned under a seven-ton boulder while hundreds of workers toiled night and day to free him. As Floyd's life slowly faded away, the scene outside the cave became a carnival. Thousands of spectators mingled with the rescuers and reporters entrenched at the mouth of the cave.

The play was produced several times in the Dallas area and over several consecutive summers within a few miles where Floyd had actually lived and died. Hatcher's play is mentioned in the epilogue of a book about the Floyd Collins incident (*Trapped* by Robert Murray and Roger Brucker, reprinted 1999), citing that though Floyd died in 1925, his influence is still felt in American culture.[37]

Although he has continued to write plays, Hatcher's career has taken a different path. A friend offered him freelance work at his animation company in 1994, and he began learning the technology of computer animation. As that aspect of the industry boomed, opportunities abounded.

"Since 1994 I have worked on several high-profile animated projects including feature films (*Jimmy Neutron: Boy Genius, The Ant Bully, TMNT*), TV shows (*The Adventures of Jimmy Neutron, Olive, the Other Reindeer, Santa vs. the Snowman*), and commercials." In 2006 he left his friend's company and has been freelancing ever since for a Dallas company called Reel FX. Hatcher feels that animation has more than compensated as an outlet for his creative side.

CATHERINE AGRELLA
August 1987

As did many of the fellows, Catherine Agrella left several items to enhance and make the ranch more comfortable: a newly matted and repaired print of J. Frank Dobie, two small braided rugs, a lamp for the front room study, and towels and washcloths — "washed and dried the Paisano way — don't be surprised at the stiff sandpaperiness of them" — an iron, and curtains in the front room, front bath, and kitchen made by her mother.[38] This is an interesting list to look back on, reminding current residents of the days of line-dried linens and before the gift of a washer and dryer. And who ever does ironing?

Before her residency, Catherine Agrella had published short stories and was completing an MFA in fiction writing at Washington University in St. Louis. At the ranch she worked on a collection of short stories and, discovering that she was interested in writing a sustained piece of fiction, began a novel.

In 1987, her short story about life at NASA appeared in *New Growth: Contemporary Short Stories by Texas Writers*, edited by Lyman Grant and Mark Busby.

DAGOBERTO GILB
February 1988

Three volumes of short stories, a book of essays, and two novels notwithstanding, Dagoberto Gilb is bound to be known for years to come for his massive anthology of

Texas Mexican literature *Hecho en Tejas*. A recipient of the Texas Book Festival's Bookend award in 2007, Gilb has been recognized not only for his own writing about the lives and loves of Texas Mexicans, he has also brought attention to Texas Mexican writers, starting with Cabeza de Vaca in the mid-sixteenth century. The anthology is primarily devoted to writers in the twentieth and early twenty-first centuries. The closing words of the introduction to *Hecho en Tejas* express Gilb's feeling that after years of being misunderstood, marginalized, or stereotyped, these writers and their subjects are beginning to enter the mainstream:

> *We have been here, we are still here.* I want this book to overwhelm the ignorance — and I emphasize the "ignore" root of that word as much as its dumb or mean or nasty connotation — about Raza here in Texas, the people who settled and were settled and still remain in Texas, who will soon be the largest population group in the state, not to mention the region beyond. Onward *y adelante!*[39]

Gilb was born in Los Angeles and held many kinds of menial jobs as he was growing up, but mainly he worked in construction, becoming a carpenter who often worked on high-rise buildings. He received degrees from the University of California, Santa Barbara, in philosophy and religious studies, though throughout his career he somewhat disdained what he felt were the pretensions of academic life.

In 1976 he moved to El Paso, where his writing career really began. In 1985, his first book of stories, *Winners on the Pass Line*, was published by Cinco Puntos Press in El Paso. (Co-founder of the press Lee Byrd later became a Paisano fellow.) Making ends meet was not easy for Gilb, and he found he could return to Los Angeles for construction jobs that paid better than in El Paso and then return for periods in which he could work on his writing.

Gilb was a Paisano fellow in 1988. Afterward, he wrote glowingly of Paisano, calling it a paradise and expressing his gratitude for the opportunity it had offered him. But it was several years before his work began to be recognized. Another book of stories, *The Magic of Blood*, was published by University of New Mexico Press in 1993. The following year, Grove Press published his first novel, *The Last Known Residence of Mickey Acuña*. Subsequently Grove has published Gilb's short stories, essays, and a novel.

In 1994, Gilb won the Texas Institute of Letters Jesse H. Jones Award for best book of fiction. *The Magic of Blood* was a finalist for the PEN/Faulkner award and PEN's Ernest Hemingway Foundation Award for the American debut of the year. Gilb went on to receive prestigious Whiting and Guggenheim fellowships.[40] His collection of essays, *Gritos*, published in 2003, covers most of his twenty-year writing career and includes some of his commentaries from NPR's *Fresh Air*. His comments about *Gritos* say a good deal about Gilb — the man, the writer, and the unswerving supporter of Texas Mexican writing.

> *Gritos*. When I turned in this collection, my publisher wasn't sure about that title. That's because it was thought the title was translated as "shouts." A part of me liked that it would be what people who don't know the Mexican tradition of a grito would think when they looked it up in a Spanish-English dictionary. If you don't know, yeah, right, it's a shout, a yell. But it's not. The most famous grito is the one from Father Hidalgo, *el grito de Dolores*, declaring Mexico's independence from Spain, defiance and freedom. A grito is what a coyote does — an animal wail of need, singular and for the group. A grito is the "Viva" at a wedding or a political rally — joy and support. A grito is most known when mariachis sing, that

loud, extemporaneous howl of triumph, or the sad — and loud, it has to be loud — lament of love lost, the orgasmic agony of love found.[41]

WILLIAM LOUIS RIPLEY
August 1988

Following Bill Ripley's father's death when Ripley was a year old, his mother and grandparents raised him on the family ranch in Mason, Texas. He was educated at Harvard and obtained degrees in creative writing from the University of Texas at El Paso (MA) and the University of Utah (PhD) He held various teaching posts during his graduate studies.

Atlantic Monthly Press published his sole novel, *Prisoners*. Its subject reflected the turmoil and violence of the drug culture of the '60s. His writing was much admired. An editor at *Esquire* wrote:

> His prose has a pop and jangle to it, each sentence an energetic production. It's possible to read Ripley's work solely for the prose. As his fiction has evolved, however, his characters have come more and more to the fore as men and women whose occasionally atrocious experiments in living merit compassion, and even admiration.[42]

Ripley resided in Austin for some time after his residency but later moved to California. He died on September 5, 2007 at his home in Lucerne, California. A celebration of his life was held at his family's ranch in Mason.

ENDNOTES

1 William Martin, faculty biography, Rice University, 2004.
2 William Martin, personal communication, ANS, July 24, 2007.
3 *On Campus*, February 2–8, 1981, 5.
4 Whitaker, "Mr. Dobie's Gift."
5 "Crossing the 'Shadow Line' between Youth and Maturity," *On Campus*, September 7–13, 1981, 20.
6 Beatrice.com, April 4, 2005.
7 Robin Bradford, "Safety in Words: The Dangerous, Graceful Life of Laura Furman," *Austin Chronicle*, April 20, 2001, 50.
8 Harryette Mullen, personal communication, August 16, 2007.
9 "Poet Completes 'Blues Baby' Volume While at Paisano," *On Campus*, February 1–7, 1982, 4.
10 Harryette Mullen, *Blues Baby: Early Poems* (Lewisburg, Pennsylvania: Bucknell University Press, 1981, 2002).
11 Review of Harryette Mullen's *Sleeping with the Dictionary* (Berkeley: University of California Press, 2002), *New York Times*, March 2003.
12 Mullen, personal communication, 2007.
13 *Mirabella* was published between 1989 and 2000 and was named after Grace Mirabella, a former *Vogue* editor-in-chief.
14 Sandra Lynn, application for Paisano, 1982–83.
15 Richard Fenker Jr. and Sandra Lynn, *Where Rainbows Wait for Rain* (Berkeley, California: Tangram Press), program and poster for world premiere, September 2, 1983.
16 Richard Brown (husband of Fellow Sandra Lynn), final report, April 5, 1983.
17 R. G. Vliet, final report, July 30, 1983.
18 "Two Paisano Fellows Named," *On Campus*, June 1982, 26.
19 As quoted by Naomi Shihab Nye, "Texas Always Remained His Own Country," *Dallas Morning News*,

October 26, 1984, 3AA.

[20] R. G. Vliet, letter to Audrey Slate, October 18, 1983.

[21] Alan Pogue, final report, July 3, 1984.

[22] Russell Lee, comments about Alan Pogue's portfolio, Center for Mexican American Studies, University of Texas at Austin, 1984.

[23] http://www.documentaryphotography.com/. Accessed January 22, 2016.

[24] University of Texas Press announcement from documentaryphotography.com.

[25] Cheryl Cessna, personal communication, written from Cleveland, Texas, August 28, 1998.

[26] Terry Galloway, Actual Lives Performance Project Announcement, VSA Arts of Texas, August 24, 2002.

[27] *Austin Chronicle*, cover and article 24–25, August 20, 1993, and *Austin Chronicle*, cover and article 28–30.

[28] Chris Huddle, *Daily Texan*, 1991.

[29] David Medina, "Onward," *Austin American-Statesman*, March 11, 1986, 14.

[30] Vicente Lozano, "The Macondo Workshop: Latino Writers Come Home to San Antonio," *Poets & Writers*, March–April 2007; Organizational History, Macondo Foundation Inc. (P.O. Box 831046, San Antonio, Texas 78283); and Alfred Cisneros Del Moral Foundation.

[31] Sandra Cisneros, final report, February 9, 1986.

[32] Rosemary Catacalos, final report, July 27, 1986.

[33] Pat LittleDog, quoted in a flyer by Cinco Puntos Press, publisher of *In Search of the Holy Mother of Jobs,* 1991.

[34] Anne Morris, "Writing her Way," *Austin American-Statesman*, September 17, 1990, B1.

[35] Pat LittleDog, final report, January 30, 1987.

[36] Tim Hatcher, personal communication, February 17, 2008.

[37] Ibid.

[38] Catherine Agrella, final report, undated, but probably early 1988.

[39] Dagoberto Gilb, *Hecho en Texas* (Albuquerque: University of New Mexico Press, 2007), introduction.

[40] Jan Reid, "Dagoberto Gilb," *Texas Monthly*, September 1995, 130.

[41] Dagoberto Gilb, *Gritos* (New York: Grove Press, 2003), introduction.

[42] Will Blythe, Associate Fiction Editor, *Esquire*, May 30, 1989—letter of recommendation.

Fellows 1989–1998

EARLY PAISANO FELLOWS, SOME OF WHOM HAD HAD THE OPPORTUNITY to actually hear Dobie speak or to meet his wife, had come of age in a predominantly rural Texas. By the end of the 1990s, the Austin that had been home to about 224,000 people when Billy Porterfield matter-of-factly purchased horses to pass along for future fellows was a cosmopolitan urban center with a population of over 630,000. A piece of property like Paisano, left undeveloped for over twenty years, on a party telephone line and inaccessible in particularly wet weather, had become an exotic anomaly. Reflecting the far-reaching changes occurring in the state itself, the majority of writers who made Paisano their home during the 1990s were urban, mobile folk. Few had been born in rural areas. A good many did not live in the state at all by the time they received a fellowship. All were conscious that as "Texas writers" they had inherited an oft-times romanticized literary landscape. Their complicated and uneasy relationship with that metaphorical landscape tended to color their time at Paisano. The gift a fellowship bestowed on writers became, in large part, not only a gift of time but a gift of *place*.

Alan Tennant

Allen Wier

Martha Elizabeth

Sheryl St. Germain

Genaro Gonzalez

Sigman Byrd

Sarah Glasscock

Ewing Campbell

Sam Haynes

Stephen Pate

Catherine Bowman

Lynna Williams

Christian Wiman

Charles Behlen

Lisa Sandlin

Marcia Buffington

Lee Merrill Byrd

James Hannah

Clancy Carlile

ALAN TENNANT
February 1989

Alan Tennant was already an established writer and
naturalist when he became a Paisano fellow. The illustrator of
The Guadalupe Mountains of Texas and author of two volumes
on the snakes of Texas, he already had four chapters written
of a book he was proposing to complete at the ranch. He
called it "The Flight of the Falcon" and wanted to recount
his flights with a seventy-year old pilot to track a falcon's
transcontinental migration from a radio transmitter attached
to it—a feat never before attempted. The book was published
as *On the Wing* in 2004. Between Tennant's fellowship and
its publication, he had a two-decades-long career conducting
natural history seminars and trips around the world.

Before the Texas Book Festival in 2004, Tennant was
asked: "You didn't conduct a bird study in the usual scientific
manner, heavy on data and theories to test. Instead, you
latched onto a gutsy pilot and took off to follow a peregrine
wherever she took you. Why?"

His answer reveals a great deal about his work and
practices as a writer:

> Because this is not a science book, it's not even
> really a bird book. This is a romance—in the
> broadest sense—about how I became obsessed
> with a femme fatale. A falcon. [Pilot] George
> Vose and I were on a quest, like following
> the Grail. Our peregrine just mesmerized us.
> For Vose it was like his barnstorming days:
> flying cross-country without much electronic
> equipment. We saw what the birds saw,
> did what they did, fighting the same winds,
> wandering. We shared their puzzlement,
> their confusion. You can read reams of fact
> in scientific papers, but that's not the same
> as living with these creatures, in the air, for
> months.[1]

In the epilogue to *On the Wing,* Tennant explains the advances in electronic tracking that have replaced the equipment and methods he and Vose used. But his flying adventures were by no means all in the past. Haunted by the tragic death of Timothy Treadwell, which is recounted in Werner Herzog's documentary *Grizzly Man,* Tennant and a friend of Treadwell's were flown onto the Katmai Glacier in Alaska, where they camped in the same area Treadwell and his companion met their end. The pair found grizzlies there, and the details of their campout are chilling. However, Tennant felt he came to understand what led the experienced Treadwell to finally reach his untimely, horrible end.

> This was the strangely interdependent world of man and primal carnivore whose images — back in the world of men — year after year won Treadwell prizes at the Telluride Film Festival. Yet this was also a cosm that meant far more to him than any mere gateway to recognition. It was a world in which, after a decade of effort to get as close to bears as any human being could, somewhere in the course of stretching those limits of mind and body Tim Treadwell actually found his ursine soul mate. She was pale-furred young Downy bear, the female cub with which he forged an intense, years-long bond of understanding. Maybe during their long, face-to-face communions, even a sort of spiritual intra-species union. For Downy, Tim finally came to feel a love almost as though for a daughter, and it was to return to look again for her, after she had vanished near summer's end, that Tim and Amy returned, much too late in the year, to Katmai's Kaflia Lakes. It was always dangerous there — a place Treadwell had termed the Grizzly Maze — and though Downy should have been there, fishing for the

last salmon of the year, what Tim and Amy found instead was the aged, hyperphasia-hungry, desperate late-season bear who broke the rules, ripped down Treadwell's Samurai mask of strength, and tore them both to bits.

Only now, seeing how he—and no one else, ever, was able to live—only now was it possible for Treadwell's life among the Katmai grizzlies to make sense.[2]

ALLEN WIER
August 1989

"Home, they say, is where the heart is," Allan Wier wrote in his fellow's report at the conclusion of his fellowship, "and mine is in the Texas Hill Country, though I've lived most of my life in other places."[3]

Wier, who was born in San Antonio and spent portions of his childhood in Louisiana and Mexico, was teaching in the writing program at the University of Alabama when he received his fellowship.

"My heroes really were Indians and cowboys," he reflected in 2012.

So when I was fortunate enough to be given a Paisano fellowship I thought that was the perfect time and Frank Dobie's ranch was the perfect place to write a western. What I had in mind was a dime western shoot-'em-up that I would have fun with, something I could complete during my time on the ranch. I set up shop—carried my computer and a chair out to a desk of planks I rigged up—in a tin-roofed shed behind the ranch house (I don't know if the shed remains, but it is still hot in there in summer and cold in winter in my memory). I ended up spending the next ten years completing the first draft, 1486 pages, of *Tehano*.

Before I had written a page, I realized that what little I knew about Indians and cowboys came from family stories or, worse, from Hollywood. I took advantage of the Barker Texas History Center at the university, and I spent more of my six months' fellowship reading than I did writing. One character I had envisioned was a wise old Indian chief in a long, feather headdress. If you grew up in Texas, the Indians most alive in your imagination are likely Comanches. One of the first things my research told me was that Comanches did not revere old age. They believed that the good die young and a young warrior riding into battle was thinking, "today is a good day to die." Not only could my Comanche chief *not* be old, he could not even in the sense I had anticipated, be a chief. Comanches did not have permanent tribal chiefs. The tribe was divided into numerous autonomous bands, and within each band a warrior might offer himself as chief of any war party he was trying to assemble...Well, I thought, at least I can describe the resplendent war bonnet my young, temporary leader of a war party will wear. Then my research revealed that Comanches did not wear feather headdresses until late in the nineteenth century, after they saw warriors from other plains tribes wearing them at various council meetings. Fashion mavens, these warriors went home and instructed their wives to sew up some knock-off headdresses. I was disappointed, but only until I learned that a Comanche warrior often wore over his head the actual, hacked-off, hollowed-out, shaggy, horned head of a buffalo. As a fiction writer, I could live with that. I also learned that until different nineteenth-century white recorders, spelling the words phonetically and with great variation, wrote down Comanche words, the tribe had no written language. That fact gave me leeway to include in my novel Comanche speech sufficient for a sense of authenticity.

And so it went, the facts fueled my imagination as I discovered the story. The more I learned, the more my cast of characters grew. Nineteenth-century Texas might have invented the notion of cultural diversity, there were so many different peoples trying to inhabit the same space. In addition to Indians and cowboys, there were Civil War veterans, African American slaves and freedmen, immigrants (especially from Germany), Tejano ranchers, North American settlers, and numerous others.

The "dime novel western" Wier had planned to start for fun at Paisano became a novel of 714 pages and seventeen major characters published by Southern Methodist University Press in 2006.

The author of *Tehano* (Southern Methodist University Press, 2006), *A Place for Outlaws* (Harper & Row, 1989), *Departing as Air* (Simon & Schuster, 1983), *Blanco* (Louisiana State University Press, 1978), and *Things About to Disappear* (Louisiana State University Press, 1978), Wier also has received Guggenheim and National Endowment for the Arts fellowships. In 2012, he said:

After one (possibly two) more semesters, I'll retire from full-time teaching at Tennessee to live in the stone house we've recently built high on a ridge overlooking Lake Guntersville in North Alabama, an enormous lake the Tennessee River runs through. We're in the foothills where the Appalachians end (or begin) and our 180 degree view goes from East to North to West....Late afternoons, I look out at water and hills beyond. My gaze inevitably follows the light that reddens the sky, my sun always riding west to set over Texas, over the Hill Country that I carry like a sepia birthmark wherever I go, over J. Frank Dobie's ranch where I started a dime novel western that took me places I'd never been where I recognized things I'd never seen. A pal of mine, the novelist Don Hendrie who died before I finished writing *Tehano*, visited us at Paisano. He stood by the old stone house and looked around at limestone bluffs and twisty oaks and fat cedars and spreading prickly pear. Squinting in the sun, grinning, he said, "I guess if you could look inside Allen Wier's head, this is pretty much what it would look like."

Texas is a place that has for me a special sense, an aura, of its own, what Henry James calls "a mystic meaning to give out." The word another Texas writer, William Goyen (whose work means a great deal to me) wrote me in a letter the year he died: "abides." Texas *abides* with and in me. I always assumed that when I retired I'd return to Texas, but Donnie has family all around us in North Alabama, and she's corrected my assumption. My daddy is buried in the Blanco cemetery, and there's a space there that I hope has to wait a good while yet for my mother to rest in, beside him. Perhaps (a goodly number of years later, I hope) I may lie me down there, as well. A Tex-patriate whose life has taken him elsewhere to live, I don't own one acre of the state, but in the landscape of my imagination there's a Texas ranch with my brand over the gate. And for awhile, thanks to the generosity of the Texas Institute of Letters and the University of Texas and to charitable folk who give of their resources and their time and energy (especially Audrey Slate and Michael Adams), for a little while I did own a Texas ranch where my family and I spent many fine days and many fine nights.[4]

MARTHA ELIZABETH

February 1990

Martha Elizabeth (for a long time she eschewed using either a maiden or married name) had been writing poetry for some time when she came to North Texas to pursue a degree in interdisciplinary studies. Following her fellowship, she published three volumes of poetry: *The Return of Pleasure* (1996), *Considering Manon* (2002), and *Night Lights and Morning Glories* (2003).

Her creative efforts took a somewhat different turn after she moved to Montana, where she earned her MFA in creative writing. Continuing to write poetry, she also took up marbling and sculpture. The covers of her last two volumes of poetry contain her artwork. She has also taken up photography.

In 1992, Martha Elizabeth married Texas novelist James Crumley. Some time after that, she found some of her old journals. These excerpts describe some of her thoughts and feelings about Paisano as well as explaining her turn toward art.

Mon. 2/5/90 Paisano

This place is going to drive me crazy — stepped out on the porch with my tea, sat a moment, saw hawks circling above the trees — ran in to get binoculars then out to east of house to see higher—then four deer ran by in the field beyond the fence—ran, bounding with an easy spring over fences, cotton-white tails erect behind them—didn't run straight by, though, or in simultaneous direction—almost as if playing a moment—then they seemed to become frightened—plane overhead or pump house door came open and banging again—and they ran on. I watched one with binoculars, clear-cut grace, rounded geometry. Prickle of tears—maybe just the wind—felt like tears, roots of tears, seedlings. I could spend every day here just watching. Sitting on the porch, I said aloud "Now I know it's real: Monday morning, and this."

I was torn between work and roaming. Just being there seemed itself an occupation. I'd find myself walking down to the creek as if visiting an acquaintance. I watched it winter to summer, watched it rise to a brown torrent and shrink to trickles and ponds. I walked in it and swam and sat watching. I walked fence lines and followed paths. I kept forgetting to make words about it, despite my plans for field notebooks fat with description. I felt reduced—restored?— to a childlike absorption. Never have I had so much room to walk, and no one to fuss at me for taking so long.

Tue. 2/13/90 Paisano

It weighs on me that I can't draw it or paint it or even photograph it. I don't know how to come close to it in words.

—that is the key problem here, my frustration with words. I wish I could get my hands on them.

There was a tree on the slope by Barton

Creek that had split itself—juniper—too heavy where it leaned out, tore down from branch to trunk to ground, a bud of broccoli torn down off the stalk, the skin peeling with it, leaving rough vertical lines exposed—torn that easily though it was wood and bark, probably that fast too—gravity, its own weight, and the angle—center of gravity held firm.

What is worth telling about? It isn't enough to want to tell something. I look at the great live oak that fills the frame of the window, so big and old that someone has propped up one of its three main sections of trunk, and I want to communicate that tree somehow. Looking at the deer this morning I understood how to draw them for a moment—how they should be drawn—but it was all only in my head....I see the shapes now more than I did, and color, beginning to perceive texture—the result is that I am frustrated in two media now, unable to reach either words or images, mind and hands childish—not childlike—baby's fists—the bitterness of not being able to abandon myself to it.

I had already taken beginning ceramics at the university in Denton, which I told myself was research for my unwritten novel about potters and painters. I always did some kind of work with my hands, but I didn't think of it as art—not as Fine Art—I didn't think it counted. I bought my first porcelain in Austin, and I fussed at myself more than once for playing with clay or a borrowed Instamatic camera or the watercolors I bought half price and had no idea how to use, instead of working or exploring and taking notes. I'm rather stunned, dipping into my earnest journals, at how hard I drove myself. I would literally run away, bang out the door and head down to the creek as if playing hooky.

I had never lived alone before. I thought time and solitude would solve everything. I typed poems to go in the mail and put together a poetry chapbook and redid my poetry collection and did the maniacal study and warm-up for writing poetry that's part focused preparation and part ritual, and I did write finished poems; I continued thematic conversations in my notes and suffered more about love and pondered story and play ideas; I waited like a forsaken bride for the grand work I thought would come given time.

The daily life of the yard went on around me, birds flitting in and out of leaves like animated shadow. The sound of bees scribbled the air in the shade of the great oak. Sometimes the wind in the trees fooled me into thinking the creek was running; sometimes it was.

I suspect I was already burned out with freshman composition papers, with workshops and readings, with playing the critical game, which boils down to Find Something Wrong With This. I didn't understand that my gift is response, not control. Art tunes me, as does nature. I kept thinking, I will never have this again! and chided myself to write more, to learn the place better, to read the books on the shelves..., And then I'd be out the door and come back to myself squatting by a milkweed watching insects stumble on the bloom.

Tue. 7/17/90 Paisano

I think I resolved today to go ahead and be an artist—I think I tend to wait for the official anointer to show up and make me legal, some combination of fairy godmother and prince —

Before he was my husband, Jim Crumley used the Dobie Paisano fellowship as an excuse to talk to me (as if he needed one), asking my advice on the application, which he never filled in, then or later. He used to say he'd go to his grave without a grant, and I'd remind him he never applied for anything. He really liked it that I'd had the fellowship. Who knew that my time at the ranch would help prepare me to be his wife! It occurs to me that it also prepared me to be his widow, pacing our Montana home deep in thought as I probably paced the cottage, this place not nearly so old but with its own maintenance challenges, in its own way historical though not a shrine — and outside the fawns are losing their spots and browse unattended where I watered yesterday, the slope impossibly greener, like the front lawn at Paisano after much-needed rain. I remember using only one door to the porch so as not to disturb the fretful bird nesting in the far light socket — explosion of wings and sharp syllables and claws, all show but a good show — she'd flap back to the nest and fix me with her eye.

Wed. 2/16/2005 Austin

We took Audrey Slate to lunch and then drove out to the Dobie Ranch. Jim left the keys in the lock of the second gate and Audrey realized too late that we wouldn't be able to get into the house. Jim and Audrey chatted on the porch while I walked the perimeter of the yard taking fast nonthinking photos with my new digital camera, chest tight — felt like

my own ghost—I wanted to be there alone
with my camera & notebook, to walk, think,
reminisce or just listen to bird calls and wind
in the afternoon sun. . . . Wish I could go back
and reassure my old self that being who I was
was all right....[5]

After Crumley died in 2008, Martha Elizabeth organized
several tributes in Montana for him and his work, including
a session at the Montana Festival of the Book.

SHERYL ST. GERMAIN
August 1990

Place can transform a writer's work. Sixteen years
after her fellowship, Sheryl St. Germain seized the chance
to explore the power of place at Paisano by organizing
a panel discussion, "Rattlesnakes, Scorpions, and Low-
Water Crossings: Dobie Paisano Fellows and the Texas
Landscape," at the Associated Writers Programs meeting
held in Austin in March 2006. Introducing herself and three
former Paisano fellows—Laura Furman, Dominic Smith, and
Scott Blackwood—St. Germain cited the warning applicants
receive about former fellows who told stories about "icy
roads, rising water, rattlesnakes, fire ants, and cars lost in the
creek." Germain said:

Rather than deter me, the warning of the
potential difficulty of living in a place where
one could have such intimacy—and danger—
associated with the physical world, excited
me. Infected with a desire to live life close to
the bone, I took the plunge and submitted an
application, though I had no experience living
close to nature and honestly did not know
how I—or my young son Gray—would fare
on an isolated ranch surrounded by scorpions,
rattlesnakes and the possibilities of flood that

could imprison us on the ranch or make it impossible for us to return for days at a time.

Both Gray, who would accompany me, and I had been born in big cities, Dallas and New Orleans, respectively. Except for early forays into the fields back of our house and brief summer trips, we had not spent much time in the country. We had never hiked or fished, and only that year had we camped for the first time. I had never had to build a fire. Neither Gray nor I had ever seen a wild anything, unless those huge Louisiana roaches or the crawfish in the gutters by our home counted for something. We were urban to the bone.

I felt full of hope when I arrived at the ranch. Here was a new place, new things to learn, and a new way of being. It included danger, but danger lurked just as powerfully, if not more so, in the city. We had to learn about this place, its flora and fauna; we had to learn to live with and not against the natural world, as we did in the city. We had to explore, not be afraid, and then the gifts of this place would be given up.

In retrospect my time on the ranch would be one of the most important experiences of my life as a writer, and would mark a sharp departure in the direction my writing life would take. The experience of living on the ranch would change me in both profound and subtle ways, ways I could not have known beforehand. I would develop a relationship with land I had never known before. After Paisano, where I would learn to fish, I would take up fishing, camping, and hiking seriously. The time at Paisano would set me on the road to my current work with nature, environment

and place; all of my books since the residency
have been concerned with investigating place
and its relationship to writing, and I now direct
an MFA program at Chatham University,
Rachel Carson's alma mater, with a focus on
nature and environment.

As St. Germain set the stage for the panel discussion that
followed, she said:

The land taught me things, mostly about
intimacy with the natural world, about the
intelligence and language of the natural world,
about the twinning of beauty and danger.

First, the isolation, darkness and silence
caused me, and my writing, to become more
reflective and focused, and to consider the
nonhuman world in a more intimate way
since there were no people nearby. I read field
guides, learned the names and habits of the
flora and fauna, the history of the land and
how it had been used. I was forced to linger.
I had lived in Dallas for ten years, not liking
it, trying to ignore where I was. At Paisano, I
finally got it, understood what it meant to love
and linger in a place.

The encounters with insects, reptiles and
animals also taught me much. The scorpions
really became intimate with me; one nestled
one fateful morning in the crotch of my pants.
One of us suffered a bit from a scorpion sting.
We saw rattlesnake skins, but the possibility
of stumbling across one filled us always with
both hope and fear, shaping our daily hikes
on the land. I watched my son learn bravery
by approaching a wild mare with a carrot.
I learned about botanical intelligence by

studying cacti, and even rabbits provided a source of insight.

The low-water crossing helped me to write a poem I had struggled with for years about my brother's addiction and my role in it; the rushing of the waters of the flooded creek, reminded me of the dangerous rushings that had filled him, and sometimes, me.

This semi desert, sparse and rich at once. I felt my writing respond to that landscape. Never have my poems been as lean as they were while I lived at Paisano. I am from a lush, overfull landscape of swamps and rivers and lakes, and my writing has always had the lushness and plumpness of my native city of New Orleans. Not while I was at the ranch; things seemed more stripped and elemental there. Every drop of water mattered. Every word mattered. In that dry, hot, and arid place it seemed even my prose became leaner, more muscular, with less of the lushness it had had before. Although the project I proposed to write while at the ranch was a book of poems about addiction, I found the stark beauty of the place led me to other places as well, especially, to the richness the natural world. In the journal I kept while at Paisano, I wrote that I was worried about my writing project, and that "I do not know what this beautiful, serene place can teach me about addiction." I wrote that I did not know what language it could give me to speak about that which is unspeakable.[6]

She then read the poem she was finally able to write that expressed her feelings about addiction:

FLOODED CROSSING

That month the Rain was strange,
Coming when we hadn't expected it—
Ten cold inches during one week
In January. I had almost forgotten
What fear was like until we faced
The wall of shouting water,
Swelling, flooding over the low
Water crossing, blocking the
Way to the house.

Stupid, I tried to ford the creek
At the crossing, refusing
To admit there was something
I couldn't do. The sucking water
Turned me back before disaster,
But I stared for a long time
At my failure.

How could I tell my son what I saw
When he asked what I was staring at?
How could I tell him I understood
Again, my brother, that last time
he pumped too much stuff into
his arms: the rushing to the creek,
something worth one's respect,
something to be afraid of.[7]

St. Germain, Furman, and Smith (Blackwood was ill) returned to Paisano for the fortieth anniversary celebration held in 2008 to renew their strong feelings about place and their writing.

GENARO GONZALEZ
February 1991

During Genaro Gonzalez's stay at Paisano, he completed about half of a novel manuscript. It was published in 1998 as

The Quixote Cult. He described it as a "semi-autobiographical account of one student activist's experiences during the Chicano nationalist movement. The action takes place in South Texas from 1968 to 1970." Though Gonzalez hadn't been sure the subject would generate much commercial interest, he felt the need to chronicle those times —

> because of their formative impact on me, of course, but also because the events of those years radically altered the society that came after. Moreover, I wanted to document them in a way that would go beyond an historical account and approximate an experiential one. For that reason I chose to write in the first person, present tense.[8]

Gonzalez has had a long career as a chronicler not only of Latino life in the border region of Texas but also as a sensitive interpreter of family relationships aside from ethnic identity.

In 2009, Arte Público Press published *A So-Called Vacation.* The father wants his high school–age sons to spend a summer doing fieldwork to earn extra money. They are not immigrants. Set more than twenty years after Gonzalez's early stories, the novel reflects on the changes that have occurred in the lives of Rio Grande Valley residents. But it also touches the same family relations he wrote about in earlier work.

In 2011, he contributed a story for an anthology on new border fiction. He has also been working on a novella that "incorporates the border only in an incidental way." He recently wrote,

> Interestingly, I'm one of the few Jurassic (i.e. Chicano) writers — possibly the only one — who continues to live in the border area and has done so for decades, but although the region has finally started catching the eye of

a mainstream publisher or two, I've moved on to other interests. At the same time the ranks of "borderlands" writers who don't live here yet sense an opportunity has increased considerably.[9]

One reason Gonzalez has not produced a great volume of work is because he has had a dual career. With graduate degrees in psychology and social psychology, he has been a professor of social and health psychology at the University of Texas–Pan American since 1979.

SIGMAN BYRD
August 1991

Sigman Byrd loved his time at Paisano: "It solidified my bond with and love of the Hill Country." After five generations in Texas, none of his family currently lives in the state, and Byrd himself would love to return some day.[10]

Byrd had been publishing poems for some time before he was chosen as a Paisano fellow. His first book of poetry, *Under the Wanderer's Star*, was chosen as the winner of the 2005 Marsh Hawk Press Poetry Prize. Since then he has published another book of poetry, *Who We Were* (Finishing Line Press, 2010).

He is on the faculty of the Program for Writing and Rhetoric at the University of Colorado at Boulder, where he teaches a wide variety of writing classes—not only poetry but also creative nonfiction. He explains that his courses "encourage the idea that creative writing, critical thinking, critical reading and writing are not just academic exercises but a way of life that continues outside the classroom."[11]

Byrd indicates that "writing poetry is still very important to me. I'm currently sending another book around to publishers. . . . My new book of poetry, *Letters to Emptiness*, is making its way to publishers."[12]

"The Child Astronomer" is from his prize-winning book, *Under the Wanderer's Star*.

Don't tell him Galileo went blind
staring at sunspots or swashbuckling
Tycho Brahe had his nose
sliced off over dueling equations,
No, he'll discover on his own one day
How even the noblest quests burn up
To nothing in so much random solar wind.
Meanwhile, let him crack open
a geometry book, the playground is empty.
Let him squint through a telescope
at all the tinseled planets and stars,
Orion, the hunter, Auriga, the charioteer,
wheeling their incandescent teams.
Don't tell him they're all growing fainter,
gods and heroes and winged horses
breaking up, accelerating out of the frame.
Don't tell him he too will become
a world of refracted light and myth,
a dazzling dream of long ago, spinning,
remote, barely visible to the naked eye.[13]

SARAH GLASSCOCK
February 1992
When writers apply for Paisano, probably few of them think about whether Barton Creek might be running high. Yet some of the most memorable moments fellows have had at the ranch included encounters with the forces of nature Sarah Glasscock, writing in 2008, declared:

> It's the summer of 2007—the summer of rain—and I think frequently about the current Paisano fellow and his or her relationship with Barton Creek. There were heavy rains in December and January of 1992 when my fellowship started. In fact, there was so much rain that I wasn't able to cross Barton Creek and move into the ranch house for two weeks.

Every day I'd drive out and check the creek to see if it was low enough to cross. That was a long two weeks, but the wait was worth it. (I also gained new respect for the power of water.) All the winter rain translated into a spring and summer of being able to float on the creek in the afternoons, thinking about the novel I was working on and all the other people who had enjoyed the creek's cool waters.[14]

While Glasscock didn't finish the novel she began at Paisano, she did participate in an unusual literary endeavor.

At the time I was also typing the manuscript for Hannah Green's book *Little Saint*, about life in the French village of Conques over the course of several centuries. Hannah was my teacher at NYU and also became my close friend and mentor. [She helped her with publication of Sarah's first novel, *Anna LMNO*.] Green died in 1995 before finishing her book. Her husband, Jack Wesley, and her editor at Random House, Sam Vaughan, and I worked together to edit *Little Saint* and usher it into the world. Although Hannah had not finished the book, we all felt that it was a complete and beautiful work.

In a front-page review in the *New York Times* in 2000, Geoffrey Moorhouse also found it a fine work.

Glasscock has been working on a novel called *The Foothills Petition*, set in West Texas. She continues to write and edit educational material for primary and middle school readers. Her short stories have appeared in the *South Carolina Review*, *Sonora Review*, *Boulevard*, and *The Pushcart Prize XV*.

She still treasures every minute she had at Paisano. "It is one of the most beautiful places in Texas, and maybe the world. In times of stress, some people take deep breaths: I just picture myself floating down the creek on a raft or sitting on the front porch and taking that Hill Country view."[15]

Ewing Campbell
August 1992

After Ewing Campbell's fellowship, he continued writing and publishing fiction. He published many individual stories and a pair of novels. After retirement from Texas A&M University, he moved to San Miguel de Allende, Mexico, and devoted himself full-time to writing. He was in San Miguel five years and while living there, his collection of short stories, *Afoot in the Garden of Enchantment* (Rager Media, 2007), was published. All the stories are set in the Spanish-speaking countries where he has taught or lived.

In 2012 he said, "We loved Mexico, but a serious health issue came up, forcing me to return to the United States for surgery." He reported that he has moved to El Paso. "I'm as close as I can get to Mexico without actually being there. Every night I look from the tablelands jutting off the Franklin Mountains right into Ciudad Juárez and imagine my return."

Looking back on how his Dobie Paisano experience contributed to his writing then and afterward, he declared,

> Honestly, the time at the ranch was instrumental in my completing work I am grateful to have written. While there, I got *The Tex-Mex Express* ready for publication and wrote the first draft of *Madonna, Maleva*. I believe my book on Raymond Carver's short fiction came out while I was at the ranch. Nothing has ever quite matched the solitude I enjoyed there, especially when the creek rose and cut the ranch and me off from the rest of the world. I loved my time there.[16]

SAM HAYNES
February 1993

When Sam Haynes arrived to take up residence at Paisano, he had read about the previous year's spring floods as being among the most severe on record. Haynes wrote in his final report:

> Expecting the worst, I stocked up on canned goods, planning for the inevitable day when the rains would leave me stranded. [Barton Creek was running about a foot deep then.] In mid-February we had our first heavy rain. I walked down to the creek every hour to check the flood gauge and watched Barton Creek rise six inches or so, but by the following day it had returned to normal. That was the only time the water level rose appreciably during my stay....By the time I left, Barton Creek was little more than a muddy trough in some places, and the road over the creek was bone dry. I suppose I was lucky, but I couldn't help feeling a twinge of disappointment, as if I had been cheated of my chance to test my survival skills.[17]

Haynes wrote: "Most of my time at Paisano was spent working on a biography of James K. Polk, the US president who is probably best known for going to war with Mexico. Although I had already done much of the research for this project before my fellowship began, having access to a major research center at UT was enormously helpful."

Shortly after his Paisano fellowship, Haynes joined the history faculty at the University of Texas at Arlington. His second book (his first was *Soldiers of Misfortune*, published in 1990), *James K. Polk and the Expansionist Impulse*, was published in 1996.

My work on the Polk book gave me the idea to write my third, which was twelve years in the making, and was released in 2010. Although *Unfinished Revolution: The Early American Republic in the British World* seems like a complete departure from my writing on the American Southwest, that's not really the case. One of the main theses of the book is that US leaders (including Polk and a host of others) feared Great Britain, and felt threatened by British alliances with the Texas Republic and Mexico. The phenomenon we know as "manifest destiny" was, I argue, the result of American insecurities, and firmly rooted in the American relationship with Great Britain.[18]

In 2008, Haynes was appointed director of the Center for Greater Southwestern Studies. The center promotes interest in the study of the American Southwest in a variety of ways such as presenting a program commemorating the centennial of the Mexican Revolution, holding workshops for teachers, organizing academic conferences, and mounting photographic exhibits on the revolution. Hayes says that the center tries to sponsor events that are of interest to both the campus community and the Dallas–Fort Worth area. With eight faculty members as fellows, the center is developing a website on the US-Mexico War based on archival materials in the University of Texas at Arlington's Special Collections, and in 2013 sponsored an academic conference on the Texas Revolution.

STEVE PATE
August 1993

Steve Pate had spent twenty-two years as a sports writer for the *Dallas Morning News* and the *Fort Worth Star Telegram* and briefly for the *National Sports Daily* when he applied for the Paisano fellowship. Although he had intended to leave sports writing, he published at least one sports book after that with Dan Jenkins (1997).

His writing went in a very different direction when he joined a Dallas restaurant owner, Matt Martinez Jr., producing two books of Tex-Mex cooking interspersed with stories of Martinez's father, Matt Martinez, the legendary Tex-Mex cook who started Matt's El Rancho in Austin in 1952: *Matt Martinez's Culinary Frontier: A Real Texas Cookbook* (1997) and *Matt Makes a Run for the Border: Recipes and Tales from a Tex-Mex Chef* (2000).

Paisano fellows have written many beautiful evocations of life at Paisano. Steve Pate's description, "Finding Violets amid the Rocks," a short article he wrote for *American Way*, the travel magazine of American Airlines in 1995, gives the essence of a writer's life at the ranch and includes one of the most intriguing happenings any fellow ever experienced out there.

About his six months, Pate wrote:

> Hey, I was prepared for everything. I stayed away from snakes and I shook my boots and I only encountered a few giant, nasty-looking, harmless brown spiders. No scorpions or tarantulas. No fires. The creek stayed so dry most of the time that I yearned for a flood. A small one. I had stocked up.
>
> But nothing, and so in the final weeks of my fellowship, I got cocky and began to feel at one with nature....I grew complacent, and so when the stench first began its cruel wiggle up my nostrils, I reacted in a manner befitting the noblest procrastinator. I tried to will the smell away.

Pate recounts that by Sunday afternoon the smell had overwhelmed the den and moved down the hallway near the bedroom. Pate had to wait until Monday to call for help from the university pest busters. When the workman came down from the attic, he said, "I'd say you had a forty-pound animal of some sort up there." Pate had to retreat to Dallas. After the crew tore into the wall, they pulled out a dead possum.

> A dead possum shaved five days off my Paisano stay, and I hate that. But Tennessee Williams once wrote, "The violets in the mountains have broken the rocks." Such words apply here. Each Dobie Fellow's personal memory of Paisano is another violet, breaking up the discomforts that accompany isolation, charred land, floods, dead-animal-in-the-wall syndrome, and other mishaps.
>
> In the months since, I occasionally think back to the dead-possum debacle. And when I do, I just sit there with a smile spread across my mind, for the incident is also a reminder of exhilarating times on that painfully honest land. Times when for me the violets were in bloom at Paisano.[19]

CATHERINE BOWMAN
February 1994

El Paso native Catherine Bowman had received a BA at the University of Texas at San Antonio and an MFA at Columbia University and spent ten years as a writing teacher in the New York City public schools when she began her Paisano fellowship soon after her first book, *1-800-HOT-RIBS* (Gibbs Smith, 1993), was published. Toward the end of her six months at the ranch, she received the first annual Kate Frost Tufts Discovery Award for Poetry, which recognized an emerging poet for a first book "that exhibits excellence in substance and style, and the promise of sustained excellence."

Since her Paisano fellowship, Bowman has gone on to write *The Plath Cabinet* (Four Way Books, 2009), *Notarikon* (Four Way Books, 2006), and *Rock Farm* (Gibbs Smith, 1996), and has been the editor of *Word of Mouth*, an anthology of poems by poets she has reviewed and featured on National Public Radio's *All Things Considered*. Her poems have appeared in six editions of *Best American Poetry*. She teaches at Indiana University and the Fine Arts Work Center at Provincetown.

Lynna Williams
August 1994

Lynna Williams was born in Waco, Texas, studied journalism at the University of Missouri, and received her MFA in fiction writing from George Mason University. She began her Paisano fellowship several years after her first book, *Things Not Seen and Other Stories* (Little, Brown, 1993), was published.

On leave from her teaching position at Emory University in Atlanta, Georgia, Williams arrived at Paisano with over four hundred pages of a novel. "I found the book here," she reflected in her fellow's report at the end of her fellowship, "and I wrote a goodly chunk of it, and the 250 pages, pared to the bone, will be a novella in my next collection of stories, I think."[20]

"Even though I grew up in Texas," Williams also recounted in her report, "as an adult my idea of the 'country' has been any place without access to at least one road show production of *Cats*. I am not, and never have been a nature girl, despite all those checks to the Nature Conservancy year after year." Echoing the sentiments of many other fellows, while at Paisano she realized she had never before been "in" nature "the way it's possible to be [at Paisano]...."[21]

After her fellowship, Williams returned to Atlanta, where she is an associate professor at Emory. Her essays have received awards from *Chattahoochee Review* and *Bellingham Review* and been anthologized in *Sleeping with One Eye Open: A Survival Guide for Creative Women* (University of Georgia Press), *From Mothers to Daughters: I've Always Meant to Tell You* (Simon and Schuster), and other collections. Her book reviews have appeared in the *Chicago Tribune*.

CHRISTIAN WIMAN
February 1995
Before his Paisano fellowship, Christian Wiman held a
Stegner fellowship at Stanford from 1992 to 1994, and was
awarded a Ruth Lilly fellowship by the Modern Poetry
Association in 1994.

Reflecting on his time at Paisano, Wiman declared:

> I can't separate clearly my experience of
> Paisano with the work that I've done here, so I'll
> just talk about the two together. I've come to the
> end of a long poem entitled "The Long Home"
> which I've been working on for a LONG TIME,
> and the last few furious weeks have blurred into
> nothing but work. ...I have worked no faster and
> no slower at Paisano than I have worked at any
> other place in the past few years, but the work I
> had to do here, bringing the poem to a close, was
> or seemed much more difficult than anything
> else that I have done, and I credit this place—
> the uninterrupted solitude, the undistracting
> distractions of turkeys, deer, or armadillos in the
> yard, the blazing hours I spent on Conversation
> Rock, reciting my poem over and over—with
> allowing, or forcing me to finish.[22]

Story Line Press published the finally completed "The
Long Home," in 1998. It was awarded the 1998 Nicholas
Roerich Poetry Prize.

In 2003, Wiman was appointed the editor of *Poetry*
magazine. The magazine, founded in 1912, introduced many
poets including Marianne Moore, Wallace Stevens, and William
Carlos Williams. In 2002 the magazine received a grant from arts
philanthropist and heiress Ruth Lilly, one of the largest grants
ever awarded to a literary magazine. Terms of the gift included
the establishment of a foundation, which has sponsored a wide
range of projects such as Poetry Out Loud.

Since then, Wiman has published a book of essays, *Ambition and Survival: Becoming a Poet* (Copper Canyon Press, 2007) and a book of poetry, *Every Riven Thing* (Farrar, Straus, and Giroux, 2010). The last essay in *Ambition and Survival* is a deeply personal account of his discovery of a life-threatening illness.

Fortunately he has received medical treatment that has enabled him to be in remission. For *Poetry* magazine's one hundredth anniversary, Wiman coedited, with Don Share, *The Open Door: One Hundred Poems, One Hundred Years of Poetry Magazine.*[23]

In 2013 he published *My Bright Abyss: Meditation of a Modern Believer*[24] and in June of that year he became a senior lecturer of religion and literature at the Yale Institute of Sacred Music and the Yale Divinity School.[25]

CHARLES BEHLEN
August 1995

In 1980, poet Harryette Mullen wrote Charles Behlen urging him to apply for a Paisano fellowship. Taking her advice that the fellowship was "made for people like me," he began applying in the mid-eighties, he recalled in 2011. "I felt like it was exactly for the kind of writer I was. I was a solitary writer. I wrote a lot about Texas. I'd been a Texas native since 1949."[26]

As he would write in his fellow's report at the end of his time at the ranch, when he arrived at Paisano, he "expected to find something that was half museum, half monument." What he experienced instead was

> ...as simple and unpretentious as my grandmother's house in Poesy, TX: cedar post porch, asbestos shingle siding, washing machine in the kitchen. My first poems were written on my grandmother's farm. I'd spread the manuscripts on the guest room bed, step

back and regard my handiwork. Middle-aged,
I spread my poems on J. Frank's worktable
and did the same.[27]

Also in his fellow's report, he admitted that when he had
arrived at the ranch he felt "like a plains Indian entering the
forest for the first time when I walked down Barton Creek.
Flatlander poets from Lubbock County should take Paisano
a little at a time." A poet whose work has often explored
uniquely Texas landscapes and people, Behlen cast his eye
over the Paisano landscape as well, noting that the ditches
and vacant lots he had explored as a boy in West Texas in the
'50's "had more life in them than Barton Creek does today.
Read in sequence, reports of past fellows chronicle the impact
that Austin development has had on Hill Country wildlife."[28]

Behlen's books include *Perdition's Keepsake* (Prickly
Pear Press, 1978), *Three Texas Poets* (Prickly Pear Press,
1986), *Uirsche's First Three Decades* (Firewheel Press, 1987),
Dreaming at the Wheel (Corona Press, 1988), *The Voices under
the Floor* (Trilobite Press, 1989), *Texas Weather* (Trilobite Press,
1999), and *Failing Heaven* (Lamar University Press, 2014). He
currently lives in Lovington, New Mexico.

LISA SANDLIN
February 1996

Lisa Sandlin arrived at Paisano between publication of
her first and second books (*The Famous Thing about Death*,
1991, and *Message to the Nurse of Dreams*, 1997, both from
Cinco Puntos Press). *The Do-Right* came out in 2015 from
Cinco Puntos Press. A Beaumont native, she received her BA
from Rice and an MFA from Vermont College while living
in Santa Fe, where she resided at the time of her fellowship

According to Sandlin's Fellow's Report, while at Paisano,
she realized the book she'd thought was finished was actually
two books. "While initially that thought was exhilarating,
it finally sank in that I had to finish two books....Meeting
a couple of people and having visitors and just keeping at

work helped that. I took to dancing at night on these broad wooden floors."[29] That book-become-two would go on to become her second book, *Message to the Nurse of Dreams* and the beginnings of her third, *In the River Province* (Southern Methodist University Press, 2004). While at Paisano, she also began work on a proposal for what would become *You Who Make the Sky Bend* (Pinyon Publishing, 2011), a collaboration with New Mexican retablo artist Catherine Ferguson.

In 2011, Sandlin remembered that at one point during her residency, she bought a large bag of corn to put out for the deer and birds that frequented the yard in front of the house. After unloading it from her car and wrestling it as far as the house's front porch, she temporarily "forgot about it, because Julie White, stage and TV actor, was reading a story of mine in Kay Cattarulla's Texas-Bound program at the Dallas Museum of Art."

> I dressed up, drove to Dallas, and heard the actors read, delighted at the performances. DMA ran two seatings, so I got to experience the whole shebang twice, and take a bow at the end of each. The highlight of my career (so far—I have to say 'so far' for superstitious purposes). I mean, how many times do we get to stand up and take a bow while three hundred people clap for us? Let's say it stands out in my life. And then Julie White told me to write something for her, and I had dinner with the actors. Thrilled to the ground, I teleported the three hours back to Austin and arrived around 4:30 in the morning.
>
> Maybe the moonlight wasn't sparkling that night. Somehow I didn't see then what I saw when I got up the next day: the porch was inches deep in cow manure, piles upon piles, and some mighty rivers. The cows— longhorns—had been in the corn, had eaten

every kernel.... So the day after that glamorous night, I shoveled shit for a good, perspective-adjusting while.[30]

"In memory," Sandlin said in 2011,

I take [Paisano] out like a picture book. The turkeys do their whirligig dances, onset of dusk makes the grazing deer invisible until a brisk flip of white tells you they've run off, the longhorns invade a rip in the fencing, I jump all over the rocks in the dry creekbed and sit on the philosopher one, wander around the quiet house and sit in every chair, get out to open the gates when I drive back in, and do jetes back to the car just because the place is so wide and solitary and I can. I feel really honored to have been able to experience Paisano, and to be in such august company as that group of fellows and fellowettes.[31]

Since her Paisano fellowship, Sandlin has received a fellowship from the National Endowment for the Arts and a Pushcart Prize. In addition to her books, she coedited the anthology *Times of Grace, Times of Sorrow* (Backwaters Press, 2002). She teaches at the University of Nebraska Omaha.

Marcia Buffington
February 1995

Marcia Buffington, an MA graduate in English from the University of Texas at Austin, had recently completed a Stegner fellowship in poetry when she arrived at Paisano in 1996 for her fellowship.

Earlier that same year, she and her husband had purchased land near Elgin, where in a few years they would move an old house that had been slated for demolition. For Buffington, Paisano was less isolated than her current living arrangements.

"For me," Buffington recollected in 2011, "living in the Dobie house was a step up in the world. The house had air-conditioning, which our place did not. It was closer to Austin. When things broke, people came out and fixed them."[32]

After her fellowship, Buffington taught for several years at Southwestern University in Georgetown. She and her family continue to live on 125 acres northeast of Elgin. "It's always a gift to have time to write," she said in 2011 in regard to her Paisano fellowship. "But the biggest impact of the fellowship for me was, ironically, a book I discovered on the bookcase in the house's living room."

That book was fellow Alan Tennant's *Snakes of Texas*. Reading it was a watershed moment for Buffington, who had always loved the outdoors and nature and been a bit of a snake buff. The meticulous attention and observation Tennant gave what might be one of the most-maligned inhabitants of Texas's natural world, along with fact that Tennant had gained his expertise through personal fieldwork and experience, impressed her.

"Tennant's book started getting me thinking about habitat loss and habitat restoration," she remembered. Though she and her husband had been keeping cattle on their own land, after her Paisano fellowship they began to investigate using their property for wildlife management. The changes they made — providing supplemental water, reintroducing native species, and basically making the land "more like it was 100 years ago" — still influence her day-to-day life.[33]

LEE MERRILL BYRD
February 1997

During the first month Lee Byrd was at the ranch she began going back through the handwritten journals she had kept for many years — more than fifteen years' worth — "journals full of prayers and complaints and accounts and little bits and pieces of stories."[34] Already the author of an award-winning collection of short stories (*My Sister Disappears*, 1993), Byrd turned these journal bits and pieces into several short stories, and eventually a novel.

The primary source of much of her stories was a fire that occurred in 1981 when her sons Andy and John were four and seven years old. Described in detail in "In a New Country," in *Spiritual Autographs: Southern Women Tell Their Stories*, 1999, the boys were caught in a fire

> inside a palm-branch fort they'd made....The doctor's first assessment brought frightening news: John, age seven, was burned on the left side of his face, on both hands, on the back of his head, in two places on his legs...Taken together, the burns constituted 35 percent of his body. For Andy, our four year old, things were even more serious. Sixty-three percent of his skin was gone—from his chest, from his back, from his left arm and hand, from his face. Half the hair on his head was gone.[35]

The boys and their parents were flown to the Shriners Hospital for Children in Galveston, which specializes in burn care, where they spent three months. Johnny and Andy emerged as strong, resilient individuals, despite their scars. While Byrd wrote about their family situation in some of her stories, it was almost ten years later that she gathered together all the elements from this experience and wrote a novel, *Riley's Fire*. Byrd said, "It was the final bringing together of all the stories about the fire that I had worked on at the ranch. They had never worked as a whole, but then suddenly they did."[36] A reviewer concluded: "Against this background of fear and pain, Byrd forges a riveting story that, in the end, is astonishingly uplifting." *People* magazine chose *Riley's Fire* as one of the Top Ten Books of 2006.[37]

Byrd is not only a writer, she is also a publisher. In 1985, she and her husband Bobby founded Cinco Puntos Press, named after their neighborhood in El Paso, Texas. Cinco Puntos publishes nonfiction, fiction, poetry, and children's literature. It has been recognized for bringing multicultural literatures of the American Southwest, the US-Mexico border region, and Mexico to a national audience.

James Hannah
September 1997

When Texas A & M University professor and author James Hannah was at Paisano, he learned

> ...that six months passes in no time. My wife and I learned how much we love the Hill Country. Enough, we believe now, to try and find some land out around Johnson City before it's sucked up into the Austin suburbs and costs $10,000 an acre...My project [compiling writing for a World War I anthology] was busy at the time doling out daily doses of despair and terror. Often pulling a surfeit of such with me, I found I lost it, it slaked away in the pools upstream on Grape Creek.... There may be other places like this for writers, photographers, artists, but I only know this particular place. And its solace is a steady and, thankfully, a lingering balm. At the close of Toby Wolff's "In the Garden of the North American Martyrs," the narrator, in a jeremiad to a roomful of disgusting academics, warns them to "mend their lives." This very place can do that. All you have to do is let it.[38]

After his fellowship Hannah, the author of *Desperate Measures: Stories* (Southern Methodist University Press, 1988) and *Sign Languages: Stories* (University of Missouri Press, 1993), resumed teaching at Texas A&M.

CLANCY CARLILE
March 1998

Clancy Carlile began his fellowship in February 1998. He died on June 4 after a brief illness. Carlile, who spent his early life in Sweetwater, was a novelist and screenwriter in Los Angeles. Author of four novels, he also wrote the screenplay for one of them, *Honkytonk Man*, which was produced and directed by Clint Eastwood in 1982. His 1995 novel, *Children of the Dust*, was given the NAACP Image Award for outstanding literary achievement. Carlile had been working on a novel about Hemingway in Paris and had plans to begin a novel about Cynthia Parker. The Hemingway novel, *The Paris Pilgrims*, was posthumously published by Carroll and Graf, in July 1999.

Carlile followed James Hannah at Paisano. In Hannah's fellow's report, he added a few words about Carlile.

> He fell ill at Paisano and died, I believe, early in his stay. I met him only once, when we came back to pack up some last things (there'd been sudden rain that kept the crossing flooded for a week or so after our scheduled departure). He was coming in as we were leaving. He struck me as a gentle and kind man. He eagerly sought our impressions of the place. He was interested in starting a vegetable garden out behind the shed where, obviously, there hadn't been one in years. Inquisitive, polite, indeed gentlemanly in his demeanor. I hope he enjoyed his days. I don't believe he had time to begin a garden. I'd like to think that maybe someday, another Dobie Fellow will get that bedraggled plot into shape. It would be a good reminder of Mr. Carlile, who lately joins the ghosts of Frank, Bertha, settlers, the nameless Indians.[39]

ENDNOTES

[1] Alan Tennant, "One Question" interview, *Austin American-Statesman*, October 29, 2004.

[2] Alan Tennant, Current Project, "The Long Strange Journey of Timothy Treadwell, The Grizzly Man," Behind the Book, *On the Wing* (New York: Anchor, 2005), http://www.alantennant.com. Accessed January 23, 2016.

[3] Allen Wier, Fellow's Report, 1990.

[4] Allen Wier, personal communication, December 2012.

[5] Martha Elizabeth, personal communication, September 2012.

[6] Sheryl St. Germain, personal communication.

[7] Sheryl St. Germain, "Flooded Crossing," *How Heavy the Breath of God* (Denton: University of North Texas Press, 1994).

[8] Genaro Gonzalez, fellow's report, 1991.

[9] Genaro Gonzalez, personal communication, November 2011.

[10] Sigman Byrd, *Who We Were* (Georgetown, Kentucky: Finishing Line Press, 2010).

[11] The website sigmanbyrd.com, which is no longer in existence.

[12] Sigman Byrd, personal communication, November 2011.

[13] "The Child Astronomer," *Under the Wanderer's Star* (East Rockaway, New York: Marsh Hawk Press, 2006).

[14] Sarah Glasscock, 2008 author biography.

[15] Sarah Glasscock, personal communication, October 2011.

[16] Ewing Campbell, personal communication, July 2012.

[17] Sam Haynes, fellow's report, 1993.

[18] Sam Haynes, personal communication, December 2011.

[19] Steve Pate, "Finding Violets amid the Rocks," *American Way*, March 1995, 54–57.

[20] Lynna Williams, fellow's report, 1994.

[21] Ibid.

[22] Christian Wiman, fellow's report, 1995.

[23] Don Share and Christian Wiman, eds., *The Open Door: One*

Hundred Poems, One Hundred Years of Poetry Magazine (Chicago: University of Chicago Press, 2012).

[24] Christian Wiman, *My Bright Abyss: Meditation of a Modern Believer* (New York: Farrar, Straus, & Giroux, 2013).

[25] Tom Bartlett, "Wiman's Rites," *Texas Monthly* (April 2013), 72, 74, 78; online at http://www.texasmonthly.com/the-culture/wimans-rites/. Accessed January 23, 2016.

[26] Charles Behlen, interview with Katherine Hester, 2011.

[27] Charles Behlen, fellow's report, 1995.

[28] Ibid.

[29] Lisa Sandlin, fellow's report, 1996.

[30] Lisa Sandlin, personal correspondence with Katherine Hester, 2011.

[31] Ibid.

[32] Marcia Buffington, interview with Katherine Hester, 2011.

[33] Ibid.

[34] Lee Byrd, fellow's report, 1997.

[35] Lee Byrd, "In a New Country," in *Spiritual Autographs: Southern Women Tell Their Stories* (Chicago: Chicago Spectrum Press, 1999) 92–93.

[36] Lee Byrd, personal communication, 2005.

[37] *People* magazine, 2006.

[38] James Hannah, fellow's report, 1998.

[39] Ibid.

Fellows 1998–2008

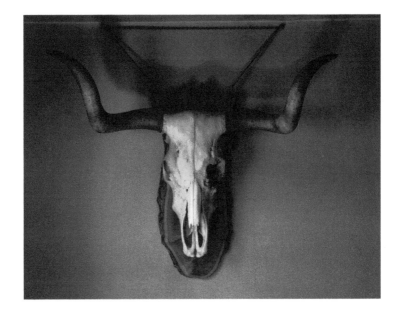

AS THE PAISANO PROJECT ENTERED THE 21ST CENTURY, THE ranch survived, and even thrived, despite the creeping suburbanization of metropolitan Austin. While the Fellows reported that light pollution from the nearby city obscured the stars, the intact, natural systems of Paisano remained an oasis for wildlife – and for creativity.

Lowell Mick White

Amy Adams

Katherine L. Hester

Thomas McNeely

Robin Bradford

Craig Arnold

Patricia Page

Mylène Dressler

Oscar Casares

Todd Hearon

Dominic Smith

William Cobb

Scott Blackwood

Daniel Rifenburgh

David Wright

Timothy Westmoreland

Sam Taylor

Vicente Lozano

Alison Moore

Mary Helen Specht

LOWELL MICK WHITE
September 1998

When Mick White sent in his final report in April 1999, he harkened back to what he wrote for his sixth grade teacher when she asked what he wanted to be when he grew up. He replied that he wanted to be a hermit. Thirty years later his wish came true. He loved the solitude and concluded that what he took away from Paisano Ranch were hope and "memories of my hermitage." White was barely breaking even driving a cab when he applied for the fellowship. He sent in a few additional words to his final report in November 2002: "When I look back at how tired and ill and discouraged I was about writing and *everything,* I can only say that Paisano saved my life."

After Paisano, White went back to driving a cab while he worked on *That Demon Life*, the novel he began at the ranch.

White described his writing career after that: "When I finished the book, I decided to go to graduate school, and I enrolled at Texas A&M, where I received my MA in 2005 and my PhD in 2010. A&M was a great experience—I taught creative writing, composition, and literature, and worked at *Callaloo,* an award-winning journal of African American art and literature."

For a graduate course, White produced an extraordinarily complete bibliography of Frank Dobie, *Mr. Texas: A Research Guide to the Works of J. Frank Dobie.* In addition to covering biographical and bibliographical work, the guide also includes sections on criticism and Dobie's legacy.

That Demon Life won the Gival Press Novel Award in 2008 and was published by Gival in 2009. It was also a runner-up for the Texas Book Award, given by the Writers' League of Texas.

A comic novel of city life in Austin, *That Demon Life* features a subplot describing the corrupt acquisition and development of a very Paisano-like ranch after the ranch's owner murders a cab driver.[2]

Also in 2009, White had a story collection, *Long Time Ago Good*, published by Slough Press. His novel *Professed* was published by Slough Press in 2013, and his novel *Burnt House* came out from Buffalo Times Press in 2018.

In addition to his teaching as a lecturer at Texas A&M from 2010 to 2012, he began teaching as the National Endowment for the Arts Writer-in-Residence at the federal prison in Bryan, Texas—"an extraordinarily rewarding job," he reported.

In August 2012 he began at Pittsburg State University in Kansas, teaching creative writing and literature.[1] He returned to teach at Texas A&M in 2016 as an Instructional Associate Professor.

AMY WILLIAMS ADAMS
March 1999

Amy Adams, born and raised in Indiana, was a James Michener Fellow in fiction and screenwriting from 1993 through 1996 and continued with a post-graduate fellowship. A screenwriter and author of poetry, fiction and historical fiction, Adams penned a screenplay based on the real-life experiences of nineteenth century Comanche child captive Herman Lehmann.

KATHERINE L. HESTER
September 1999

Katherine L. Hester, a native of Dallas who received her MA in English, concentration in creative writing, from UT Austin, was awarded the Paisano fellowship after publication of her first book (*Eggs for Young America*, Penguin, 1998).

In 2012, she reflected:

> Even now, almost twelve years to the day after my residency, I still have dreams about Paisano. In fact, when I stop to think about it, I've probably had more dreams located

squarely on those dusty, blue-green acres than
I have anywhere else in the world. In those
dreams, I'm arriving there for the first time.
I'm more-than-happily taking up residency
again, though this defies all logic. I'm visiting
current fellows. I'm walking up the road from
the house to the mailboxes. I'm—and this is
by far the most reoccurring of my dreams set
at the ranch—standing on the gallery outside
the house, the realization dawning that a
McDonald's, or a subdivision, or an interstate
(fill in the blanks) has just been built just on
the other side of the creek. Austin has grown
and grown and *grown* until it lies just beyond
the yard in front of the house, and the world is
not the better for its proximity.

Hester arrived at Paisano in September 1999.

Friends joked that the ranch might be the safest
place to hunker down if all hell broke loose on
New Year's Eve. Having been warned about
the possibility of being flooded in if Barton
Creek rose too high, I'd already stocked the
pantry at the house with food and water—I
figured I was ready.

In the end, vandalism of the mailbox on Rawhide Trail
was the only excitement at Paisano on the eve of the twenty-
first century.

In 2012, Hester summed up her time at the ranch:

People say—*being at Paisano gave me time*, and
this is the truth, of course. We're a productive
society, even us writers, and we tend to think
of time as being valuable mainly because of
the tangible production it allows us. But I've

come to feel that the importance of Paisano isn't *time* (as valuable as that might be) so much as it is the fact that the ranch lies *outside* time. The time a writer spends there isn't—can't be—real life. You can't (by honest means at least) ever go back to Paisano, though I've heard of former fellows who drove out and parked their cars at the outer gate and snuck across the fence, they missed it so. You can't own Paisano, or change or keep it. But for six months, you get to be your writer-self there, however you define that, and to the exclusion of all else.

These days, what I remember most fondly about the time I spent at Paisano isn't how productive I was (though I was, and was hugely grateful for the opportunity to be so), but one particular night when I drove home from having dinner with friends in Austin.

While I was at the ranch, I always kept the radio in my car tuned to KGSR at the far right end of the dial. That particular night, I hit the inner gate just at that particular moment of Hill Country dusk when the sky is neither blue nor rosy but the tenderest imaginable combination of the two. When I got out of the car, an armadillo was dumbly nudging its way through the brush on the other side of the gate. The faintest breath of air was rustling the live oaks. As I pulled the hasp of the padlock on the gate and undid the chainlink, I realized that the song spilling from the open door of my car was *Knocking on Heaven's Door*.

If any of us could stay at Paisano longer than six months, I'm sure we'd find a way to mess it up—start building mental McDonald's restaurants and subdivisions across the creek.

I love the place Paisano has taken in my
memory, as my best writerly Shangri-La.[3]

Hester's first collection, *Eggs for Young America*, was
awarded the Katharine Nason Bakeless Literary Publication
Prize for Fiction and named a *New York Times* Notable Book
of the Year. Her short stories have been published in *Five
Points*, the *Yale Review*, *Southwest Review*, and elsewhere and
collected in anthologies such as *Prize Stories: The O. Henry
Awards* and *Best American Mystery Stories*. She lives in Atlanta,
Georgia, with her husband and two daughters.

Thomas McNeely
May 2000

Tom McNeely described himself as a "fledgling
writer, thirty-two years old" when he received his Paisano
fellowship. A graduate of the University of Texas who had
been living in Boston, his first published story had appeared
in the *Atlantic Monthly* the year before. His time at Paisano
gave him "a chance to enter a fictional world, and to think
about the processes of fiction, in a way that has been
impossible in my everyday life."

McNeely's fellowship also gave him an opportunity to
reflect on his place in the natural world. "The sunsets, the
trees, the cliffs and rabbits and longhorns and deer are not
self-conscious in their artistry," he noted. "(At Paisano),
nature, which I have never thought much about, or stopped
to take the time to notice, dwarfed me and my worries. It has
been good to feel part of a larger whole, and more than the
pages I've written here, I hope I can take this back with me."[4]

In 2012, he reflected further:

It is really hard for me to measure how much
Paisano influenced my work, because its
influence is so pervasive. While I was there,
I wrote the first draft of a novel that I am still

reworking. The landscape at the ranch crept into the book in ways that would not become evident until years, and a couple of drafts, later. Also, the book now centers on an imaginary horse. The image for that horse, which also didn't appear until a few drafts later, comes directly from a picture of a ghostly white horse that hung in front of me each day as I wrote in the gallery.[5]

In 2001, McNeely was awarded a Stegner fellowship in fiction. In 2008, he received a literature grant from National Endowment for the Arts. His stories have appeared in the *Atlantic Monthly*, *Ploughshares*, *Story Quarterly*, *Epoch*, the *Virginia Quarterly Review*, and other magazines and have been anthologized in *The Best of the South*, a collection of stories from the second decade of Algonquin's *New Stories from the South*. As of this writing, he lives in Cambridge, Massachusetts, with his wife and daughter. The novel that he worked on at Paisano, *Ghost Horse*, won the 2013 Gival Press Novel Award.

ROBIN BRADFORD
September 2000

Robin Bradford grew up in Oklahoma but has lived in Texas since the mid-1970s. In addition to publishing stories, articles, and reviews in journals and newspapers, she has work in *It's a Boy: Women Writers on Raising Sons* and *Three-Ring Circus: How Real Couples Balance Marriage, Work, and Family*. She was awarded a community sabbatical from the University of Texas Humanities Institute, which allows nonprofit workers time off to work on projects relating to their work. She has written about the spiritual crisis she experienced after helping numerous Hurricane Katrina survivor families. In 2007 she completed yoga teacher training at Dharma Yoga, a Buddhist-influenced studio.[6]

Bradford lived at Paisano with her husband Jim Williams

and her three-and-a-half-year old son Cope. In an article for the *Houston Chronicle* magazine adapted from her fellow's report, Bradford wrote:

> On New Year's Eve we stayed home, making party hats and noisemakers out of construction paper, plastic containers and dry beans. When I put Cope to bed around ten, Jim went out for firewood and discovered an animal hiding there. It turned out to be a little, shivering dog. We fed the black and white spotted terrier some Christmas turkey and finally got her inside. We made her a bed in the kitchen, amazed at how far she must have traveled to find us. When Cope woke the next morning, we told him there was a surprise in the kitchen. We had talked about getting a dog when he turned four, and that was just a couple of months away.
>
> He immediately suggested the name "Lucy," which we had no idea he'd heard before. It was the perfect name because it was only one letter off from "Lucky," which we knew we were.
>
> That was two years ago. I never imagined I would grow up to feel so alienated from nature…At the ranch it was easy to see how tiny I was, how little control we have over anything besides making sure there's enough gas in the car. I saw why people who live close to the land are deeply religious. How else to explain why things happen? Limbs break, creeks flood, deer die in the woods and disappear except for their perfect bones.
>
> As spring teased its arrival, I explored the small creeks, hidden veins of life, tangled and green, that had not existed when we arrived.

Lucy was my companion. Low-hanging cedar raked through my hair, and the deer paths I followed wandered in lazy circles. I realized that the Hill Country I thought I knew, dry limestone bluffs clotted with over-pollinating cedar and spiderlike live oaks — what you can see from the car or walking the fence line — is only the obvious, unimportant part. To get to the truth about something, you have to be brave enough to get lost inside it.[7]

Bradford has an extensive website, www.robinbradfordwriter.com, in which she writes about her work, her writing, and other aspects of her life. She regularly posts comments on a variety of subjects.

In 2012, Bradford wrote: "I am still working and writing. Cope is fifteen now starting high school and Jim is teaching tai chi."[8]

CRAIG ARNOLD
March 2001

Before he began his residency at Paisano, Craig Arnold had already held a number of distinguished writing fellowships including the Amy Lowell Poetry Travelling Scholarship, a National Endowment for the Arts Creative Writing Fellowship, and the John Atherton Fellowship in Poetry from the Bread Loaf Writers Conference. His book of poems, *Shells* (Yale University Press, 1999), was selected by W. S. Merwin for the Yale Series of Younger Poets.[9]

He was a visiting writer at the University of Texas at Austin the semester before he arrived at Paisano. He completed his second book of poetry, *Made Flesh* (Ausable Press, 2008), at the ranch.

Following Paisano, he held the Alfred Hodder Fellowship in the Humanities at Princeton and in 2005 was awarded the Rome Prize in Literature from the American Academy of Arts and Letters.

He completed his PhD in creative writing at the University of Utah in 2001 and taught poetry at the University of Wyoming beginning in 2004.

Arnold's distinguished career as a poet and teacher was cut cruelly short. In 2009, Arnold was at work on *Volcano Pilgrim: Five Months in Japan as a Wandering Poet* while on an US-Japan Friendship Commission's Creative Artists Exchange fellowship. He had registered at an inn on the tiny (population 150) island of Kuchinoerabu-jima, about 30 miles off the coast of Japan's southern Kyushu Island. On April 27 he set out for a solo hike to explore an active volcano on the island. He never returned. After extensive searches by Japanese officials and assistance arranged by the Wyoming congressional delegation, it was reported that he likely fell from a high and dangerous cliff.[10]

The evocative cover of "Texas," in the *Houston Chronicle* magazine of August 19, 2001, shows Arnold and his young son headed on the barely visible trail through the high grass toward the cabin at Paisano.

PATRICIA PAGE

September 2001

Patricia Page is a freelance writer of fiction, nonfiction, children's stories, textbooks, and business and technical publications. Her first novel, *Hope's Cadillac*, was published in 1996 and was chosen by Barnes & Noble for its Discover Great New Writers program. A memoir, *Shadows on a Nameless Beach* (2006), is about her struggle to come to terms with her son's suicide.

Her short stories have appeared in the *New Yorker*, *Glimmer Train*, *Epoch*, and other publications. Besides her Paisano fellowship, she has had residencies at Yaddo and the Centrum Center for the Arts.[11]

In 2012, when asked about particularly memorable Paisano experiences, she wrote:

My most memorable day during my tenure

at Paisano was, tragically, a memorable day for people around the globe. I awoke a little before dawn, as usual, and walked out into the old-fashioned, stone-paved gallery to watch the sunrise. Venus was still in the sky, sitting just above the curve of a crescent moon. The early morning breeze was up, soft and fresh, captured expertly by the orientation of the gallery. As the eastern sky began its rosy yawn, a canyon wren commenced a song I'd titled "Bird Singing Water," a cascade of two descending notes tumbling end over end, an aural waterfall. A few mosquitoes made their presence known, then a cricket chirped, and when enough light had penetrated the bountiful canopy of the live oaks, I opened my journal and wrote: "I am a long way from the paranoid culture of missile defense systems and biological warfare."

Not such a long way, as it turned out. At 9:15, the phone rang, and I left off writing to go inside to answer it. The voice was my sister's: "Patti! The World Trade Center and the Pentagon have been attacked!"

For days afterward, I was unable to write. I swam in Barton Creek, its waters so clear that deep spots look shallow, and walked the bluffs. I watched a garden spider trap and wrap a grasshopper in about three seconds flat. I witnessed a territorial dispute between two turtles at the low-water crossing until one of them retreated downstream. I startled a deer, prompting its peculiar sneezing sound as it crashed off into the junipers. Here at Paisano, I was just another species of fauna. And, I realized, I was happy. Strange to say that, in the wake of a disaster as momentous as September 11, I should have felt guilty or at least embarrassed, but what I mostly felt was grateful to be on those unspoiled acres, where human touch had been so blessedly light, where the beauty and endurance of the natural world could take up residence in our minds and bodies to restore well-being, and where the waters of Barton Creek like a muscle rippling through the land, could strengthen the spirit.

Over the next days, I continued to listen to developments on the radio and I continued to watch the sunrise each dawn from the gallery, but my notebook pages remained blank until one morning, a book title elbowed its way into my thoughts—*The Sun Also Rises*, and all at once the importance of that workaday adverb hit me. *Also*, yes, the sun also rises, despite disaster and tragedy. I uncapped my pen and began to write.[12]

Mylène Dressler
March 2002

Mylène Dressler, a native of the Netherlands, held her Paisano fellowship between publication of her second and third books (*The Deadwood Beetle*, Putnam, 2001, and *The Floodmakers*, Putnam, 2004). She wrote her first novel (*The Medusa Tree*, MacAdam/Cage, 1997) while finishing her doctorate at Rice University in Houston.

"I'd always believed myself an experienced nature-dweller, hiking and mountain biking being my great loves when I wasn't at home writing," Dressler wrote in her final report.

But now of course I know that visiting the land, and living as part of it are two very different things; and I will forever feel a sense

of wonder at having witnessed and been part
of the cycles of birth and death, flower and
fall, and drought and flood that mark this
surprising place.[13]

Dressler was living at the ranch during the July 2, 2002, flash
floods that left twenty-nine Texas counties disaster areas and
experienced those cycles of drought and flood more intensely
than fellows generally do.

Dressler's time at the ranch "may have been the greatest
gift I have ever been given," she remembered in 2012, noting
in particular the physical beauty of the land and the fact that,
because the property was "tended to," fellows could enjoy
the land rather than shoulder responsibility for its upkeep.
"I cried when I arrived and cried when I left."

When Dressler received her fellowship she was
extraordinarily grateful, but later she would wonder if she also
might have been "cocksure." She had received the fellowship
after a successful second book, at a time in her career when
she thought that in some respects she had "arrived." When
she got to the ranch, she immediately plunged into work on
a new novel. "Every day I would sit down in that front room
and I wrote and wrote and wrote," she recalled in 2012. Two
months into her fellowship, when she began to reread and
assess the work she had already completed (over a hundred
pages), she realized it was "dreadful."

"It couldn't be saved. It was coming out of the wrong
place...I felt terrible...and I also felt terrible that I had wasted
two months of this great gift."[14]

But Paisano, she would discover, was a "very nourishing
place." After taking a little time to regroup, she started over.
She was a month into a new novel when the July 2 flooding
occurred. The title she had given the work she had begun?
The Floodmakers.

After I found my car wedged between two
boulders downstream of the house, I called

my husband and told him I had bad news
and good news. The bad news was that the
Jeep Grand Cherokee was no more; the good
news was that I had received a sign from the
heavens that my new novel was on the right
track.[15]

"Paisano is such an immense place—it exposes a lot if
you let it," she pointed out. "There was fog the day I left—it
was like Brigadoon. It came into my life, and then it left."

In addition to her Paisano fellowship, Dressler has received
a Fulbright fellowship and Georgia's 2007 Carson McCullers
Fellowship in Writing. Her work can be found in French,
Dutch, and Turkish editions; she has taught in the United
States, Mexico, and Europe. She served as the visiting writer at
Guilford College in Greensboro, North Carolina, in 2012.

Oscar Casares
September 2002

A native of Brownsville and graduate of the University
of Texas at Austin, Oscar Casares had worked for eight years
at GSD&M advertising agency in Austin when he decided to
commit himself more fully to his fiction writing. He went on to
receive his MFA from the University of Iowa Writers' Workshop
in 2000, the year before his Paisano fellowship. Several months
before his arrival at the ranch, Casares sold his debut short story
collection, *Brownsville*, to Little, Brown and Company.

"It was a weird time," he reflected in 2012,

I'd only been writing for five years, most of
this without anyone knowing what I was
doing, and suddenly it felt like I was in this
three-hundred-acre bubble with people taking
some interest in what I might be doing out
there. The book was released a couple of weeks
after I left the ranch, so whatever interviews
or press there was associated with the book
happened at Paisano.

The timing of book release and fellowship garnered media attention both for Casares and for Paisano. Much publicity for *Brownsville* mentioned the fellowship and included photographs taken at the ranch.

In the years since he held his residency, Casares has been candid about the effects of the ranch's isolation on him:

> So when people learned that I'd be staying alone on this huge ranch they all wanted to know what kind of "protection" I was taking with me. My now former brother-in-law suggested a shotgun, even offered to give me lessons. An old high school friend said it ought to be handgun, and more specifically a .357, just in case. He didn't exactly offer lessons, but he did show me how to do a proper gangsta-grip. I didn't want to believe staying at writers' retreat required a firearm, so I blew off all their advice and showed up with just my laptop and a box of books I planned to read. It wasn't until that first night alone on the ranch that I started getting a little paranoid about something happening out there and what I might do. The house is like a couple of miles from the main road, so it's not like some crazy person was just going to stumble upon the ranch, right? So, if it's midnight and there is a crazy person wandering up to the front door, chances are he's not there to ask for a cup of sugar. Which is to say, if someone goes out of their way to find you out there at that hour, it's for no good reason. But of course I had rejected the idea of bringing along a gun and now had to find some other means of protection. I considered keeping the axe in the bed but thought it might get tangled up in the sheets right when I needed it most. Later I set

the axe on the floor, leaning it up against the foot of the bed, where it stayed for like five minutes until I imagined the killer—because now he wasn't just a crazy person anymore— sneaking into the room when I was sleep. Then I decided under the bed, with the axe handle sticking out a couple of inches, was my best option.[16]

Casares's second book, *Amigoland*, received a starred review from *Publishers Weekly* and was selected by the 2010 Mayor's Book Club in Austin for that year's citywide reading campaign. Since 2003, his essays have appeared in the *New York Times* and *Texas Monthly* as well as on *All Things Considered* for National Public Radio. He directs the New Writers Project, a master of fine arts program in the English Department at the University of Texas at Austin, where he lives with his wife and two children.

Todd Hearon
March 2003

Todd Hearon, a native Texan and graduate of Baylor University, moved to the East Coast for his graduate work (MA, Boston College; PhD, Boston University). He remained in the east and since 2003 has taught literature and creative writing at Phillips Exeter Academy, where he is the Charles Lynn and Mary Chase Stone Instructor in Humanities.

A published poet and prize-winning playwright even before his Paisano fellowship, during his time at the ranch Hearon wrote the first draft of a novel; his wife, Maggie Dietz, also a poet, finished a number of works there as well.

Over the years since then, Hearon has published a large number of poems and has garnered many prizes. While at Boston College he cofounded the Bridge Theatre Company, a troupe dedicated to classical and contemporary verse drama. He won the Paul Green Playwrights Prize for his full-length play, *Wives of the Dead*.[17]

His first book of poems, *Strange Land*, won the Crab Orchard Poetry Series Prize and was published in 2010 by Southern Illinois University Press. He has received the PEN New England Discovery Award, the Friends of Literature Prize from *Poetry* magazine and the Poetry Foundation, and the Rumi Prize for Poetry from *Arts & Letters*.[18]

His wife Maggie was the 2002–2003 George Bennett Fellow and writer-in-residence at Phillips Exeter. She directed, with former Poet Laureate Robert Pinsky, the Favorite Poem Project. The project included three published anthologies with Norton, a DVD archive, and study guides. Her first book of poems, *Perennial Fall*, appeared in 2006 from University of Chicago Press.

In 2011, one of Hearon's poems from *Strange Land* was set to an original score and performed in a musical premiere concert, *Three Horizons*. Held in Philips Exeter Academy's Phillips Church, the effort included performances by the academy's Concert Choir, whose students sang the poems.

According to a report in the Academy's news bulletin, Hearon said he was surprised and delighted with the translation of his work:

> I'd never thought to hear my poem (or rather a part of it) sung, and this itself was transformative. Kevin Siegfried (the composer) worked to contribute tone and tempo in ways that I thought very much matched my own sense of the poem. This is something that poetry on the page cannot typically do, and I was pleased to be included in a process that served, for me, as a rich and ongoing analogy. Music and poetry: they have always been sister arts (as have been poetry and painting). I love thinking about the analogous lines between them, how they light each other up.[19]

DOMINIC SMITH
September 2003

Dominic Smith grew up in Sydney, Australia. He holds an MFA in writing from the Michener Center for Writers at the University of Texas at Austin. At Paisano, Smith finished the manuscript for his novel *The Mercury Visions of Louis Daguerre*. A scene in the novel that describes the sound of lions calling at night was directly inspired by the haunting noise of the rescue lions calling from the Austin Zoo, just a mile from the Paisano front porch.

Since the fellowship, he has published three novels, most recently *The Last Painting of Sara De Vos*. *Bright and Distant Shores*, his third novel, was chosen by Kirkus Reviews as a "Best Book of 2011" in Australia, where Dominic grew up and where the book was also published. The novel was shortlisted for the Age Book of the Year and the Vance Palmer Fiction Prize, two of that country's foremost literary prizes. His awards include a New Works Grant from the Australia Council for the Arts, the Sherwood Anderson fiction prize, the Gulf Coast Prize, and a Pushcart nomination. His short fiction and articles have appeared in various journals and magazines, including *The Atlantic Monthly*, *Texas Monthly*, and the *Antioch Review*.

Smith has taught creative writing at the University of Texas at Austin, Southern Methodist University, and Rice University. He lives in Austin and serves on the graduate faculty of the Warren Wilson MFA Program for Writers.[20]

In March 2006, Smith was a panelist at a session of the Associated Writers Program held in Austin on "Rattlesnakes, Scorpions, and Low-Water Crossings: Dobie Paisano Fellows and the Texas Landscape" with Sheryl St. Germain, Laura Furman, and Scott Blackwood.

During the session, Smith related his fellowship to the subject of the novel he was working on:

> The physical location of my daily life at Paisano and the setting within my novel could

not have been more different on the surface. The novel is set in mid-nineteenth-century Paris. In the 1840s Paris was a city of social turmoil, a café society where the bohemian set challenged the artistic status quo, but also a place where an emerging middle class could be seen...department stores were coming into vogue. You could buy luxury items from all over the world on the Right Bank.

It was interesting for me to ponder what was going on around Austin, which lies just fourteen miles northeast of the Paisano front gate, during the same period my novel takes place.

In 1839, Louis Daguerre, the protagonist of my novel, invented the world's first practical form of photography, the daguerreotype. That same year the town of Waterloo was purchased by the republic of Texas, renamed Austin, and made the new seat of government.

In 1840 Austin was a town of unpaved streets and log cabins. Nonetheless, France, under the reign of King Louis-Philippe, sent a diplomat to found the French legation (which was built just a few blocks to the east of us and is still standing). France saw the young nation of Texas as an important trading partner. Louis-Philippe was the same king that awarded Louis Daguerre a national pension and the Legion of Honor for his photographic invention.

So Louis Daguerre and Texas had some interesting overlap for me. Just as the daguerreotype was becoming a worldwide phenomenon, being praised by the likes of Walt Whitman and Samuel Morse, Texas was being embraced as a young republic. In 1840

Paisano was not yet a ranch. It was a wild tract of land through which Barton Creek flowed.

James S. Burton was the first owner of the Paisano tract, after he surveyed 160 acres of it in 1860; it was later expanded to its current 254 acres. Burton sold it to Frederick and Lucy Kunze in 1863 and they built a log cabin.

The original cabin is hidden within the walls of the present Paisano house, though a part of it can be seen since a renovation was completed in 1979.

In the main bedroom of Frank Dobie's literary retreat there is a viewing window that displays the 3-foot thick walls of the original 1863 cabin.

There is something about seeing the rough-hewn walls of the cabin through a viewing window in the Paisano house that kept me connected to the nineteenth century as I worked on my period novel. It was a house within a house, a distant era packaged within a modern one, and that seemed like a compelling metaphor for the novel. Every day I faced the problem of how to package the middle of the nineteenth century into a novel that was being written in the first years of the twenty-first century.

By the time Paisano was a ranch, Louis Daguerre had been dead for nine years and the daguerreotype invention had been used all over the world for almost two decades, including in Texas. Among the first images to be daguerreotyped here were the Alamo and Sam Houston. But by 1860 other forms of photography were beginning to eclipse the success of the daguerreotype.[21]

WILLIAM J. COBB
March 2004

Born in Texas City, William J. Cobb attended Southwest Texas State University (now Texas State University) and the University of Texas at Austin and received his PhD from the University of Houston's writing program. His first book (*The Fire Eaters*, W. W. Norton) was published in 1994; his second, a book of short stories (*The White Tattoo*, Ohio State University Press) was published in 2002.

Cobb worked on a third "and hopefully final" draft of what would become his third book, *Goodnight, Texas*, while at Paisano and felt at the end of the stay that it had been "the best writing experience I've had in some time."[22]

In 2012, he reflected:

> My fellowship came at a good time, when I was burned out from teaching and needed some time to write...People don't realize how demanding the role of being a writing professor can be, how full your days can become, with no time to write.
>
> I was most definitely an "ex-pat" Texan when I visited Paisano, having taken a professorship at Penn State in 1995, and it affected my experience in a variety of ways. For one thing, I think all my time away made me appreciate what I like most about Texas and the Austin area all the more. We had a long, beautiful spring that year, and where I live in Central Pennsylvania, spring doesn't usually arrive until the end of April or early May: In the Hill Country the flowers started blooming in February (or at least it seemed that way), but I know that by March we had bluebonnets, firewheels, Mexican hats, and Indian paintbrushes along the roadsides and in the meadows of Paisano Ranch.

... The bird life was amazing. In late April we started hearing a lovely trilling sound outside our bedroom window, and soon came to find a family of eastern screech owls lived in the elm oak beside the patio. If you shone a flashlight over the fields, you could see just their glowing eyes as they hunted insects. We liked to say those were the souls of Comanches floating over the fields. I have a long list of Paisano birds sighted, which includes the remarkable sighting (by my wife) of a juvenile whooping crane (traveling along the Colorado River flyway, no doubt), ospreys, painted buntings, black-billed cuckoos, and a golden-cheeked warbler, which is extremely rare. The chuck-will's widows could be so loud at night we'd have to close the windows to get some sleep. We had a trio of longhorn steers that came to visit us regularly, and although I'm sure we weren't supposed to, we left the gate open so they could come inside and eat the sweet grass close to the house. My wife even hand-fed them now and then. They liked her cornbread the best.[23]

Cobb directs the MFA program at Penn State. He lives in Pennsylvania and Colorado, and his fourth book, *The Bird Saviors*, was published by Unbridled Books in June 2012.

Scott Blackwood
September 2004
Scott Blackwood attended the University of Texas at Austin as an undergraduate and received an MFA in creative writing from Texas State University. He received his Paisano fellowship between publication of his first and second books (*In the Shadow of Our House*, Southern Methodist University Press, 2001, and *We Agreed to Meet Just Here*, New Issues Press, 2009).

"Paisano, as many people will note, changes lives," he reflected in 2012.

> I don't say this lightly. Without my Paisano, I would not have had the time, with a full-time administrative job, a newborn and a fourteen-year-old, to get my novel *We Agreed to Meet Just Here* finished for years (I'd already been working on it six years at that point). As so many of the other Paisano fellows know, timing is everything. In fact, the experience greatly changed the writing of *We Agreed to Meet Just Here*. Originally, the book was a novel in stories but at page 80, in my first month at Paisano, I knew that the form I'd originally planned for it wouldn't work. It was headed for failure. I had to rethink the whole thing. But the genius of Paisano is that it allows for mistakes—it encourages you to take more chances because if you follow one trail to a dead end, you have the time and (hopefully) equanimity to trace your way back through the thicket and start again. So Paisano—and the many walks and swims I took there—became part of my process. I feel very fortunate to have had those open-ended days near the creek, occasionally joined by water moccasins and the then still-living longhorn (is there anything as strange and disconcerting as the sound of a steer munching on grass in the pitch dark? Or the same steer being summoned to the porch when you start up burgers on the grill?). Finally, reimagined sections of Paisano appear in *We Agreed to Meet Just Here* as the character Sonny Farbrother's home, complete with dinner-time roars from the Austin Zoo's lions echoing off the creek bluffs. And honestly, the spirit of the

place is all through the book and still present (when I can summon it, like the steer to the porch) in my writing life.[24]

We Agreed to Meet Just Here would win the AWP Prize for the Novel and the Texas Institute of Letters Award for best fiction. It was also a finalist for the PEN USA Literary Award for fiction. Blackwood teaches in the MFA program in creative writing at Southern Illinois University and received a Whiting Award in 2011.

Daniel Rifenburgh
March 2005
Daniel Rifenburgh, a native of Elmira, New York, attended the University of Louisville and served three years in the US Army during the Vietnam War, working as a military journalist. He holds a BA from Florida Atlantic University and an MA from the University of Florida. He received the Robert H. Winner Memorial Award from the Poetry Society of America in 1996. His first book, *Advent,* was published in London by Waywiser Press in 2002 and received the Natalie Ornish Award from the Texas Institute of Letters. After some years of college adjunct teaching, he began driving an eighteen-wheeler flatbed rig, hauling steel out of the Port of Houston. His collection of poetry, *Isthmus,* was published in September 2013.[25]

In 2013, Rifenburgh described the genesis of his second book of poetry:

> It's been eight years since my sojourn at Paisano Ranch, and only now can I hold in my hands the volume of verse, *Isthmus,* I began crafting there. Perhaps I would not even today have this present accomplishment if I had not received a Dobie Paisano fellowship and been forced, for six months, to confront that looming black hole of uncreation, my invisible,

nowhere-to-be-found second book.

At Paisano, I made a start. I recall I availed myself of my UT library privileges and borrowed several books by my former teacher, the poet Donald Justice, who had recently passed away. I wrote a long elegy for Don entitled "After Justice," for I was experiencing not only grief at his passing, not only the anxiety of his enormous influence, but something akin to a long hangover following his death. So, I did the therapeutic thing and tried to get it all down on paper there at Paisano. I think that freed me finally to go forward. The resulting book was dedicated to Don and carries this epigraph from his work: "Come back now and help me with these verses. / Whisper to me some beautiful secret that you remember from life." I felt Don's spirit was with me there at the ranch, whispering, sharing, helping.

It was very strange, coming from inner-loop Houston where I lived with my family, to be so isolated at Paisano Ranch, particularly given its proximity to Austin. I felt from the beginning that it was fitting to allow the strangeness of that isolation, the pure weirdness of being quite alone, to bathe over me, to fully experience it. My only companion and compensation was my black Lab, who made the situation tolerable. To say we bonded is to understate our relationship.

I attempted to take most every opportunity to explore the land that is Paisano Ranch. I spent most of my days romping over the landscape, even walking up through the middle of Barton Creek in tennis shoes, accompanied by my dog. I got to know the ant colonies, the rattlesnakes and wild turkeys, the cacti, scorpions, feral longhorns and the amazing wildflowers. The ranch is thoroughly beautiful, particularly in spring, and I considered it a supreme duty to enjoy its beauty. I did get one poem directly from all of this romping and stomping, "Wild Turkeys at Paisano," and it pleases me that others seem to like it.

One unlooked-for benefit of the fellowship was getting to know something of J. Frank Dobie, the man behind the ranch. Most of his books are in the little library there and I had occasion to read them. They are of widely varying quality, but his most novel-like book (and, really, it is a novel), *Tongues of the Monte*, seems to me a buried masterpiece of American literature. Dobie was such an earnest, unpretentious soul he was a little ashamed, I think, of fully deploying the tropes of fiction to sew his Mexican adventures together, yet he gritted his teeth and did so. His experiences in the wilds of long-ago northern Mexico are both magical and thrilling. The work combines the best of a proto-Carlos Castañeda (*Don Juan, Or a Yaqui Way of Knowledge*) folklorist with the deep characterization of Owen Wister's *The Virginian* and, in its passion and violence, nicely adumbrates Cormac McCarthy's Border Trilogy. That it stands four million down on Amazon's bestseller list is lamentable. It's a terrific read, brimming with action and fascinating detail.

Without the possibility of knowing Dobie personally, I at least got to know something of him through his work, and am glad to have done so. The fellowship that bears his name is a fine testament to his legacy, and also embodies the noble generosity and idealism of both the Texas Institute of Letters and the University of Texas.

I am forever grateful for my time at Paisano and I'm glad to know other writers are getting the same shot at being alone with themselves and their work. I think it's particularly useful for that writer who has just had a first success, a first book, and is drawing a blank as to what comes next. That's a dicey place to be. At that time, it's good to look long at a pocked, tough old cactus and see the fresh, stunningly beautiful scarlet flower it puts forth. *O, yeah: in springtime, at Paisano.*

WILD TURKEYS AT PAISANO
From their roosts
Among the cedars
Wild turkeys come
Down to the morning meadow,
Stepping lightly through gray mist
Like living brushstrokes
Upon a silk panel.

I count five
And they are larger
Than one imagined,
Yet can fly
For brief spans,
And will,
When, of a sudden, they spy
An interloping human.

There they rise now, seeing me,
And go wheeling
Like the turning measures of a verse
Over the next line of oak and cedar
To settle in a meadow unseen

On the cool reverse of earth's
Upright, Chinese screen.[26]

David Wright
September 2005

David Wright grew up in Borger, Texas. He holds a
BA from Carleton College and an MFA from the University
of Massachusetts at Amherst. Before he started teaching
creative writing he was a player and coach on various
American football teams in Paris and London.

His first book, *Fire on the Beach: Recovering the Lost Story
of Richard Etheridge and the Pea Island Lifesavers* (2001) was
described by the *Washington Post* as "adding significantly
to our understanding of the many essential ways in which
African-Americans have served their country." The book was
a *New York Times* Notable Selection and one of the *St. Louis
Post Dispatch's* Best Books of 2001. The television version, *The
Pea Island Story*, won a Salute to Excellence First Prize from
the National Association of Black Journalists.[27]

He has published essays on Malcolm X, Martin Luther
King, Ernest Hemingway, and James Baldwin. He has
received the Zora Neale Hurston/Richard Wright Award.

Wright has continued to work on the novel he began at
Paisano. It has had several different incarnations. At first, he
thought he had finished it, but was advised to do another
draft. Then he received a Fulbright to Brazil in 2011 and
completely rewrote the novel. He is now calling the novel
All the Best Things Thus and making plans for its publication

He is also working on a novel about the 2005 Paris riots.

Wright is a tenured professor of English at the
University of Illinois. He is on campus only in the fall. He
spends the other eight months (when he is not abroad) in
Austin. "Paisano made me realize that I want Austin to be
my home."[28]

Timothy Westmoreland
March 2006

Timothy Westmoreland, a native Texan, received his BA degree from the University of Texas at Arlington and an MFA from the University of Massachusetts at Amherst. He has taught creative writing at the University of Massachusetts at Amherst, Amherst College, Hampshire College, Southern Illinois University, and Indiana University.

His first book, *Good as Any* (Harcourt Brace, 2002) is a collection of short stories that was widely reviewed and recommended as the work of a promising young writer. He was featured in *Book* magazine's article "Writers You Need to Know." Amazon.com selected *Good as Any* for its top five list of 2002 Best Books of Fiction by New Authors.

Westmoreland was a guest on NPR's international program *Studio 360* and has also appeared on Voice of America radio.[29]

When he returned for the fortieth reunion at Paisano, Westmoreland recalled:

> My time at the ranch was marked by a punctual, nightly event. The longhorns would come up into the yard and peer in the kitchen window at me. I loved them very much, and I took to feeding them bread. Each time I left the ranch I'd stop in at the HEB and buy several loaves of bread for them. It became such a habit that if I didn't come out to feed them they would use their nose to bump the kitchen door to let me know they were ready for a treat. If I was out of town late, the two of them would be waiting for me on the gravel where I parked my car. It was like being a teenager again and having my parents worry over me. So on Saturday when I learned that they had died, I was unexpectedly brought to tears. I'm soft hearted where animals are concerned. (Tom

McGuane has a sentence about animals that
touches me: "There is a special grief for the
innocent caught up in Mankind's murderous
follies.") It seems that I was one of the last
(or the last, I'm not sure) fellows to have the
pleasure of their company. I am sorry for the
other fellows that won't get that nightly knock
at the door.[30]

Sam Taylor
September 2006

A native of Florida, Sam Taylor received his BA from
Swarthmore College and his MFA in writing from the
University of Texas at Austin. While there, Taylor held a
Michener fellowship in poetry. He has published poems in a
wide variety of literary journals and his collection of poetry,
Body of the World, was published by Ausable Press in 2005. It
is now available from Copper Canyon Press.

Whereas most Paisano fellows came to the ranch from
more urban environments, Taylor arrived after several years
living in a remote wilderness refuge, the Vallecitos Mountain
Refuge in the Carson National Forest in New Mexico, where
he was a caretaker. At the refuge he was without phone,
electricity, or internet. Sometimes snowed in for months at a
time in the winter, Taylor said living at Paisano

> ...represented a transition to city living...
> This adjustment back to the world of so-called
> civilization dominated my living and writing
> experience. I had become quite sensitive living
> in the silence of the wilderness over the past
> few years, and even within the seclusion
> of the ranch, I was constantly aware of the
> pulse, roar, and hum of the city around me.
> Nevertheless, Paisano was a perfect place
> to make a gradual transition back into the

world of the 21ˢᵗ century, as it allowed me
to work in the relative seclusion of a natural
landscape, while also offering access to the
city, the internet, and the UT libraries, as well
as billboards and strip malls, and *America's
Next Top Model*.[31]

Since 2011, Taylor has been an assistant professor of
English and creative writing at Wichita State University. His
second poetry collection, *Nude Descending an Empire*, was
published by the University of Pittsburgh Press Pitt Poetry
Series in 2014. Poems from it have appeared in the *New
Republic*, *Hudson Review*, *Agni*, *Michigan Quarterly Review*,
and *Poetry Daily*.

VICENTE LOZANO
March 2007

Vicente Lozano is a systems administrator for the
Undergraduate Writing Center at the University of Texas at
Austin. When he was thirteen, his father retired from the Air
Force and moved the family back to the Texas Gulf Coast,
where his Mexican American ancestors settled in the 1880s.
He received a BA and MA in English and a Master of Library
and Information Science from the University of Texas at
Austin.

For many years, Lozano has pursued his family's
complicated border history, drawing on Chicano scholarship,
archival material, and family gossip.

Lozano's writing plan took an interesting turn after he
left Paisano. He described this dramatic change in 2013.[32]

My six months at Paisano were very much a
"Big Bang" time. In those six months I managed
to sketch out three ambitious books with
seven intertwining story lines that spanned
112 years and roughly 358 pages. I felt like I

would never have that amount of time again, and so, after a month of research at the Center for American History (itself a great luxury) I bore down pretty relentlessly.

Since then, it's as if the material has cooled off, and it became a sprawling map for disentangling and simplifying. Where I was on fire with trying to create a grand unified theory that made sense of my family history, time has given me a more removed and maybe compassionate perspective. One that is less about fierce wrongs righted, and more about the mystery of the times people happened to find themselves, and how they did the best they could.

For a while it was necessary to get away from the South Texas material. They were ghost stories I was tired of channeling. I spent several years writing satire and absurdly comic things, some about Austin and others that are even more nonsensical. Think I needed to rediscover my sense of play.

With the help of an agent I've grounded all seven stories and focused on a beginning one: of a political rally in 1937, over three days.

Three days ago, while cleaning up writing folders, I looked back on all of the material I generated out at the Dobie ranch. It was nice to see how the history of my family obsession grew and then sort of exploded during those long rainy days out at Paisano. It made feel like an opportunistic magpie who will keep revisiting that pile of shiny and messy words again. Maybe that is the way it was always meant to be. …

A final piece of news that makes me smile: a year ago (2012) my wife, Alyssa Harad, published her memoir, *Coming to My Senses*. Published by Viking, it's the story of how she went down the perfume rabbit hole and fell in love with the world of perfume. The book is set during the year of our wedding, 2007. Also the year I was out at Paisano. She mentions visiting me at the ranch to plan our nuptials. Can't tell you how much it tickles me to have ended up as a character in a book on the way to publishing mine. It's fitting, somehow.

ALISON MOORE
September 2007

Alison Moore was born in Massachusetts. She holds an MFA in creative writing from the Program for Writers at Warren Wilson College and has taught English and creative writing at the University of Arizona. She is the author of three books: a collection of short stories entitled *The Middle of Elsewhere* (Phoenix International/University of Arkansas Press, 2006); *Small Spaces between Emergencies* (Mercury House, 1992); and *Synonym of Love* (Mercury House, 1995).[33]

Moore describes the genesis and outcome of her fourth book:

> Since I left the program in 2008, I received a National Endowment for the Arts Fellowship in fiction in 2010 to finish the novel I worked on at Paisano. The result was *Riders on the Orphan Train*, a historical novel published by Roadworthy Press of Fayetteville, Arkansas, in 2012. The book is part of the outreach program for the National Orphan Train Complex Museum and Research Center. My husband Phil Lancaster and I tour the United States, primarily the Midwest and Southwest, with our multimedia program with live music,

video, and a dramatic recitation from my novel in museums, libraries, and performing arts centers. In 2012 we received the Charles Loring Brace Award for preserving the stories of the orphan trains.

In the summer after leaving Paisano, I received a research fellowship from HRC to do some preliminary research on the orphan trains that came to Texas. In 2013, I wrote a grant for the National Orphan Train Complex for funding from the Texas-based Ayres Family Foundation and received the funding. In 2014, this grant was used to create research materials for online use on the Texas orphan train story.

The Paisano fellowship came at a crucial point in my writing career. It gave me time away from touring to delve deeply into the material I needed to develop the novel. It also gave me wonderful research opportunities in UT libraries and the ability to audit a graduate seminar in American studies called "The End of American Innocence—1900–1920" that was key in giving me a cultural/historical context for the time period of my novel.

We're still on the road, and in 2014, we gave the keynote presentation for the National Federation of Genealogy Societies conference in San Antonio.[34]

MARY HELEN SPECHT
March 2008

A native of Abilene, Texas, Mary Helen Specht received a BA in English from Rice University and an MFA in creative writing from Emerson College in Boston, where she won the department's fiction award. Her writing has been nominated for multiple Pushcart prizes and appeared in numerous publications, including the *New York Times*, the *Colorado Review*, the *Michigan Quarterly Review*, the *Southwest Review*, the *Florida Review*, *Southwestern American Literature*, the *Texas Observer*, and *Night Train*, where she won the Richard Yates Short Story Award.

Specht's short stories explore what she describes as

> ...primarily a "post-western" Texas where characters try to piece together an identity amongst the remnants of what Texas used to be and is still known for in the rest of the world: Ranches have become pleasure or retirement spots, neon longhorn saloons tourist traps; a peculiar brand of Austinesque Texas mythology has gained strength; in small West Texas towns, kids are more likely to be in a heavy metal band than know how to ride a horse even though the idea of themselves as cowboys still holds a powerful authority.

A past Fulbright Scholar to Nigeria, Specht is an assistant professor at St. Edward's University in Austin, Texas.[35]

Specht kept a personal journal during her fellowship.

> March 11: The sunrise glowed through the east kitchen window by the cupboards as I boiled water for tea and oatmeal. (My grandmother says, "If it can stick to the pan like that, imagine how it can stick to your ribs.") After I walked to the cabin and back, I settled in at the table in the gallery, writing and watching the birds. I named the first male cardinal at the feeder A. C. after A. C. Greene, one of the first Paisano fellows and, like myself, an Abilene native. The purple martin house stood empty like a relic. The work I planned to do unfurled in front of me, no hurry, nothing

to rush off to, nothing to get in the way.

March 15: This morning the wind blew just right, and I could hear the rushing of the creek from where I sat on the porch reading my late grandfather's copy of Dobie's *The Longhorns*, signed by Dobie with the image of his cattle brand. My grandfather was also the one who taught me to tap, tap, tap the stones with a stick so as to warn the rattlesnakes I was on my way. I wish he were alive to see this place, to know that I was here.

March 16: The finches, still cloaked in winter olive, have finally discovered my feeder, and they crowd around it, fighting for a turn. The numerous issues and frustrations over how to move forward with my Nigeria book are somehow cradled in Paisano's wonder, in its reminders of how life goes on, and that even to be a bird is a beautiful thing. Before going to bed, I stepped onto the porch, and the moonlight illuminated the stone edge where the overhang didn't reach, and the light was like a milky picture frame.

March 18: Rain. And then it stopped. The road has become a crossing for turtles and frogs, and one cardinal stands in the glistening tree like a ruby leaf. I'm working on my chapter set in Nigeria's own rainy season, dilapidated vehicles clogging muddy streets.

April 9: On my way back from a walk up to the bluffs along the creek, I was lost in thought and didn't notice something crossing the road in front of me until it hissed and rattled. An adult diamondback rattlesnake. I turned and walked back the other direction, heart in my throat.

April 24: A few clouds, buttery sun rays:

I waded and swam out by Conversation Rock, scaring large trout and even one water moccasin that went zigzagging away from me through the water. The crayfish are beautiful, almost translucent sitting on the creek bed.

Today I thought about how much of the life around me at the ranch I never see, but only know by its evidence. Fox tracks in the dirt. Turkey scat in the yard. Deer corn eaten up. The call of whippoorwills and owls in the night. And I thought, maybe melodramatically, that this was also like the life of a person who lives alone. The friends whom I occasionally meet in Austin for dinner or who come out to visit in the evening only see trace evidence of my real life. Returning to the States from Africa has been hard on me, and I spend many nights on the porch nursing a broken heart, nursing feelings of loss and frustration over all that I left undone. A friend told me recently on the phone: you seem fine. As if to reassure me. I am fine, but I also wanted to say: You have no idea about the minutes and hours of my life. You see only a track in the dirt. You hear my voice in the trees, but don't know the first thing about my life out here.

May 4: My heart grows big watching the pages of my book accrue day by day. When I go in town for dinner, friends offer to let me crash at their places but I resist. I like driving back here, unlocking the gate in the moonlight, and then waking up early to walk and write. And I guess I've never really thought about the difference between boredom and loneliness before—I am never bored here, although I am sometimes lonely. I wish I had someone with whom to share the daily wonder of this place, the wonder of myself growing inside it.

June 11: A pair of painted buntings have taken up at the feeder. They are dazzling jewels. The Mockfords were kind enough to have me over to dinner—he came for me in his 4-runner Mule, and I brought wine and watermelon. They were charming hosts, and we looked from their balcony over all the new construction and development. On the way back, I offered to get out of the Mule to open the gate, but Mr. Mockford, in his gruff way said, jokingly, "I doubt a girl from Abilene would even know how."

July 22: I woke at dawn after a fitful sleep, an unsettled feeling in my stomach because of losing my hard drive the day before. I walked from the west gate toward the Mockfords' and, at some point, heard a rustle to my left. It was not unusual for me to startle deer on my morning walks. Sure enough, a doe came bounding out of the brush, crossing my path at high speed with something hanging from her mouth. But, then, there was more noise. A second and maybe third deer? No, a coyote, wolfish and big, was on the chase. When he saw me, he stopped six feet away, and our eyes met. Then, he rushed on.

I thought (once my heart calmed down): this is a little like my time at the ranch. I am only a blip in this world, something the coyote sees once out of the corner of his eye before continuing on his way. I am one in a long line of humans blessed with the gift of this ranch for only a small window of time. And, in the end, that's all right.[36]

ENDNOTES

[1] Lowell Mick White, fellow's report, 1999; personal communication, June 2012.
[2] Lowell Mick White, *That Demon Life* (Gival Press, 2009).
[3] Katherine L. Hester, personal correspondence, October 2012.
[4] Thomas McNeely, fellow's report, 2000.
[5] Thomas McNeely, personal correspondence with Katherine Hester, March 14, 2012.
[6] Robin Bradford, biography for Paisano's fortieth anniversary celebration.
[7] Robin Bradford, *Houston Chronicle Magazine* (March 3, 2003), 4, 15.
[8] Robin Bradford, personal communication, August 2012.
[9] "Craig Arnold," https://en.wikipedia.org/wiki/Craig_Arnold. Accessed January 23, 2016.
[10] "UW Poet and Professor Believed to Have Died after Fall," University of Wyoming website, News, May 8, 2009, http://www.uwyo.edu/uw/news/2009/05/uw-poet-and-professor-believed-to-have-died-after-fall.html. Accessed January 23, 2016.
[11] Patricia Page, biography for Paisano's fortieth anniversary celebration.
[12] Patricia Page, Paisano reminiscences, December 20, 2012.
[13] Mylène Dressler, fellow's report, 2002.
[14] Mylène Dressler, telephone interview with Katherine Hester, April 2012.
[15] Ibid.
[16] Oscar Casares, personal communication with Katherine Hester, March 4 and May 2, 2012.
[17] Todd Hearon's Poetry Foundation biography, http://www.poetryfoundation.org/bio/todd-hearon. Accessed January 23, 2016.
[18] *Agni Magazine*, Boston University, online.
[19] "Phillips Exeter Academy English Instructor Todd Hearon's Poetry Set to Music," http://www.exeter.

edu/news_and_events/news_events_8170.aspx. Accessed January 23, 2016.

[20] Dominic Smith, personal communication, November 27, 2012.

[21] Panel discussion, "Dobie Paisano Fellows and the Texas Landscape," Associated Writers Program, Austin, Texas, March 2006.

[22] William Cobb, fellow's report, 2004.

[23] William Cobb, personal correspondence with Katherine Hester, May 14, 2012.

[24] Scott Blackwood, personal correspondence with Katherine Hester, June 11, 2012.

[25] Daniel Rifenburgh, *Isthmus* (Houston, Texas: Mutabilis Press, 2013).

[26] Daniel Rifenburgh, personal communication, October13, 2013; "Wild Turkeys at Paisano," from *Isthmus*.

[27] David Wright, biography for Paisano's fortieth anniversary celebration.

[28] David Wright, personal communication, August 9, 2013.

[29] Timothy Westmoreland, biography for Paisano's fortieth anniversary celebration; announcement of Paisano fellows, 2005–2006, AWP Chronicle, September 2005.

[30] Timothy Westmoreland, personal communication to Michael Adams, March 14, 2006.

[31] Sam Taylor, fellow's report, 2007.

[32] Vicente Lozano, personal communication, September 2013.

[33] Alison Moore, biography for Paisano's fortieth anniversary celebration.

[34] Alison Moore, personal communication, October 2013.

[35] Mary Helen Specht, biography submitted October 2013.

[36] Mary Helen Specht, excerpts from Paisano journal, March–July, 2008.

Ten: The Fortieth Anniversary

On a lovely March morning in 2008, buses arrived at Paisano, bringing former fellows to the ranch to celebrate the fortieth anniversary of the program. A few of the annual meetings of the Texas Institute of Letters had been held out there, but this was the first time the creation of the fellowship program had been celebrated. The celebration was planned and carried out by the graduate school staff under the direction of the new program director Michael Adams. A handsome program was designed by Maria Ramirez. Kathleen Mabley wrote an extensive article about the celebration for the graduate school website.[1]

A large tent was set up in the front yard. After a welcome by Adams and short remarks by executive vice president and provost Steven Leslie, vice provost and dean of graduate studies Victoria Rodriguez, and William V. Davis, president-elect of the Texas Institute of Letters, brunch was served. Special recognition was given to the Ralph A. Johnston Foundation (Johnston's daughter, Mrs. Jerry Andrews, received the award), the Houston Endowment, and Audrey Slate, the director of the program from 1974 to 2007. Music was provided by the most recent fellow, Alison Moore, and Phil Lancaster as well as Mariachi Tamazula.

In an addendum to her fellow's report, Moore captured the spirit of the scene:

> A week after I left the ranch, I returned to find three hundred people in the front yard. Forty-three former fellows, a bevy of UT folk including the provost, a delegation from the Texas Institute of Letters, and some family members of J. Frank Dobie gathered for the fortieth anniversary of the program. All of the fellows' publications were displayed on tables, thick volumes and chapbook-thin. We mingled and met like long-lost relatives or survivors of an arduous journey, some a little shy, some boisterous with camaraderie.
>
> After brunch and mariachi music, Michael Adams took to the podium and by the time he finished reading what he'd written about the history of the program and the cast of characters with very human hopes and fears that had lived and written on the ranch, the assistant provost was in tears, as were many of the rest of us. Suddenly we were real to everyone else, written about, though not everyone was still living. We comprised several generations, from José Cisneros in his

ninety-eighth year, telling us all that Paisano meant true freedom to him, freedom to create art, not on commission or contract but by heart-driven choice and desire. There were fellows one-quarter his age, the ink not yet dry on their University of Texas MFAs who entered the great post-workshop void without Michener money and weekly deadlines determined to persevere on their own. Some were well known: Steven Harrigan, Oscar Casares, Laura Furman. In greater numbers were the emerging and mid-list mid-career all the way to the relatively obscure. But we had all been woven together in a narrative, pulled out of our separate writerly solitudes and circumstances into a common inheritance with a shared language of living on this particular piece of land and learning to trust the writers we were still becoming because of it. We looked at each other knowing we'd been changed in different ways by the same thing, by the gift of time in Texas given by a man we've never actually met but who no doubt stood just outside the gate he'd left open on the way out, amazed by all he'd set in motion.[2]

The writers who gathered on the property on that spring day at the beginning of the Paisano project's fifth decade sprang from rural roots and urban environs; they were born and raised in Texas and they were just passing through; they were cab drivers and journalists and academics. They stood at the brink of new careers; they recognized the perils of a writer's sophomore slump; they were grizzled old-timers able to take a philosophical long view of their profession—in short, they mirrored the transformations that, over the past forty years, had changed the state of Texas, the state of Texas writing, and the state of the literary world.

By the Paisano program's fortieth anniversary, writers had begun to "ply their trade" in a world increasingly defined by its far-reaching connectivity. Barton Creek might rise, but the writer who sat on the porch at Paisano in 2008 was no longer truly isolated. The lag time between an event and a writer's knowledge of it had dwindled to almost nothing. And as a writer's interior "world" and the larger one became increasingly connected, writers became increasingly cognizant of the need to sometimes step out of the cultural currents that shaped them. The Paisano that had been first "the Wende Place" and then just another Hill Country place was now an artistic Brigadoon, a Shangri-La. As the fellowship project entered its fifth decade, the property Dobie had so loved had become a sanctuary for writers in the truest sense of the word—a sacred place of refuge and protection, honoring both literary history and the land itself.

ENDNOTES

[1] Office of Graduate Studies website: http://www.utexas.edu/ogs/about/archives/paisano.html. Accessed January 23, 2016.

[2] Alison Moore, "Aftermath," from *Time in Texas*, revised fellow's report, October 10, 2013.

Afterword
by Michael Adams

FOR OVER THIRTY YEARS, AUDREY SLATE KEPT WATCH OVER THE Dobie Paisano Project. Her genuine joy and love for both the ranch and the fellows motivated her to write their history. For Audrey, their history was important for the literary community, the University, and the state of Texas, but in providing the reader a profile of each ranch-writer, she was also giving us a profile of the ranch itself—its unique personality and presence. And she wrote with the inspiration from her knowledge of the valuable gift Paisano bestows upon all who, however briefly, call Paisano home.

The opening of the Paisano gift begins at the gate and Katherine Hester tells it best: she was at the gate with her car radio tuned to KGSR. It was at the "moment of hill country dusk when the sky is neither blue nor rosy but the tenderest imaginable combination of the two. When I got out of the car, an armadillo was dumbly nudging its way through the brush on the other side of the gate. The faintest breath of air was rustling the live oaks. As I pulled the hasp of the padlock on the gate and undid the chain, I realized that the song spilling from the open door of my car was "Knocking on Heaven's Door." And so be it. Katherine had already learned that beyond the gate was truly a heavenly gift—a world that inspires writing and changes lives. No hyperbole, just fact. And the fact is that, for each fellow, this future of change was entering into them the moment they locked the gate behind them.

The first presence that greets each fellow beyond the gate is the rush-in-the-blood fear, in varying degrees, of that first night—the aloneness in the middle of 250 acres of darkness, thick curtains of trees, two miles away to the nearest help, the obvious fact that no one could hear you if you yelled, the cries of coyotes that seem alarmingly too close, the squeaking and cracking of the house itself, the rush of something in the bushes outside, the shadow of something darting across the floor, the glowing eyes from the darkness. And when the rescue zoo arrived up the road with MGM's Leo the Lion look-alike, there was the nightly roaring, movie-starish and regal, that sent one fellow to put a hatchet under the bed. Others brought family or friends to help take away, literally, the NATURE of the ranch. Some didn't sleep at all. Call it what you will, exhilaration, fear, excitement, menacing enchantment, it was clear you were in someone else's territory—and someone who could harm. And yet every fellow wouldn't have had it any other way.

The second presence that greets the fellow, especially first morn, is the huge blanket of peace and a fragile quietness they can feel. Almost immediately they are drawn beyond their will to the creek—Barton creek, which is the soul of Paisano, the sacred world where fellows spend most of their time whether it be in drought when the creek becomes the bed of bleached bones of some serpentine Leviathan or be it flooding with a fury and grandeur that becomes a kind of wild communion. And when they understand that they and the creek are surrounded by the fields of flowers and grasses and plants and ancient trees crowding together on this island of Texas earth, they begin to feel the mystery and preciousness. And then they know they are feeling what others have felt before them. And they begin to understand. They were becoming a member of a rare family that has been touched in some way by what Barton Creek historian Ed Crowl calls "an oasis of natural wildness."

Once you are within the deepest part of the Paisano canyon, the fellow realizes that he or she is walking on the same trail, even stepping into same footprint that 50 or more fellows have stepped into. This was the same world still protected and hidden within the busy world from which they came. In this sense, Paisano was a kind of miniature eternity all to itself. And in this sense, each fellow was living within the eternal home of the creatures who made the noise, followed the game trails, defecated on the road, drank from the creek, and reproduced themselves once a year.

Each fellow was first met at the same steel gate with the same steel carved, faded-orange Paisano, holding its own against the battering elements, opening up to the same world. Each fellow would be startled by the beauty and innocence of the same doe that Steve Harrigan and his baby girl saw through the kitchen window years earlier. Steve put the moment into a poem, knowing that this was a profound pause in time that she would never remember but that he would never forget.

And after all these years, they are all still there. The same chicken snake that lives under the house. The same huddle of turkeys lodged in the same tree. The same blue heron, (christened "Charlie" by a fellow after her father) patrolling up and down the creek, always floating or gliding, never flying, maybe a swoop now and then. The same lost turtle on the road. The same ugly possum, the same skunk with its purse of stink, the same cougar gliding in extra-slow -motion among the caves within the rock walls above the creek. The same huge prehistoric porcupine, his body loaded with thorns. The same night birds singing you asleep, the same morning birds celebrating the dawn. The same family of deer grazing in the back yard. the same coyote turd lying on the same spot on the low-water crossing, the same lizard, same throat-inflating chameleon, the same army of Monarchs on their same miraculous journey, the same flock of cardinals that like a living American flag zoom through the front yard when mating is in their blood. And, of course, there is the always-present Paisano, racing, darting, occasionally just standing photogenically with a snake squiggling in his mouth You get the point. Every year a new fellow gets to know the same world known by another fellow decades years ago. And before leaving, every fellow encases a host of special memories.

All of these are the magic and definition of Paisano that each writer lives among. A fauna society no one else in the world knows about—or so it feels like. It's even on record that some fellows have either climbed the fence and come back home or lingered in their car at the gate, wanting to feel the nearness of the little eternal world just down the road.

Audrey's book, then, is a voice celebrating a special place for dreaming writers and an important piece of Texas history. It is a choir of voices, writer after writer, singing just as enthusiastically as the night birds and morning birds that become the magic and beauty that is Paisano. There are too many of these voices to offer here like gifts, but just a few will give the reader an alluring sense that there is a place on this earth that inspires, heals, comforts, and teaches.

Patricia Page was safe in her forest harbor when The World Trade Center was destroyed on September 11th. The news brought her to her knees. She was unable to write. So she swam the creek, walked the bluffs, "watched a garden spider trap and wrap a grasshopper in about three seconds flat. I witnessed a territorial dispute between two turtles at the low water crossing until one of them retreated downstream." And despite the horror that had just struck the world, she realized "I was happy. What a strange thing to say…I should have felt guilty or at least embarrassed, but what I mostly felt was grateful to be on those unspoiled acres, where human touch had been so blessedly light, where the beauty and endurance of the natural world could take up residence in our minds and bodies to restore well-being, and where the waters of Barton Creek like a muscle rippling through the land, could strengthen the spirit."

Her notebook pages remained blank until one morning, despite disaster and tragedy. She uncapped her pen and began to write—with a "strengthened spirit."

James Hannah wrote that Paisano could mend a life-- "all you have to do is let [her] do it." He was working on a compilation writings for a WWI anthology that was full of "despair and terror." But it would all be "slaked away in the pools upstream on Grape Creek." There he found a "steady solace and a lingering balm."

Daniel Rifenburgh was enduring a profound grief at the loss of his dear friend and poet Donald Justice—a grief so deep that he needed to turn to the therapy that writing an elegy at Paisano could offer. It was an act that freed him from the grief, and the result was a book that carried the epigraph from Don Justice's work: "Come back now and help me with these verses / Whisper to me some beautiful secret that you remember from life." Daniel tells us, "I felt Don's spirit was with me there at the ranch."

Scott Blackwood was lucky to live at the ranch when the still-living longhorn could always be summoned to the porch by starting up the burgers on the grill. In his novel *We Agreed to Meet Just Here*, the lions at the zoo, as part of that Paisano's spirit, made a cameo appearance with their dinnertime roars echoing off the creek bluffs, but as Scott tells us, "the spirit of the place is all through the book and still present (when I can summon it, like the steer to the porch) in my writing life."

Mary Helen Specht placed in her beautifully written

diary a collection of beautiful moments. "Today I thought about how much of the life around me at the ranch I never see, but only know by its evidence. Fox tracks in the dirt. Turkey scat in the yard. Deer corn eaten up."

"It was not unusual for me to startle deer on my morning walks. Sure enough, a doe came bounding out of the brush, crossing my path at high speed with something hanging from her mouth. But, then, there was more noise. A second and maybe third deer? No, a coyote, wolfish and big, was on the chase. When he saw me, he stopped six feet away, and our eyes met. Then, he rushed on. I thought (once my heart calmed down): this is a little like my time at the ranch. I am only a blip in this world, something the coyote sees once out of the corner of his eye before continuing on his way. I am one in a long line of humans blessed with the gift of this ranch for only a small window of time. And, in the end, that's all right."

Gary Cartwright needed the "spiritual fellowship" Paisano offered: "needed to lean against Dobie's rock." Sandra Cisneros said it "altered her destiny." For Tom McNeely, nature dwarfed him and his worries as he began to feel "part of a larger whole" which gave him peace.

Martha Elizabeth received restored, a childlike absorption: "I wish I could go back and reassume my old self that being who I was was all right.

For Sheryl St. Germaine, "It was one of the most important experiences of [her] life as a writer." Her "intimacy of the natural world" taught her about the "intelligence and language of the natural world, about the twinning of beauty and danger."

Allen Wier found that the ranch gave him a special word--abide. It was the sense that he forever would carry his own personal Texas with him: "[An] aura of it abides and lives within me." Billy Porterfield confessed that after Paisano he "would never be the same. " Lowell Mick White found something close to saving grace. Ewing Campbell encapsulated the Paisano experience as "therapy of the creek." Mylene Dressler tells us: "that visiting the land, and living as part of it are two very different things; and I will forever feel a sense of wonder at having witnessed and been part of the cycles of birth and death, flower and fall, and drought and flood that mark this surprising place." Her time at the ranch "may have been the greatest gift I have ever been given."

The distinguished and wise photographer Jim Bones— savior and nurturer of the precious land—has eternalized Dobie's small paradise of Texas in both prose and glorious prints. His plea is to never forget: "Paradoxically in wild pursuit of life, we leave the greatest mark in what we leave untouched. So save for the children's sake a little unspoiled land, and love and grace and green leaves may in time heal the wounded earth."

The last day for every fellow is the saddest day. As if they had been struck with a swift unease—as the car tires crunch the grave of the road, it seems to be going too fast, too fast, too fast. And on their first night back home or in some strange hotel on the way back, the now-new-world seemed too noisy, too busy, too artificial—Oh where was the coyote? Where was the pure breeze? Where was the soft earth, and yes, even? Where were the snakes (home in their garden?)— in short, Where was eternity? Where was Paisano? It was already drifting into memory—and loss. Yet, ever true to those who loved her, eventually the sorrow would be consoled by the mercy of their own imagination.

If the song that welcomed Katherine Hester at the entrance gate was "Knocking on Heaven's Door," then surely the leaving must be an old country song altered (dare I say altared?) just a bit:

I'm driving out backwards so I'll think I'm driving in.

Post-Afterword
by Diane Wilson

NOW I NEVER KNEW AUDREY SLATE, BUT HER CARE AND LOVE FOR Paisano Ranch changed my life. I owe her a lot. She kept it going for 40 years, and Michael Adams kept it going after that, and because of them it was there when I got a chance to go there.

I drove to Austin from the Gulf Coast like a bat out of hell and found out it was hot as hell in Austin, too. No difference, except it was muggier on the coast. I was delirious to get to the ranch, but the ranch wasn't the first thing on the agenda. Nope. First thing on the agenda was the University of Texas campus for some business about a library ID—even though I didn't want to go to the library. I wanted to see that ranch! Get me to the Paisano ranch!

I drove to a UT parking spot but had to get past a security guard first. He had been there thirty years he said. Where's my ID? Where am I from? Then he asked me what's the matter with my truck. It sure was making some mighty strange noises. Oh yes, I said, it makes noises, but a mechanic told me not to worry. Worry when the noise stops. The security guard laughed at that. He was a very friendly guy and walked alongside my rusty truck to make sure I got where I was going and to make sure I got a shady spot, too.

I wound my way through a shady road that had buildings on both sides, climbed one set of stairs, climbed back down. Wrong building. Finally, I entered a building close to the legendary Tower where a sniper shot some people a number of years ago. It was the only landmark I knew at UT. I had written instructions from the Paisano fellowship folks that I had to get a library ID and then a clearance for getting in the library—yes yes, even though I didn't want to go to the library. I wanted to stay at the ranch and never leave. They would have to drag me out kicking.

A receptionist asked me if I found my way okay and I said, yes, I met a great security guard. She asked who the guard was, and I said I don't know but he sure was friendly. The receptionist laughed and said, Oooh yes, Mister Garza. He is friendly. He will talk your leg off.

Around 2 pm and after much squirreling up and down the shaded sidewalks of the university, we finally headed for the ranch—fifteen miles outside of Austin. Margaret Borden, from the UT Graduate School, was the lead in her air-conditioned car and I followed in my rat trap truck. Twice, Margaret stopped and called me on the cell phone and asked if I wanted to get something to eat before I got to the ranch. I said, "No, no. The ranch! The ranch." I was half afraid they would jerk away the invitation to write at Paisano and Margaret was half afraid I would starve since there was nothing to eat at the ranch.

Yes, you could say I was eager. I had 55 years of kinfolks living and roaming within two miles of my double-wide trailer in Seadrift and an ex-husband who resembled the Unabomber in my back four acres. So, I was eager for some peace and quiet. Also, I was raised in the country my entire life and there wasn't a single thing about country living that frightened me. (This was a question the Paisano folks asked their new boarders: Are you afraid of living alone in the country?) Hell, no! The only thing that scared me was Austin traffic. Holy Mackerel! Don't ever drive I-35 in Austin! Anyhow, the whole drive to the ranch I was mumbling to myself, "Oh sweet Jesus, give me some quiet." Then I hit two locked entrance gates and got four phone calls in a row. Low and behold, my cell phone worked hunky-dory out there. At home in Seadrift, I got one bar on the phone at the most, but here on the ranch—15 miles from Austin—I got four bars.

Margo wasn't kidding when she told me there was NO food in the house. She asked me what snacks I brought to tide me over until I went to Kroger's grocery shopping later in the week and I said that I brought coffee and a little quart jar of tequila. The bottle broke so I was using a mayonnaise jar. The refrigerator was clean as a whistle. One little bottle of grapefruit juice was stuck in a side bin and that's what I had for supper the first night.

The next morning, I woke up early. There were no clocks in my new bedroom, but the sunlight was streaming through all three windows. So, I was up and raring to do something. Mainly, I scouted the shelves for a coffee pot. Writing was going to have to wait on four cups of strong coffee—at least. But I was not in a panic if I didn't find a coffee pot. If worse comes to worse, I'd make shrimper coffee like I did out on my shrimp boat. For those that don't know, shrimper coffee was just like cowboy coffee—except its cooked over a two-burner stove on a shrimp boat or the exhaust pipe. I finally drug out a tiny plastic Motel 6-looking coffee pot from deep inside a bottom shelf. Looked like the thing could only give me one cup at a time. Dang it! I was gonna be brewing coffee all day long!

I loved this ranch house. My kind of house and my kind of

country. I knew I wouldn't get lost outside, but I was getting confused in the house. There were six rooms—not counting the two bathrooms—and what seemed like a hundred doors. And electrical outlets. I had never seen that many outlets in my life! And I was trying very hard to be careful with the newly renovated floors. What a terrific varnish job! Plus, new ones in the hallway blazed like the evening sun. Yikes! Take off your shoes, Diane!

Sarah Bird, the writer before me, and I were the first writers to try out the new, remodeled Paisano Ranch on its 254 acres of hill country. Guess I wouldn't be writing home about all those scorpions I'd heard so much about. Wait, take that back. I saw two climb out the sink drain while I was brushing my teeth. But the best entertainment around for your buck were the daddy long legs spiders that congregated in the hundreds of thousands in the eaves of the ranch house.

To be honest, I had no idea of the literary legacy I'd lucked upon when I sent in my application for the Paisano writing fellowship. I lived my entire life in a very isolated, rural fishing village on the Texas Gulf coast and I didn't know two writers in the whole state of Texas. I certainly didn't know much about the Paisano Ranch, although I'd heard stories about the wild long horn cattle that roamed around there. I couldn't wait to see them. But nope—those longhorns over Frank Dobie's mantel piece were the last of the longhorns. Well, shoot! So, I didn't see any cattle. No deer. No bobcats or javelinas except during the night, I heard the loud roar of a lion in the zoo a few miles away. Then once, after a flood, I found tusks jutting from a boar skull. Wild turkeys were the only thing I saw in abundance and nothing seemed to bother them too much. They strolled around like they had all the time in the world to munch on the short grass in the front yard. I started collecting the turkey feathers and twined them in my hair.

In the beginning, it took a solid week before the birds came out. I guess my loud truck scared them off. Anyhow, I got a big blue jay the first time. I thought it was a blue jay.

Back home I'd say, that's a blue bird. I knew a bird watcher from Houston and took him out on the bay and he pointed at a white bird and said, what's that and I said, that's a white bird and then he pointed at a brown bird and said, what's that and I said, that's a brown bird. The bird watcher looked at me with a curious look on his face and said, you sure have a simple method for bird watching.

Well, yeah. That's what country living did for you.

First week at the ranch, the water well went kaput. One minute it was on, and the next minute it was off. I went around the house and checked for any empty glasses that had water and put them in the kitchen so I could have coffee water in case things went bad. And they got bad. And not just a little flip switch thing going bad in the well house. I know, because I checked out the well house. Water was everywhere. Pouring out the pump shed and into the yard. I was a little leery about gripping wires and fiddling with them in the middle of all that water, so I called the emergency guy at UT. (There was a very long detailed list of who to call in case of any emergency you can imagine)

And he said, Paisano? What's that?

A ranch, I said. I'm a writer here.

UT? he said, and I said yeah, UT.

Well, he would talk to the working guy when he came in. Three hours later and around 8pm or so, I called again, and he said, well, the guy was working on another problem they had at UT. Then he said the water is low out there at the ranch, anyway. I said, Well, it's a little more than low. Water is shooting everywhere. Well, he don't know nothing about fixing water. So, I never hear anymore from those guys. The next day at 10 am there is still no water and no mechanic, so I call the emergency number for water problems and it's a new guy. You're out of water? Paisano? Yeah, he knows the place. How long? Two days? Yeah, I said, and the water pump gauge says overload and its shooting water when I turn it on. Ooooh he's gonna send a guy right out there. Three hours later. I'm watching through the window. Where was that dang plumber? Then here came a road runner. The Paisano! Long tail. Big spiky hairdo on top. And it ran. Never walked or strolled. It ran. Ain't I lucky. No water but I sure had a paisano.

It was a full week at Paisano and I had something of a schedule. I got up early — before the sun came up and before the birds started talking in the trees. I made coffee and sat on the front porch as the sun made it over the trees. I propped my feet up and drank two full cups of coffee. Then I moved my metal rocking chair a couple of inches to keep the sun out of my eyes. Nothing rushed around here. I had three months. Gonna be a great day for me and the turkeys.

I read a couple of directives about wooden chairs on the front porch. Please do not leave them out in the yard. Please. Please. There wasn't a single wooden chair in the yard. All metal. Guess the wooden chairs rotted in the yard. Paisano writers, apparently, were bad at following directions.

I switched from flip flops to tennis shoes because the walk up the rock road had some terrific little stones and when I took the grass path with the dew still in the grass, I would slip and slide in my rubber flip flops. So far, I hadn't made it to the first gate. I was sure that made me a sorry specimen of a walker. But I was taking it slow. Not trying to kill myself here. I had three months to make it to that first gate and beyond.

In my walks I discovered three piles of stones marking three different trails. I checked out two trails but the third was gonna have to wait until it was cooler. It was a good little hike up through some cactus, cedar trees and some knee-high grass to the bluffs. I figured when that first norther came through, I would give it a try. Also, fewer snakes. I saw my share of snakes for sure. Apparently, Paisano was famous for snakes. Read the historical account from one of the families of the original owners and they said they'd sleep on the veranda and more often than not would wake up to a rattlesnake curled up in the quilt with them. He also told about the time his mother and aunt came into the yard from the west side of the house and he said a dozen snakes lit out like lightning bolts.

First week in September a hurricane blew in from the gulf at Brownsville and took a little ride to Austin. It was raining kittens, puppies, and alligator gar. I was told and told how high that creek in front of Paisano got when it flooded. Well, it did. I heard it first about 2 am. Sounded like the Gulf of Mexico was at the front veranda. But nope, that wasn't the Gulf out there. It was Barton Creek at flood stage. I could hardly wait until it got light enough to go take a look.

At the first peep of daylight, I headed for the noise. Couldn't see but I sure could hear. The water was everywhere, thundering through the creek, boulders, bluff, disappearing the road, and heading up through the cedar trees. A high-water sign that had been on the edge of the road and marking 1 to 5 foot over flood stage was nowhere to be seen.

Since the water well went dry that first week at Paisano, I had a daily habit of bathing and washing my hair in the creek. I toted milk jugs down and filled them up so I could flush the toilets and wash the dishes. Well, no more dry well. I'd bet money on that one. So, I went down in my truck with all my water jugs and set on the hood and watched the creek flow like the Guadalupe River at high stage. I expected to see snakes squirming like crazy. When hurricanes and high tides hit the gulf coast, usually water moccasins and rattlesnakes start moving. But no snakes so far. I wondered how the lion in the zoo next couple acres over was taking all this rain. Hadn't heard a peep from that lion all morning.

It was a solid week of water across the road. I took a dozen trips down there to check the level. Brush, dead trees, logs, uprooted grasses, and one long dead snake skin slid past. The high water marker in the road was flattened like a pancake and a mountain of debris hung on the top, I had a hard time figuring what it was when I first saw the sign laying in the water. I was thinking a dead body. I expected to see one float past any ole day.

Still no water inside the house although there was plenty

outside. I went back and forth to the pump house, flipping little switches in the hope that the water pressure from the creek flooding would get the pump working again. But nope, a blue electrical flame shot out at me. Leave me alone! Well, thank you very much, I WILL. Plumbers had been out here four times. Still no water. They said they would bring a huge 3,000-gallon water tank that would solve all the water problems. But the road was under water.

I put a big rock in the middle of the road to mark where the creek water had flooded to. I doubt anybody would believe how deep and wide the creek got. A rancher a little north above me called on the house phone. I had no idea that phone worked. First time it ever rang. He wanted to know if I was all right and I laughed and told him how excited I was about the creek rising. I'm sure he thought I was a geeeen—uuuu-ine writer nut from that Paisano Ranch.

Two weeks after the hurricane blew through, the water was still over the road. The road was now mossy with so much water running over it and it was slick as greased lightning. One thing that I've noticed: with all the writers coming out to the ranch, very few leave their initials anywhere. I didn't see names carved in the wood in the house or on the trees. Didn't even notice much on the old 1850's cabin out on the property.

But I did find a string of messages and initials in the mossy cement with a foot of water running over it. I've taken a tumble a time or two and spent time reading them.

After the rain came the mud, and after the mud came the UT trucks with my 3,000-gallon tank of water. Water water. I took a bath for the first in the house since I've got here. I washed the dishes using water from the faucet instead of river water. My truck was full of water jugs. That's where I stored everything. I finally had to write "river water" on the sides with magic markers because I couldn't figure which was bottle water from a store and which was river water. I'm pretty sure I made coffee with river water, at least once. It didn't taste too bad. Much as I loved having the water in the house, I missed taking a bath in the creek. I had spent at least two hours every day sitting in that creek. I won't lie. Sometimes half nude. But I didn't worry. The road going up to the gates was torn up. Rough rocks were jutting everywhere and the fine gravel on the road had been washed off and into the ditches. A low riding car was liable to lose a muffler on that road. Or knock a hole in the oil pan. Michael Adams, who was the director out here, said they were sending someone out to fix the road. Well, I hoped not.

After all the rain, there was a magnificent crop of wildflowers. Tiny lilac blooms and tall bushes with a string of yellow blossoms were sprouting throughout the ditches and climbing into the cedar trees. When I walked to the cabin after that first rain there was hundreds of rain lilies shooting up. Wild blue verbena cropped up in the rocks.

Seven hen turkeys, that usually wound their way around the house, walked down the creek road with me that last week. A snapping turtle, 12 inches across, was sunning on a rock slab and splashed into the water as I reached the creek. Then I walked to my swimming hole and saw another turtle with his head out of the water. I had never seen such turtles before! Yellow sun flowers were blooming everywhere, and water was crystal clear. I was told (and believed to be true) a musician who died had his ashes spread on the grounds.

Now the writing. Paisano Ranch was all about the writing. I haven't mentioned that much. I have a philosophy that you can either write a book or talk about a book. You can't do both. Only so much energy to go around. Anyhow, my book began and was near finished at the ranch. I never had that much uninterrupted time to write in my entire life. I remember once, when I was younger and still had five young kids, begging my then husband with $5 an hour if he would let me write. (Five dollars an hour was a lot of money in those days). Nope.

I liked to wallow in a book. Roll in it. Smear the words and ideas around. Get it in my ears, between my toes, and hope to sweet baby Jesus it showed up in my dreams (It did!).

I didn't take notes or write outlines. I immersed myself like I was a swimmer, and the book was the deep blue sea. Then I took a dive. Usually, I had no idea where I was going with that book. I never had an ending. Maybe just two words— end or beginning—and they were always a big surprise.

We are in a world now where places like Paisano are in danger—from global warming, from pollution, from development. Which means we need to fight for it and protect it, the way Audrey Slate did, and Michael Adams did. Paisano Ranch is a magical place and has been behind so much great Texas literature, and it must be saved and preserved for future writers. When I was there, I had to trust in the magic and that was the one thing Paisano gave me. Three months to let the magic work.

Acknowledgments

Audrey Slate was friend to a wide swath of people in the Paisano universe and she would have wrestled with proper acknowledgment, knowing the many contributions that have made the fellowship the successful endeavor that it is. This manuscript was at copy editing stage at her passing in December 2017 and we hope we haven't left anyone out.

First of all, a deep, heartfelt thanks to all the Paisano Fellows of the past and of the present, especially those who were able to contribute their time and unique reflections to this book.

Posthumous and generous thanks to Michael Adams, Director of the Dobie Paisano Fellowship, the University of Texas at Austin, and Marla Akin, senior program coordinator at the James A. Michener Center at the University of Texas at Austin. Audrey relied on you time and again and your friendship, encouragement and kindness over many years helped make this book a reality. Jim Magnuson, former director of the Michener Center, is thanked for supporting the fellowship through thick and thin, including the use of office space in the Michener Center (Dobie's former residence) on East Dean Keeton Street.

The Office of Graduate Studies, the University of Texas at Austin, is the home of the fellowship and its co-sponsor. We thank the deans and staff past and present for their support of the Dobie

Paisano Fellowship and the stewardship of the ranch. In particular, Audrey would have wanted to recognize past Deans W. Gordon Whaley, William S. Livingston, and Theresa Sullivan. Audrey's family wish to thank Dean of the Graduate School Mark J.T. Smith, Senior Associate Dean Marvin L. Hackert and Brian Van Reet for supporting and keeping Paisano in the forefront.

We are equally thankful to the Texas Institute of Letters (TIL), co-sponsor of the fellowship. For the past fifty years, TIL has supported the fellowships financially and was instrumental in raising funds to acquire Dobie's retreat. The Houston Endowment and the Ralph Johnston Foundation are thanked for their continuous and generous funding, without which there would be no fellowships.

Very special thanks to Paisano Fellows Jim Bones, Alan Pogue and John Christian for permission to use their images made at Paisano, and kind thanks to Wanda Gamble for the use of Glenn Whitehead's Paisano artwork.

Audrey and her family thank Pamela Booton, Lowell Mick White, and Diane Wilson, Alamo Bay Press, for agreeing to publish this book and believing in it. Further thanks to Catherine Hester and Susan Spicer. Without their help and wise counsel, this book would not have been completed. And last but not least, thanks to the genial Stephen Harrigan for his thoughtful foreword to this book.

Friends and family rooted her on over time as she completed this book. I know she enjoyed the enthusiasm and encouragement of her children and grandchildren. In the end, Audrey would have asked for forgiveness for anyone she missed in the previous accounting.

John H. Slate, 2023

About Audrey Nelson Slate

"She speaks with wisdom and faithful instruction is on her tongue."

Audrey Nelson Slate, Ph.D, was born October 10, 1926. She was born and raised in Ponca City, OK and took degrees from Oberlin College, the University of Oklahoma, and the University of Wisconsin. She resided in Austin from 1959 to 2007, where she served in several capacities, finally as Assistant Dean in the Office of Graduate Studies at the University of Texas at Austin. She was the author of *The Association of Graduate Schools: A History (1994)*.

Beyond motherhood, her greatest role was coordinator of the Dobie-Paisano Fellowship. For 33 years beginning in 1974, Audrey managed the judging of the fellowship and was the caretaker of J. Frank Dobie's ranch. Over the decades she handed the keys over to dozens of award-winning authors and poets and advised fellows on how to deal with creek floods, snakes, coyotes, failing appliances, and more. In 2007 she was inducted into the Texas Institute of Letters for her help in making the Paisano Fellowship one of America's great literary prizes.

She retired in 1997 but managed the fellowship until 2007, when she moved to Dallas to be closer to family. Slate died December 1, 2017.

Photo Credits

Printed in the USA
CPSIA information can be obtained
at www.ICGtesting.com
LVHW061513200324
774829LV00025B/40